Muslim Worldviews and Everyday Lives

Muslim Worldviews and Everyday Lives

el-Sayed el-Aswad

ALTAMIRA
PRESS

A DIVISION OF
ROWMAN & LITTLEFIELD PUBLISHERS, INC.
Lanham • New York • Toronto • Plymouth, UK

Published by AltaMira Press
A division of Rowman & Littlefield Publishers, Inc.
A wholly owned subsidiary of The Rowman & Littlefield Publishing Group, Inc.
4501 Forbes Boulevard, Suite 200, Lanham, Maryland 20706
www.rowman.com

10 Thornbury Road, Plymouth PL6 7PP, United Kingdom

British Library Cataloguing in Publication Information Available

Library of Congress Cataloging-in-Publication Data
El-Aswad, el-Sayed, 1949–
Muslim worldviews and everyday lives / el-Sayed el-Aswad.
p. cm.
Includes bibliographical references and index.
ISBN 978-0-7591-2119-5 (cloth : alk. paper) — ISBN 978-0-7591-2121-8 (electronic)
1. Muslims—Attitudes. 2. Islam—21st century. 3. Islamic sociology. I. Title.
BP173.25.E42 2012
297.2'7—dc23

2012017885

™ The paper used in this publication meets the minimum requirements of American National Standard for Information Sciences—Permanence of Paper for Printed Library Materials, ANSI/NISO Z39.48-1992.

Printed in the United States of America

To those who advocate peace, *salām*

Contents

Figures

Notes on Transliteration and Translation

The book follows the transliteration system of the *International Journal of Middle East Studies* for Arabic words. Except for proper nouns, all Arabic words are in italics. Colloquial words or terms and phrases are transliterated as spoken and pronounced by individuals; nevertheless, in certain contexts where it is necessary, their meanings, in parentheses, are written in standard Arabic form. An extensive glossary of the Arabic words that are used frequently in the text can be found in the back matter. All translations from Arabic to English are the author's.

Acknowledgments

This work has taken more than ten years to research, prepare, and complete. The book has not been funded by any specific organization or academic institute. Serving tenure at universities in the United States, Egypt, Bahrain, and the United Arab Emirates has given me the opportunity to conduct focused and in-depth ethnographic studies, for which I am grateful. I hope the reader finds reading this book as enriching an experience as I have had through interacting with people in their homeland and diasporic communities.

I would like to thank my family for the great support and unique ways in which they contributed to the production of this book. My wife, Maryam, provided editorial assistance. My son Kareem introduced me to a number of Muslim American youths in both the Bloomfield Hills and Dearborn communities, offering invaluable insights into Muslim American lifestyles. My son Amir aided me in fashioning the five maps found in this book by using Adobe Photoshop and Adobe Illustrator.

Friendly interlocutors from Bahrain, Egypt, the United Arab Emirates, and the United States have openly and sincerely provided me with valuable personal narratives and views concerning their myriad and rich experiences with Islam. Special thanks go to the late Shaikh Hasan al-Shinnawi, the former patron head of the Shinnawiyya Sufi Order and former president of the Supreme Council of Sufi Orders in Egypt (1997–2008); Shaikh Said al-Shinnawi, the current head of the Shinnawiyya Sufi Order in Tanta, Egypt; Shaikh Muhammad Musa, the religious leader and former Imam of the Muslim Unity Center in Bloomfield Hills; Ayatollah Abdul Latif Berry, the religious leader and Imam of the Islamic Institute of Knowledge in Dearborn, Michigan; and Shaikh (Sayyid) Muhammad Baqir al-Kahsmiri, the chair of the Imam Mahdi Association of Marjaeya

(IMAM) in Dearborn, Michigan. Without their assistance, this work would not have come to fruition.

The comments and feedback of scholars, namely Muhammad Aman, Dale Eickelman, Hasan El-Shamy, Amy Evrard, Nicholas Hopkins, and Dan Varisco, in addition to those of anonymous peer reviewers, have enriched and deepened the scholarly discussion of the book.

I would like to thank the students of Dartmouth College and the United Arab Emirates University for the insightful discussion on the topic of *Islamic Dreams* conducted on November 14, 2011, through a videoconference, which Professor Dale Eickelman and I organized. The videoconference provided a lively cross-cultural exchange concerning the impact of the unseen world, including dreams and dream visions, on Muslim everyday lives.

I would like to express my gratitude to Wendi Schnaufer, executive editor at AltaMira Press, for providing meticulous editorial attention throughout the process of production of this book. Also, thanks go to Jehanne Schweitzer, senior production editor at Rowman & Littlefield Publishing Group, and to Michele Tomiak, copyeditor.

With appreciation,
el-Sayed el-Aswad
Bloomfield Hills, Michigan

Introduction

Worldview, Ideology, and Geography

In the past two decades, students and scholars from a variety of disciplines have shown sincere interest in understanding Islam and Muslim cultures located around the globe. This book tackles a critical topic encompassing such interrelated themes as Muslim worldview, ethnocosmology, emic interpretation of sacred tradition, geography, folk culture, and identity transformation. It is critical to understanding the place Muslims now occupy in the world and presents new grounds for ethnographic and cross-cultural inquiries of Muslim worldviews and ethnocosmologies in their visible and invisible spheres.[1] It endeavors to bring to attention the impact of sanctified and nonsanctified worldviews on the construction of identities and aspirations of Muslim communities in various local, national, and transnational contexts.

What distinguishes this book from contemporary books on Islam is its concern with the ethnography of the worldviews of Muslim societies with their seen and unseen spheres as well as with their social and symbolic implications. Another unique feature is its strategy of addressing Muslim worldviews. The strategy presumes that discursive and nondiscursive actions or everyday practices, rituals, prayers, and lifestyles are core means for grasping the worldviews of ordinary Muslims around the world. Worldview is based on assumptions concerning the structure of the universe. It includes the society as well as the human and nonhuman beings and forces, both perceptible and imperceptible, that constitute the integrated parts of the universe or cosmos (el-Aswad 2002, 2). From this perspective, I maintain that except for books dealing with the worldviews of certain Muslim intellectuals or classical texts from the medieval ages (Heinen 1982; Izutsu 1964; Nasr 1964), contemporary monographs addressing the worldviews of ordinary Muslims are scant. Compared with rich ethnographic and cross-cultural studies dealing with worldviews of different societies (Barth 1987;

Chevannes 1995; Gill 2002; Howell 1984; Stoller 1989; Wagner 2001, among others), few monographs (el-Aswad 1988, 1990b, 2002, 2005f; Geertz 1960) address worldviews and cosmologies of Muslim societies. Although certain aspects of local Muslim worldviews have been addressed, specifically and as related to, for example, gender (Delaney 1991; Doumato 2000; Ruffle 2011), piety (Deeb 2006; Flaskerud 2010), and ritual or performance (Joll 2012; Netton 2000; Torab 2007), there is not an integrated and holistic treatment of overarching Muslim worldviews. Further, Islam presented in this book is different from the Islam portrayed in newspapers, television, or biased monographs as a fanatical, distorted, and radicalized reality. As such the book looks at the majority, who are politically "moderate," as well as the cultural variations that are dispersed not only in the Middle East but also around the globe.

The book explores the dynamic relationships between Muslim worldviews and sociocultural practices of Muslim communities in various geographic locations. The significance of religion in a materialistically oriented and globally dominant and changing world has been a nexus of current debates in anthropological and sociological circles.[2] It is also apparent that there is an imperative motivation for why Islamic discourses gradually dominate contemporary global and local events.[3] At the same time, one of the most important aspects of globalization[4] has been the spread of religious networks, virtual and real, that perpetuate the connectivity of religious and cosmological beliefs. By providing a wealth of historical, geographic, and spatial accounts of Muslim worldviews, this book seeks to contribute significant insights to the scholarship of Islam and Muslim societies as well as to question derogatory misconceptions of non-Muslim societies toward Muslims and vice versa.

WORLDVIEW AND IDEOLOGY

For the purpose of theorizing Muslim worldviews, this introduction develops a distinction between worldview or cosmology and ideology. While ideology implies certain economic and political orientations related particularly to power, worldview indicates belief systems and related symbolic actions. Worldview or cosmological belief system is an interpretative and integrative paradigm encompassing the assumptions through which people view the world in which they live and with which they interact. Worldview is comparable to "*Weltanschauung*,"[5] "meaning system," "patterns of thought," "perceptual framework," "cognitive orientation," or what Charles Taylor (2004, 249) calls "social imaginary," where the focus is on the way ordinary people imagine their social world. It is not expressed in theoretical terms but is manifested in images, stories, and legends. The main concern here is not merely with the intellectual aspects of the cosmological order but also with the social and subjective domains in which individuals locate and define themselves in their relations to others. Worldview or social imaginary, shared by large groups of people, is generated by people's aspiration to reach a unified comprehension of the world, drawing together facts, principles, assumptions, generalizations, and answers to ultimate questions. It constitutes the common understanding that makes possible common practices and a widely shared sense of legitimacy.

Muslims' perceptions of themselves and of the worlds in which they live have been given less attention by scholars than their economic activities and political ideologies represented mostly in the Islamists, who see in Islam a political ideology capable of solving society's problems. Here, people's worldviews are treated not as an ideological system but as a system of meanings generated and enacted in different courses of public and private scenarios dealing with seen and unseen domains of local communities. Islam is dealt with as a cultural matrix of ethno-cosmologies and worldviews of ordinary Muslims and not a political ideology. Ideology "is essentially linked to the process of sustaining asymmetrical relations of power—that is, the process of maintaining domination" (Thompson 1984, 4).[6] Islamist movements that apply the ideology of political Islam are not essentially religious groups concerned with issues of doctrine, beliefs, and faith, but political organizations manipulating Islam as an ideological force to gain power over others. Rajaee (2007, 4) states, "An ideology is a project with a clear blueprint that requires only mechanical implication. . . . Islamism has betrayed many of the tenets of Islam as a divine message; as a way of life; as a civilization, polity, and state; as a religion; and as a body of thought composed of a moral and ethical system." Further, the politicization of religion is a fundamental feature of "the secular," where the allegedly well-built relationship between religion and politics contests the interest and importance of religion itself (Asad 2003, 193, 199). Olivier Roy (2004, 40) states, "The failure of political Islam means that politics prevail over religion, as is obvious in Iran."

To give another example, the uprisings and revolutions that have been occurring since January 2011 in Tunisia, Egypt, Yemen, Bahrain, Libya, and Syria were not religiously organized, or at their core caused by Islamist politicians or militants, but rather were politically and socially motivated. However, recently I heard some Shi'i people, ordinary and intellectuals alike, suggest that such uprisings, in addition to natural disasters such as the tsunamis that struck Japan, are signs of the expected return of Mahdi, the Twelfth and last Shi'i Imam, who is believed to be alive but in occultation.[7]

The distinction between worldview and political ideology does not mean that a Muslim worldview has no potential political role in Muslim societies. The idea that the book is unconcerned with politically oriented Muslims or Islamists does not negate the fact that religious worldviews and traditional cosmologies have a great impact on grassroots political activities.[8] In his insightful study of the rise of political ideologies in traditional societies (Maya, Upper Egypt, and Ogoni), Tschirgi (2007), applying el-Aswad's approach (2002) for studying religious-traditional cosmology, states, "Here is the fundamental explanation of how and why ideologies based on traditional cosmologies attract sufficient followers to enter into conflict against objectively hopeless odds." The book, moreover, does not address the political ideologies and activities of Muslims as such; rather, it offers a differing view from the current global debate concerning political Islam. Such an approach might increase cultural understanding and rational dialogues between Muslims and non-Muslims, leading to the establishment of effective and peaceful policies.

Although cosmology as a scientific field is generally concerned with secular domains, its holistic paradigm and its concern for order are inseparable from views about the cosmos more closely associated with religious considerations. Furthermore, as Durkheim noted, "there is no religion that is not a cosmology at the same time that it is a speculation upon divine things" (Durkheim 1965, 21). Taking religion as an aspect of life, this book examines how far religion impacts societies and how far societies influence certain religious worldviews and practices. Religious concepts and beliefs are not just parts of the worldviews or cosmologies, however; they also contribute in making up certain core elements of these worldviews.

Worldview is concerned with people's place in the universe, setting boundaries between nature and culture on the one hand and the local and global on the other. Though worldview represents a cultural phenomenon, it is not treated as forming an ideology. Rather, as in Durkheim's sociology, it is seen as constituting social facts or collective representations. Worldviews, contingent on cultural traditions, are clusters of ideas, beliefs, shared meanings or understandings, and practices that render social life possible (Foltz 2003; Redfield 1968; Smart 1995). Thus, this book proposes that the use of the terms "worldview" and "cosmology," rather than exclusively "religion," may augment dialogue and enlarge the circles of perspectives that complement, contrast, or go beyond religious beliefs per se.

All in all, the term "worldview" or "cosmology" emerges as an encompassing and useful tool for the comparative task of anthropology (el-Aswad 2002, 2003a; Herzfeld 2001, 192). Societies construct and alter worldviews, but worldviews also shape and impact societies. Within the Arab context, for example, it is worthwhile to note that the Arabic word *al-kaun* (the universe or cosmos) is derived from the root k-u-n, which means to be, to exist, to take place, or to happen within temporal and spatial dimensions. It refers to the dynamic process of being and becoming (*kaynūna*) as opposed to the word *'ālam*, which means the world as being settled or fixed (el-Aswad 2002, 2). The cosmological belief system, influenced by Muslim culture, determines the appropriate time and place in which people conduct certain practices and rituals. Though latent, shared worldviews and cosmological beliefs have played a decisive role in the social history of Muslim communities and have manifested themselves powerfully in critical historical moments of these communities.

Comparative and cross-cultural studies of Muslim worldviews, real or imaginary, are woefully scant. In most of the contemporary literature on Islam, Muslim communities have been scrutinized either within the Arab world or within non-Arab countries with Muslim majorities such as Indonesia (with the world's largest Muslim population), Turkey, Pakistan, and Iran. Further, Muslim minorities living in the diaspora have been investigated as being isolated communities dissociated from their homelands. The grave problem, however, is that social inquiries of Muslim communities have paid less attention to issues of cultural diversity, transformation of identities, and reconstruction of worldviews than to issues related to economic and ideological domains or radical Islamist politics. It is a matter of social cosmologies and religious orientation that give social, private, economic, and political domains themselves a subordinate position within the larger whole. The research presented here fills these gaps through cross-cultural inquiries of worldviews of Muslim communities in Arab and non-Arab societies. Many of the real and imagined Muslim worldviews are examined both locally and globally.

Worldview, embodied in the practices and discourses of large groups of ordinary people, reveals inner meaning systems made of assumptions and images in accordance with which the universe, including the society and person, is constructed. Worldview deals with such issues as the creation of the world, the place of humans in that world, potential means for improving social conditions, fate, death, resurrection, the afterlife, magic, envy, blessing, invisible beings (souls, spirits, angels, *jinn*), and unseen forces without and within humankind. Religious worldviews of both Muslim intellectuals and grassroots, which endow them with a unique imaginative sense of engagement with a spiritual, transcendent, and superior reality, accentuate the theme of a divine higher power surpassing any other. Such a belief represents an inexhaustible source of spiritual, emotional, and social empowerment.

This book is not concerned with orthodox Muslim worldview,[9] textual in nature, but rather with the enacted and lived worldviews of ordinary Muslims. This book examines Muslims' folk worldviews without getting into the problematic consequences of applying the misleading jargon of "folk Islam." Muslim worldviews are addressed not within the principles of orthodox Islam, but within the views and values of grassroots (or folk) Muslims, both Sunni and Shi'a,[10] in the homeland and diaspora.[11] Such a strategy aims at creating a better cross-cultural understanding of Muslim communities.

Muslim worldviews are not constructed solely by religious scholars (*'ulama*) or literate intellectual elite; rather, they are latent in Islamic tradition, embedded in popular imagination, and triggered through people's everyday discourses. Likewise, access to sacred texts in Islam is not restricted to specialists in religious knowledge. Any person able to read, however basically, has access to scriptures, both individually and collectively.[12] Further, Muslim worldviews do not form a monolithic bloc but represent uniquely ordered syntheses of multiple differing views (el-Aswad 2002; Varisco 2005).[13] In the study of worldviews, the focus is on the way the folk or ordinary people perceive and imagine their social, trans-social, and transcultural surroundings, and this is not often expressed in doctrinal or theoretical terms but is embodied in images, symbols, narratives, and myths.

It is difficult and perhaps even impossible to understand Muslims' modes of behavior and thinking without paying attention to their multiple worldviews, interpenetrating domains, and points of reference correlating with cultural constructs that render different experiential worlds, real or imaginary, comprehensible. Contemporary Muslim worlds are characterized by ethnic, cultural, and ideological diversity. Muslim cosmologies include, for example, those of the Sunni (including the Salafiyya or Salafism, a Sunni purist–reform movement calling for a return to Islam as understood and enacted by the pious forefathers), the Shi'a, and the Sufi (those adhering to a mystical form of the faith), in both local and transnational contexts. In addition, there is the Wahhabi worldview or Wahhabism, a movement within the Sunnis established in Saudi Arabia by Mohammad ibn Abd al-Wahhab (1703–1792), which regards the Qur'an and Hadith as fundamental texts and considers Sufism, mysticism, and Shi'ism as forms of non-orthodox Islam (el-Aswad 2005d).[14]

Islam, however, is confronted not only with multiple cultures or worldviews of different Muslim communities but also with Western attempts at imposing its essentially secular worldview through the process of globalization. Increases and changes in transcommunication, global flows of culture, capital, and material forces have recently and concurrently opened new venues for Muslims to rethink certain modes of both their worldviews and social lives.

This book critiques literature that imposes Western worldviews or ideologies on Muslim worldviews. Muslims in most of the Western media, especially since the events of September 11, 2001, are stereotypically and uncritically depicted as fundamentalist, intolerant, violent, terroristic,[15] and as the threatening "Other."[16] With the exception of a few Western scholars[17] who seek to understand and present Islam objectively, most Western scholarship and media have portrayed Muslims in terms of global terrorism, Islamic jihadism, Islamism, fascism, and authoritarianism. These global depictions of Muslims, creating so-called Islamophobia,[18] have not only aggravated sociopolitical problems in the Muslim world such as poverty, unemployment, homelessness, violence, and the "brain drain" caused by migration, but have also generated serious questions concerning indigenous cultures and identities of Muslim diaspora.[19]

The grave ignorance about Muslims and their stereotypical images in scholarship and the press the world over is held responsible for the emerging conflict between the West and Muslims as represented in Samuel Huntington's theory (1996) of the clash of civilizations, critically refuted by Edward Said (2001a) as the clash of ignorant Orientalists. There have been plenty of theories and scholarly books dealing with topics such as the *Islamic Threat*, *Islamic Fundamentalism*, *Islamic Imperialism*, and *The Theory and Practice of Islamic Terrorism*, to mention some.[20] Suicide bombing, for instance, for many Americans and Europeans, has become an icon of the Islamic "culture of death" (Asad 2007, 5). The problem in the ideology of New Orientalism is that the fight against violent political Islam is viewed as a fight against Islam as a whole (el-Aswad 2008a).

Throughout its cosmic history, Islam has never advocated terrorism or antagonism, nor has it blindly rejected modern or secular modes of life. Without essentialism, Islam has managed to assert its encompassing worldview, casting doubt on the extreme form of secular modernity though accepting its moderate form and technological-scientific culture. The cosmologies of Muslim societies are not based on evolutionary, materialistic, and separatist models but on the cosmology of spirituality, sanctification, unification, and creation (without nullifying secular worldviews) and are influenced by various interrelated factors. The first factor is the exegeses of the religious scholars (*'ulama*) concerning the constituents and construction of the universe or cosmos. These exegeses, unlike revelation, are not divine, sacred, or unchanging. Rather, they are limited by the time, context, and culture in which they appear. The second factor is the tradition of Sufism and related beliefs derived from varied Sufi orders. The third factor concerns ritual performances and related symbols and emotions substantiating religious and cosmological concepts. The fourth factor pertains to local tradition and specificity of local communities as related to their histories, social structures, locations, and ecological features. These factors, inseparable in the context of social reality, are expounded in this book for theoretical purposes.

WORLDVIEW AND GEOGRAPHY: GLOBAL AND LOCAL CONTEXTS

Cross-culturally, this work seeks to identify what the world looks like from the points of view of certain Muslim communities in different locations or geographies. Geography includes sacred and mundane places and spaces that shape Muslim lives and identities. Places are constructed in people's memories and affections by repeated encounters and complex associations through which a sense of place involves a sense of being (Butz and Eyles 1997).

Drawing on ethnographic and cross-cultural materials dealing with the notions of spirituality, sanctity, secularity, modernity, authenticity, connectivity, and seen and unseen domains of social life, I examine how religiously constructed images of the world influence the daily actions of people belonging to various Muslim communities in the homeland such as Bahrain, Egypt, and the United Arab Emirates as well as in Muslim diaspora in the United States.[21] These ethnographic accounts are examined and compared with scholarly literature dealing with non-Arab Muslim communities in the Middle East and Southeast Asia so as to highlight the similarities and differences between them (see figure). The connection between spirituality, represented in both Sunni/Sufism and Shi'a esotericism, and certain geographies has been documented in various Muslim communities. Further, I tackle the emergence of the cyber-Islamic environment (Bunt 2003, 2009) caused by globalization and electronic communication promoting connectivity among Muslim communities. This new cyberspace or cybergeography serves as a global Muslim space for generating a global discourse concerning Muslim worldviews and praxis.

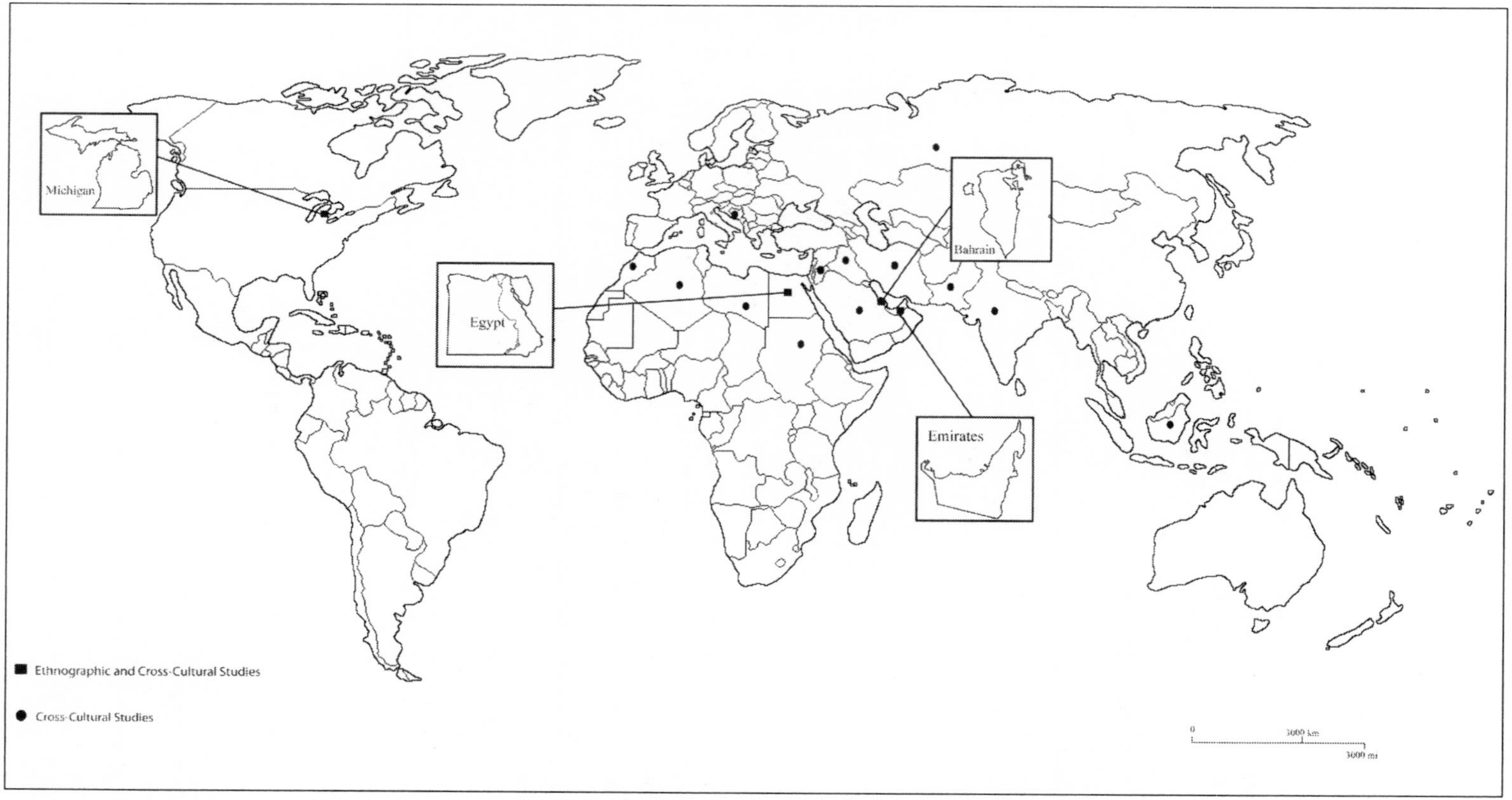

The world: Ethnographic and cross-cultural areas.

Modern and traditional means of education and communication have contributed a great deal to the preservation, continuation, and geographic distribution of Islamic tradition. The divine text as well as the exegesis of Muslim tradition have become accessible through various public and private channels, including, for example, simplified books, mass media (newspapers, radio, television, satellite, websites, and electronic mail), audio recordings, Friday sermons, formal or informal religious sessions in mosques or houses, religious ceremonies, daily prayers, and funerary rituals.

Although Muslims have impacted the worldwide landscape, the research here does not claim to examine the geography of all Muslim countries or map the global Muslim population, but rather seeks to understand the relationship between Muslim cosmologies or worldviews and certain territories of spiritual significance in the sense that both worldview and geography indicate the heterogeneity of Muslims' experiences and identities, notwithstanding certain common features among them. Thus, my point of departure is fundamentally cosmological insofar as cosmology or worldview encompasses a totality of the universe, geography, society, and person. It is not only religious beliefs and behaviors that drive Muslims or other people in their multifarious ways. Human thoughts and actions are shaped by beliefs and values derived from perspectives and orientations of a wide variety (Valk 2009, 4).

METHODOLOGY AND THEORY

Along with library research, archives, government documents, oral history, and textual traditions, I used in-depth interviews, participant observations, and long-term observations to collect data. Ethnographic studies were conducted in more than ten rural and urban communities in the aforementioned countries. Specifically, ethnographic data were drawn from the city of Tanta and the villages of Shibshir al-Hissa and al-Rajdiyya (Egypt);[22] the city of Manama and villages of 'Arad, ad-Dayh, and al-Duraz (Bahrain);[23] the city of al-Ain and the village of Um Ghafa (United Arab Emirates);[24] and Dearborn and Bloomfield Hills (Michigan, United States).[25] Traveling between these countries and working in their academic institutes have kept me in touch with the communities there. The material was obtained through more than fourteen fieldwork studies of varying intervals conducted between 2000 and 2010. These short and long intervals helped me to observe and assimilate differences and similarities between these communities as well as the changes in their social, economic, political, religious, and cultural activities, especially in the past decade, during which there has been an unprecedented spread of globalization.

To delineate the various aspects of social and religious practices in different urban and rural communities, I participated in numerous religious and social gatherings and other acts of devotion in the mosques and other places, including those of Sufi orders (*ṭarīqa*). Further, I visited the shrines of both Sunni and Shi'i local saints[26] and partook in Shi'i rituals (including 'Ashura) and social practices conducted in specific gathering places such as *ma'tams* and *ḥusainiyyas*. In Bahrain and other Shi'a majority countries, the *ma'tam* (also called *ḥusainiyya*), exclusively a Shi'i public domain, consists of a large hall used for social and religious gatherings as well as for special events such as death rituals and marriage ceremonies. For the Shi'a, the *ma'tam* is one of the most significant and equitable means of informal public representation. Both mosques and *ma'tams* function to substantiate beliefs.

The mosques and other religious places of the communities were among key means through which I discussed religious principles, concepts, and values with religious leaders (*shaikhs*) and their followers. In addition to Friday sermons, which are structured and delivered in classical Arabic, there are two kinds of informal religious teachings delivered by both Sunni and Shi'a: one held at the mosque, the other held at a house. Religious teachings, however, are not confined to mosques and *ma'tams* but are sometimes taught at the houses of religious leaders or their followers where religious narratives, texts of the holy Qur'an, and interpretations of scripture are read and commented on. I participated in both kinds of religious sessions. Despite the fact that the number of those who attend religious sessions at houses is less than that of those who attend them at mosques, home sessions are more intimate and longer lasting than mosque and *ma'tam* sessions.

This work, applying the heuristic tools of ethnography and phenomenological inquiry that incorporate objective description and subjective interpretation, examines the inner perspectives and social imaginary of Muslim communities living in different regions. Phenomenology is "the study of human experience and of the ways things present themselves to us in and through such experience" (Sokolowski 2000, 2).[27] An experience is an outcome of people's awareness of what is happening to them. According to Wilhelm Dilthey, "Whatever presents itself as a unit in the flow of time because it has a unitary meaning, is the smallest unit which can be called an experience. Any more comprehensive unit which is made of parts of a life, linked by a common meaning, is also an experience, even when the parts are separated by interrupting events" (Dilthey1976, 210).

Phenomenology is concerned with wholeness, with examining entities from many sides, angles, and perspectives until a unified picture of the essences of a phenomenon or experience is achieved (Moustakas 1994, 58). According to Charles Peirce, "Phenomenology ascertains and studies the kinds of elements universally present in the phenomenon; meaning by the *phenomenon*, whatever is present at any time to the mind in any way" (quoted in Rosensohn 1974, 2; italics in original).[28] Peirce argues, "If belief is taken in the active sense, it may be discovered by the observation of external facts and by inference from the sensation of conviction which usually accompanies it" (Rosensohn 1974, 27). This means that phenomenology searches for meanings from appearances and arrives at essence through intuition and reflection on conscious acts of experience, leading to ideas, concepts, and understandings (Moustakas 1997, 58).

In dealing with Muslim worldviews and belief systems, however, several scholars have categorized them within binary oppositions such as visible (*ẓāhir*)/invisible (*bāṭin*), apparent/hidden, external/internal, and material/spiritual.[29] Although such a dualism has been criticized and refuted as representing a Western dichotomous heritage (Geertz 1960; Gilsenan 1982), my presentation here is that these categories are fused together, stand in relation to one another, and are represented in people's everyday experience rather than in stringent and abstract binary oppositions. Along with phenomenological perspectives, the theoretical construct utilizes Dumont's idea of hierarchical opposition (1986), distinguished from the binary symmetric opposition of Levi-Strauss (1963) in which two opposites have equal status, in that it is asymmetric and refers to the opposition between a whole and a part or level of that whole. Hierarchical opposition necessitates the attachment of a value to one of two opposites. That is, a highly developed idea, to which a value is attached, contradicts and encompasses a lower idea (Dumont 1986, 227). Further, Dumont (1986, 8) has argued that "hierarchy is implicit in various aspects of people's cosmology and social life."

Dumont's method that seeks to delineate hierarchies of relations within a whole or system is akin to the mode of comparison by "proportioning" that means "the relation as to magnitude, degree, quantity, or importance that exists *between portions, parts, a part and the whole, or different things*" (Tambiah 1990, 125–26; italics in original). Rappaport also points to hierarchical levels of meaning in which high-order meaning, based on unification with the other, the cosmos, or the divine, may be experienced "as effects of or as *parts* of, that which they signify" (Rappaport 1999, 72; italics in original).[30] Analysis of ethnographic material shows that hierarchical logic does not negate the distinctive character of a part within the system.

It is imperative to discuss some fundamental components of Islamic worldviews to consider their impact on people's daily interactions. What makes a worldview sacred or secular is not its subject matter, but rather the sources from which its nuclear notions and assumptions are deduced. Fundamentally, Muslim sacred worldviews are drawn from the Qur'an and the Prophet's tradition. Islam has been perceived as encompassing different worldviews and practices within one unifying global entity or overarching Islamic worldview, a holistic view embedded in the Qur'an and the Prophet's tradition.

There is a significant theological dispute between Sunni and Shi'i; however, this dispute is not found in the basic doctrines and practices that include the five pillars of Islam. These pillars, the testimony of the oneness of Allah and Muhammad as His prophet (*ash-shahādatain*), praying five times daily (*ṣalāt*), almsgiving (*zakāt*), fasting during the month of Ramadan, and participating in the pilgrimage to Mecca (*hajj*), must be observed by ordinary Muslims regardless of their sect, occupation, education, or exegeses of religious scholars (*'ulama*). The basic religious doctrine of the unknowable or invisible (*al-ghaib*) upon which the entire Muslim worldview is built and that has a profound impact on Muslims' daily lives can be defined as the belief in Allah, His angels, His books, and His prophets as well as to such concepts as fate and the hereafter.[31]

The invisible encloses what is spiritual, unknowable, imperceptible, and existent withstanding its absence, while the visible comprises material, natural, objective, historical, and geographical components. The concept of invisibility is expressed in what Muslims call "the world of absence" or "invisible world" (*'ālam al-ghaib*) as opposed to "the world of presence" (*ālam ash-shahādah*). There are two kinds of *al-ghaib*. The first kind is the absolute or complete *ghaib* that relates, for instance, to such ultimate events as the end of the world, resurrection, and the nature of souls or spirits. Second is the relative or partial *ghaib*, bestowed by God on prophets and saints (*walīs*), especially in foretelling certain matters related to past and future events.

Theoretically, this book shows that the binary of visible/invisible can be articulated as "in/visible" because what is "visible" indicates, is encompassed by, or is a product of what is "invisible." These categories can be better understood through scrutinizing relations within and among cosmological and conceptual orders in their wholeness as well as through relating their relevance to social and historical circumstances.

In addition to narratives of past events as well as certain nations, people, prophets, miracles, and creatures mentioned in the Qur'an, there are Qur'anic verses describing seen and unseen elements embedded in the universe, ranging from the heavens, stars, sun, earth, mountains, oceans, and rivers to paradise, spirits, angels, and *jinn*.[32] These elements and associated sanctified cosmic images have been fused with local worldviews triggered by Muslim imagination. Focusing on *jinn* as an example demonstrates various forms of local or folk worldviews. Within the context of rural Egyptian worldview, *jinn* encompass certain unseen creatures, good and bad, created of fire. Devils and *'afārīt* or *'ifrits* (sing. *'ifrīt*) also belong to *jinn*. They are believed to be as real as humans. However, rural Egyptians differentiate between devils (including Satan), which are entirely evil, and *'afārīt*, which are not entirely evil in the sense that they do not harm people if the latter do not interrogate them (el-Aswad 2002, 154–55). The same distinction is found among the Javanese,[33] where *setan* and *ḍemit* (which resemble *'ifrits*) are different. Like *'ifrits*, *ḍemit* can bother people if they bother them, but *setan* are completely evil (Geertz 1960, 24–26; Woodward 2010, 36).[34]

Religious meanings are essential factors in maintaining and accentuating the notion of sanctity, especially when it is applied to mundane or nonreligious domains. For instance, statements concerning ecological features as well as economic, political, and social activities may be sanctified by associating them with religious propositions (Rappaport 1979, 1999). When a worldview is sanctified, it becomes as real as the natural world. Within this context, a sanctified worldview helps people cope with social problems as well as with personal suffering by providing explanations and solutions, real or imaginary, that make life comprehensible.

By associating different aspects of life with sacred propositions, religious cosmological order expands its domains to encompass secular or mundane and social cosmologies. Cosmologically, the belief in the sacred or divine "invisibility" (*al-ghaib*) strengthens the visibility of Muslim worldview and identity, challenging the hegemony of so-called global culture. I argue that it is the power of the imagined, internalized, and sanctified invisible within and through which people's daily actions can be understood. Islamic grassroots programs have flourished, giving rise to powerful mass social movements. Religion or religious cosmology is far more complex than what the mainstream media suggest (Eickelman and Anderson 2003). This complexity is related to a large extent to the reemergence of religious cosmology as an important player in the public arena.

ABOUT THE BOOK

Chapter 1, "Muslim Worldviews: Unity and Diversity," delineates the relationship between translocal or universal Islamic worldview and local variants of Muslim worldviews. The contemporary Muslim world is characterized by cultural, ethnic, and ideological diversity. It can be assumed that Muslims share a family of worldviews that relies on shared principles, but they interpret and employ the entailments of these principles in diverse manners.

Socioculturally, the main concern of this chapter is to demonstrate how ordinary people belonging to different communities (rural and urban) and sects (Sunni and Shi'a) within and between different countries understand and develop their worldviews and traditions. Although Muslim worldviews share some common features (based on the Qur'an and the tradition of the Prophet Muhammad), they are different and drawn from various sources, as is the case among the Sunni and Shi'a, for example.

The underlying principles of the popular understandings of Sunni Muslim worldview as comprehended and enacted by Egyptian and Emirati people are treated in some detail in chapter 2 ("The Worldview of the Sunni"). The essential thesis here is that Sunni Muslims in such geographically, demographically, economically, and politically different societies as Egypt and the United Arab Emirates are deeply influenced by an overarching Islamic worldview, notwithstanding the differences in the folk exegeses of certain elements of Sunni worldview. The chapter argues that the economic disparity between Egypt and the UAE is mirrored in the dissimilarity of some significant constituents of their worldviews or cosmologies as presented in the different interpretations offered by individuals belonging to these countries.

The connection between the unseen/theoretical or doctrinal and the seen/social levels of worldview is addressed in chapter 3 ("The Esoteric Worldview of the

Shi'a"). The chapter deals with the worldview of the Shi'a of Bahrain, an Arab Gulf country with a Shi'a majority. Comparative material from Shi'i communities in Iran and Pakistan that highlights the esoteric dimensions of religious experience of Bahraini Shi'a is provided. Further, the chapter focuses on the social side of the Shi'i worldview, illustrating the impact of religious practices on the visible sociopolitical lives of Bahraini Shi'a. The narrative shows how the Shi'a manipulate observable ways of innovatively enacting and embodying their esoteric beliefs as articulated in iconography, art displays, folk dramas, consecrated places, religious discourses, and calendrical rituals, including 'Ashura.[35]

The relationship between Sufi beliefs and practices in local contexts and in broader national or global (Muslim) worldviews is considered in chapter 4 ("The Mystic Worldview of Sufism"). The chapter, refuting the ideological dichotomy between scriptural or orthodox and mystical forms of Muslim experience, demonstrates the complex interplay between expressions of Sufi belief in the local setting and the most common religious worldviews aiming to attain deeper understanding of Islam. The chapter discusses the impact of regional Sufi orders (such as Ahmadiyya and Shinnawiyya) and related saint cults on the inhabitation and perpetuation of geography and local landscape of Egypt's delta, among other places. It examines the relationship between the worldviews of the adherents of Sufi orders concerning the spiritual world and the world of kin and geography. Also, it discusses the shift from biological genealogy, narrow and vertical in nature, into a spiritual genealogy, broader and horizontal in nature. Sufism is socially and ethically relevant because it emphasizes the use of spiritual diplomacy, negotiation, and tolerance in dealing with social problems.

Chapter 5 ("Muslim Worldviews, Imagination, and the Dream World") explicates the significance of dreams to both Sunni and Shi'i Muslims in various places, including Egypt and Bahrain. It focuses on the place of dreams in Muslims' worldview with their seen and unseen dimensions. It also demonstrates the sociocultural conditions that bring about moral and social support to certain dreams for constructing and reconstructing reality. The role of imagination and dreams in accentuating Muslim beliefs and practices is addressed. There is a mutual substantiation between the dream world and Muslim worldview in the sense that certain dream visions are justified or sanctified by religious worldviews, while some significant aspects of worldviews, especially those related to invisible domains, are validated and substantiated by dreams.

Chapter 6 ("Multiple Worldviews and Multiple Identities of the Muslim Diaspora") expounds the nature of Muslim worldviews and identities (of both Sunni and Shi'a) in American society through an exploration of discourses and practices related to traveling, migration, and movement at global and local levels. It addresses various experiences of Muslims living in the communities of Bloomfield Hills and Dearborn, in metropolitan Detroit, Michigan, with a particular emphasis on personal narratives of both men and women of different ages and socioeconomic backgrounds.

Muslim migrants or Muslim minorities experience profound changes in their outlook and orientation as they move from the state of belonging to the homeland to that of belonging to the new land, generating a unique sense of hybrid or multiple identities. In addition, the chapter tackles the geography of Muslim cyberspace, demonstrating the role of cybercirculations, including Internet and cyberforums, in both maintaining and changing certain elements of Muslims' worldviews and daily lives from traditional to modern forms.

The main findings of the book, focusing on meanings and practices related to Muslims' local and global patterns of worldviews or cosmological paradigms in different communities in the homeland and diaspora, are considered in the conclusion. There are multiple perceived and imaginary worlds from which possible worldviews emerge. From a cross-cultural perspective, the discussion tackles the similarities and differences between Muslim worldviews. The movement between local and global spheres has played a major role in creating a particular sense of Muslim immigrants' cosmology and identity attached to both local and global communities.

Overall, this book examines to what extent Muslim cosmologies cope with or resist cultural hegemony and globalization. It shows how these cosmologies provide better images of Muslims, enabling them to overcome overwhelming negative images or stereotypes. In the past two decades, along with the advent of globalization, there has been a tremendous change among Muslims, in general, and Muslim immigrants in the United States, in particular, manifested in the transition from static to dynamic views of space and time as well as from a limited number of alternatives to unlimited options and open possibilities. The future of Muslim cosmologies is not a matter of purely local or regional concern but is bound up with the future of tradition in Islam as a whole.

1

Muslim Worldviews

Unity and Diversity

Worldviews are assumptions concerning the structure of the universe. They include the society as well as the human and nonhuman beings and forces, both visible and invisible, that constitute the integrated parts of the universe or cosmos (el-Aswad 2002, 2). Worldview, denoting both the things individuals believe in as well as the act of believing, concerns people's images of the way things are (Geertz 1973, 45, 89). It influences the attitudes people have toward nature, space, time, and self and is a holistic conceptualization of how the world is shaped and ordered. As such, worldview, based on assumptions that human thought is both social and public, can be used as a hermeneutic and analytical construct aimed at better understanding human actions.

Overarching Muslim worldviews typify the majority of Muslims, whose worldwide population is more than 1.5 billion.[1] Although Muslim worldviews share common features based on the Qur'an (the Word of Allah), revelation (*waḥy*), and the tradition (Hadith and praxis) of the Prophet Muhammad, they are different and drawn from various sources.[2] To delineate the relationship between universal or translocal Islamic worldviews and local variants of Muslim ethnocosmologies, this chapter focuses on how ordinary people belonging to different communities or sects and different Sufi orders within and between different countries understand and develop their cosmologies and traditions while adhering to common and shared worldviews. The information in this chapter is based on ethnographic inquires in three Arab countries, Egypt, Bahrain, and the United Arab Emirates, in addition to scholarly literature dealing with other Muslim societies.

Islam comprises various sects of which the two largest are the Sunni and the Shi'a. The Sunni, derived from the Arabic word "Sunnah," meaning the tradition of the Prophet Muhammad, is the largest branch of Islam, constituting 90 percent of the religion's followers stretching from Indonesia to Morocco.[3] The Shi'a are the second-largest denomination of Islam[4] and include those whose forebearers supported 'Ali ibn Abi Talib, cousin and son-in-law of the Prophet, who was to be the fourth caliph but was killed in AD 661.[5] Shi'a Muslims are divided into various divisions (the Twelvers, Ismaili, Zaydi, Druz, Nizari, and Bohara among others), of which three are dominant. The Twelvers (Ithna 'ashariyya)[6] is the largest and most influential. The other two predominant Shi'a factions are the Ismailis and the Zaydis, who dispute the Twelver lineage of imams and their beliefs.[7] Essentially, the Shi'a tend to focus on the biological genealogy of imams tracing the line to the Prophet through Fatima (the Prophet's daughter) and 'Ali (the Prophet's cousin and husband of Fatima). The Twelvers of the Bahraini Shi'a are the focus of this chapter.

Differences in religious views give rise to local dissimilarities of actions and performances found among relatively similar cultures. In other words, these religious views, mediated through broad worldviews, yield differing sociocultural frameworks. The interaction between Islamic doctrines and local traditional beliefs is a recognized attribute of Muslim communities. An example of these dissimilarities and the contrast between Sunni and Shi'i worldviews is represented, respectively, in their differing emphases on individualistic/independent versus emulation/dependent and Imamate conceptions of faith. While both Sunni and Shi'a emphasize that the relationship between humans and God is direct or without any sort of mediation, the Shi'i doctrine of Imamate (spiritual leadership) and related practices of emulation, *taqlīd* (Lawson 2005, 526–27),[8] not observed by the Sunnis, constitute major differences between them. These differences are reflected in practices and attitudes toward charity, almsgiving, marriage, religious rituals, regional conflict, welfare policy, and other aspects of economic and social life that exist between and within local Muslim communities.

This chapter discusses the impact of imagined worldview, with its visible and invisible realms, on the daily practices of Muslims in various countries with specific focus on Egypt and Bahrain because of their respective Sunni and Shi'i majorities. More specifically, it addresses both the unity and diversity of Muslim worldviews by concentrating on five paradigms. First is the doctrinal paradigm, where the focus is placed on the way Muslims, in theory and practice, deal with the doctrine of the unity or oneness (*tawḥīd*) of God. Second is the communal paradigm, showing the way Muslims relate to each other through the encompassing worldview of the *ummah*, or universal Muslim community. Third is the ontological paradigm, explicating how the world is constructed and how its elements are categorized within Muslim frameworks. Fourth is the spatial paradigm, dealing with sacred geographies and sanctified places with which Muslims identify themselves. Fifth is the temporal or calendrical paradigm, which regulates Muslims' discursive and nondiscursive actions, including rituals, prayers, and other practices.

THE DOCTRINAL PARADIGM

Muslim doctrinal paradigm concerns the unity of God. Various interpretations of Islamic tradition refer to the balanced and perfect order of the natural world as a sign of the oneness, omniscience, and majesty of Allah (Burkhalter 1985, 229). The quintessential religious faith or belief concerning the oneness of God, who created and transcends the universe, is highly emphasized and enacted by Muslims in various communities. Except for the religious scholars, or *'ulama*, most of the ordinary Muslims I interviewed were not well versed in Islamic theology; rather, they adhered to an accepted system of beliefs and enacted them in their daily practices. This characteristic fits the strategy of this study, which deals with worldviews not in their theoretical forms but in their everyday expressions. In an interview, after I asked him to define himself beyond his nationality, a young Egyptian Sunni man said, "I am a Muslim, and this is enough for me." Likewise, I addressed the same question to a young Bahraini Shi'i man who recounted, "I am a Muslim and I am blessed to have Islam as my religion." In both cases, it seems there was no indication of sectarian identification notwithstanding the differences I observed later.

The Arabic word "Islam," meaning both submission to Allah and the maintenance of peaceful relationships with people, is a core concept in Muslim identities and worldviews. The submission to Allah and Islam is embodied in the Muslim utterance of the two testimonies (*ash-shahādatain*) that there is no God but Allah and that Muhammad is His Messenger (*lā ilāha illā Allah, Muhammad rasūl Allah*), which is a phrase commonly used in practices of worship and when adhering to religious, moral, and social codes, and which reflects the firm belief in the Qur'an as the Word revealed by Allah. It is a phrase commonly used in contexts of social and mundane discourses or secular daily interactions, including disputes, debates, economic transactions, tragic events, sorrow, travel, and so forth. To say "there is no God but Allah and Muhammad is the Prophet of Allah" is not merely to confirm a religious testimony (*shahāda*), which is the first doctrinal condition for a person to be a Muslim, but to act and establish a relationship with God as well as to entrust or commit oneself to a pattern of life that captures both this world and the other world diligently and seriously.

An Egyptian interviewee, for instance, recounted that when he traveled or even made a phone call he used the phrase "*lā ilāha illā Allah*" to the person with whom he was engaged, expecting him or her to respond by saying, "Mohammad is the Messenger [*rasūl*, or Prophet] of Allah." The reverence with which Muslims hold their beliefs also explains their practice of whispering the *shahāda* in the ears of both newly born and dying individuals. Further, it is not uncommon to hear Muslims say that Muhammad is the "master of the two worlds" (*Sayyid al-kaunain*), with reference to seen and unseen dimensions of existence. Similar phrases of veneration have been used in comparable social contexts by Muslims belonging to different societies. One day, for example, on a visit to a Shi'i friend in the village of Shahrakkan in Bahrain, I heard the phrase "*qudrat qādir*" used with reference to a beautifully risen cake that was offered to me out of hospitality. I was puzzled because I knew the meaning of that phrase was "the divine power of God." To put an end to my confusion I asked my friend if the cake was actually called "*qudrat qādir*." He affirmed this, saying, "Yes, because only Allah can make it rise in such a nice way."[9]

Islam holds that human beings, endowed with the ability to choose between right and wrong, need guidance, *hidāya*. God has provided that guidance through the Qur'an and the *Sunna*, or tradition of the Prophet. Both Sunni and Shi'i Muslims follow the Qur'an and Prophet's tradition but differ in their worldviews regarding the religious implications of Muslim leadership (as represented in the concept of *imām*).[10] For both Sunni and Shi'i Muslims, the Arabic word *imām* means "leader" with reference to any person who leads others in prayer. However, the concept *imām* is used differently by the two groups. For the Sunni, the *imām*, synonymous with the word "caliph," is the leader of an Islamic community as well as the person maintaining the *shari'a* (Islamic law). "Imam" is also used by the Sunni as a formal title, like "the Grand Imam of al-Azhar," or as an honorific title, such as Imam Shafi'ī and Imam Mālik, founders of two of the four Sunni schools of law. For the Shi'a who believe in the Twelve Imams, the term "Imam" is used exclusively to refer to one of the twelve successors of the Prophet Muhammad (Sachedina 1981; al-Tabataba'i 1977).

While both Sunni and Shi'a believe in the oneness of God (*tawḥīd*) and that Muhammad is the messenger of God, the Shi'a emphasize the Imamate or *imāmah* of 'Ali who is *walī* (friend) of God.[11] The phrase "'I witness that 'Ali is *walī* Allah" (*ashahadu anna 'Alian walī Allah*) is used in the Islamic Shi'i call for prayer (*adhān*) but not in Islamic Sunni *adhān*.[12] While attending a funeral among the Shi'a of Bahrain (figure 1.1), I heard a *shaikh*, addressing his speech to the dead person buried in the grave, say, "O slave of God, if the two angels of the grave ask you about your God, say 'Allah,' if they ask you about your prophet, say 'Mohammad,' if they ask you about your religion, say 'Islam,' if they ask you about your Imam, say "Ali and his eleven infallible sons 'Imams.'" Then he mentioned the name of each Imam. On mentioning the name of the twelfth or hidden Imam, al-Mahdi, the *shaikh* raised his right hand above his head as a bodily sign of reverence.

In brief, Shi'i Muslims believe in the doctrine of Imamate (spiritual leadership or *walāyah*) of the Twelve Imams, including the hidden Imam (al-Mahdi) and his occultation (*ghaiba*), and the related concepts of dissimulation (*taqiyya*) and emulation (*taqlīd*).[13] Both Sunni and Shi'a believe in the Mahdi as the redeemer or savior who is expected to reappear and restore justice before the Day of Resurrection or Judgment (*yaum al-qiyāmah*). However, the Shi'a Muslims accept traditions from their own Imams as being of spiritual and divine inspiration (Amir-Moezzi 2011, 18). The majority of Sunni Muslims I interviewed did not know or understand the concept of emulation (*taqlīd*). In contrast, it is

Figure 1.1. Shi'i cemetery, Bahrain (left: Mr. al-Khal; right: el-Sayed el-Aswad).

extremely important for the Shi'a to have and follow a cleric or religious scholar or *marja'iyya* (*'ālim*, *shaikh*, or *marja'* [pl. *marāji'*]). The *shaikhs* and *marāji'* are believed to mediate hierarchically between the hidden Imam and the ordinary Shi'a, providing them with necessary advice (Lawson 2005, 526).

For all Muslims, *shaikhs* are chosen and identified on the basis of their competence in religious knowledge, whether achieved through formal education (*al-Azhar* for the Sunni and *Ja'fari* for the Shi'a) or through self-education.[14] For the Sunni, there is no particular dress or symbol, except for their religious knowledge, that distinguishes informal *shaikhs* from other people. However, formal Sunni *shaikhs* wear cloaks and turban, *'umāmah*, a red fez wrapped with a white sheet. Within the Bahraini context, for example, Shi'i people further differentiate between *Sayyid* and *shaikh* or *'ālim*. As opposed to the *shaikh* who is a person of religious learning, a *Sayyid* is a descendant of the Prophet's family (*ahl al-bait*), wearing a black turban, especially when certified in religious knowledge (el-Aswad 2010c). The word *Sayyid* (fem. *Sayyida*), used by the Shi'a as a mark or title for a person belonging to the Prophet's family, is often confused with the common proper name of a man, Sayyid, who is not descendant of the Prophet's family. Because of my name, el-Sayed (Sayyid), I was frequently asked by Shi'i persons whether I was related to the category of *Sayyid* (as being related to the Prophet's family), and my answer was "no," which generated some humorous conversation.

A *shaikh* or *marja'* often makes decisions when a Shi'i person has special concerns related to religious, social, economic, and even political issues.[15] Such a concept is unknown among the Sunnis. Even for the Sunni Sufis, the role of the *shaikh* is to lead the student into the Sufi path or the Prophet's presence; once the disciple has established contact with the Prophet, he has no further need of his *shaikh* (Hoffman-Ladd 1992, 621). A *marja'* has a book (or books) (*risālah*) and representatives in various locations. A Shi'i person can check the book of his/her *marja'* to find an answer for a specific inquiry. If the book does not have the answer, the person then consults with the nearest representative in person or via regular mail or e-mail, asking for advice. Some *shaikhs* or *marāji'* have their own websites to facilitate connectivity with their devotees.

The oneness of God, along with the unity or oneness of existence, is the core idea of Sufism and mystic thought.[16] For Sufi Orders (*ṭuruq*), such as the al-Ahmadiyya and Shinnawiyya in Egypt, Naqshbandiyya in central Asia or worldwide (Buehler 1998; Weismann 2007), as well as others in Bosnia, Libya, Indonesia,[17] and the Sudan (Karrar 1992), Sufi leaders are believed to seek to achieve mystical connection with the universe as well as unification with God through love, humility, and rational discourse.[18] Surveys of Islam and Muslim life in the Balkans in general and in Bosnia Herzegovina in particular regularly stress the impact of Sufism on Bosnian Islam, where there is belief that divinity somehow lies within people. Sunni Muslims in Bosnia Herzegovina practice Islam with an apparent Sufi orientation, not detached from everyday activities, where Sufi traditions are parts of their lives (Raudvere 2008, 53).

THE COMMUNAL PARADIGM

In their social life people generate strategies to understand and reconcile, in one unified picture or paradigm, the multiplicity of possible meanings related to cultural events. Communal worldview is centered on a vision that Muslim societies are united, whether actually, ideally, or virtually, in one universal community (*ummah*). The Arabic word *ummah*, derived from *umm*, which means "mother," is a term used by Muslims to denote the worldwide or universally unified community of the faithful that goes beyond a mere geographical community or nation. The *ummah* constitutes a significant component of the worldview or framework through which Muslims identify themselves and view the world or other people with whom they interact. The *ummah*, a transregional communal identity, is a binding element of individual Muslims in various geographic locations. Put differently, regardless of their ethnic, cultural, or national backgrounds, Muslim people perceive themselves as being fully part of the *ummah* or Muslim community.

In an interview with Saqr, an Emirati businessman leading a local charity organization, discussing the concept of *ummah* as related to his activities, he recounted, "We, the Muslims, are *ummah wāḥida* and we did not invent it. It is mentioned in the Qur'an." As if he were prepared to respond, he recited a verse from the Qur'an, "You [Muslims] are the best community *ummah* evolved for Mankind, commanding what is righteous [*ma'rūf*] and forbidding what is wrong [*munkar*]."[19] Also, Saqr emphasized his thesis that despite the differences between diverse peoples (*shu'ūb*) and tribes (*qabā'il*), with reference to another Qur'anic verse,[20] the Muslim world is still unified in terms of religious, social, ethical, temporal (past, present, and future), and spatial (global) domains. This sense of Muslim communal identity or *ummah* is also symbolized and enacted physically and spiritually in the *hajj* pilgrimage to the Ka'ba, in Mecca, creating a unique collective sentiment that goes beyond any economic, political, ethnic, racial, or sectarian division.

Muslim community is a dynamic concept unifying multiethnic, multicultural, and pluralist communities within an overarching Muslim worldview that advocates peace (*salām*), dignity, and human rights of Muslims and non-Muslims. However, these idealistic features, emphasizing not ethnocentric views but ethical and dialogic aspects, render the *ummah* a utopian community. It is common to hear Muslims in their daily discourses and activities call, "O people who declare 'there is no God but Allah'" (*Yā ummat lā ihaha illa Allah*), for help or warn their peers of the negative consequences of misconduct or social conflict. I heard this phrase used in various contexts when Muslim communities or countries were on hostile terms with each other, as was the case with the Iraq-Iran war in the 1980s, the Iraqi invasion of Kuwait in the 1990s, and recently with the internal conflict in Libya since 2010.

Within the larger Muslim *ummah* there are noticeable differences among particular Muslim communities. Some of these particular communities include Sufi orders such as Ahmadiyya, Shadhiliyya, Shinnawiyya, and Tijaniyya, among others, that endow people with certain identities that can be recognized locally, regionally, and globally throughout the Islamic world.[21] The networks of these Sufi orders, notwithstanding the distinctive features of each one, provide a significant foundational bond for the Islamic world. Others include Shi'i communities oriented toward solidarity based on the concept of precautionary dissimulation (*taqiyya*) through which the Shi'a in action with their Imams aim to secure the safety of the individual and the community against outside threats or an unfriendly majority (Clarke 2005, 47). According to Shi'i worldviews, the entire Shi'i community, through *taqiyya*, provides means for its religious, social, and political survival in anticipation of the final return of the Imam, when the *taqiyya* will come to an end (Clarke 2005, 52).

Technological and communication advancements have made the world a more connected and interdependent global village. Increases and changes in transcommunication, global flows of culture, capital, and political power have recently and concurrently changed certain perceptions of the Muslim *ummah* as well as certain modes of social life in the Muslim world and elsewhere. In this globalized world, the primary instruments of Muslim community are social-cyber networks of regular people, scholars, and students who interact across the vast territorial reaches of the Islamic world, operating in transnational zones of shared discourses. I take social-cyber networks to mean both public and private (actual and virtual) mediums that establish the religious and social bonds necessary for maintaining basic community relations. As cultural mediums, social-cyber networks encompass cultural, personal or private, and public aspects and go beyond instantaneous tangible practices or rituals to include continuous reciprocity of material and immaterial symbolic codes between people. Sociologically, social-cyber networks strengthen social ties and facilitate communication for maintaining Islamic communities at both local and global levels (el-Aswad 2004a, 2007b).

The collective identity of the Muslim *ummah* is depicted in a new, modern, digital, or virtual *ummah*, represented in an imagined community in cyberspace.[22] Global religious networks inspire competing visions of community (Uddin 2006, 157). There are a large number of social and religious websites called *Ummah* or Muslim forums (*muntadayat*) that stem not only from official departments, formal institutions, or business organizations but also from informal groups or individuals constituting what can be called Muslim cyber-grassroots. These Muslim forums constitute unique dialectic channels between the global and the local or the universal and the particular. In this context, social and religious *muntadayat* provide the participants or viewers with the means to engage with Muslim culture in general with social implication in particular. Traditional ideas of what is religiously or legally accepted (*ḥalāl*) or forbidden (*ḥarām*), food, marriage, kinship, friendship, among other things, are addressed in new fashions through the proximity created by cyberspace. Most of these forums advocate the unity of the Muslim *ummah* recognizing at the same time the diversity of Muslim communities. For example, the basic goal of a website named "Iqra: A Voice of Muslim Ummah" is to "present Islam as a global way of life, not merely a ritual of regional worship practices." It also states, "Unity of the Ummah is stressed and is our main focus. This is not to be done by belittling the values of diversity. Diversity in lawful ways is encouraged."[23]

In brief, Muslims have become interested in faraway countries and events, enticed by the proximity provided by advanced means of communication, mass media, and expedient transportation. This novel experience has strengthened Muslims' identity and provided them with a unique view that has given them a positive and constructive community image.

THE ONTOLOGICAL PARADIGM

Despite the fact that this book deals mainly with ordinary Muslims' worldviews concerning the universe and ontological reality, it is hard to ignore the fact that cosmology is among the central themes of the Qur'an.[24] However, this does not mean I rely on the analysis of Muslim textual traditions including Qur'anic exegeses (*tafsīr*). Textual traditions express the thought of Muslim intellectuals or authors in certain periods of history but do not explain the exceptionally rich and diversified worldviews of everyday Muslims. Very little is known not only about the worldviews of ordinary Muslims, but also about the impact of these worldviews on their daily lives.

An adequate conceptualization of the world and people's place in it is founded, not on the analysis of specific concepts,[25] but on an "adequate inquiry of people's ontological views" (Heil 2003, 3). The construct of the world implies the idea of the "structure of religious consciousness," which states nothing at all about things as they really are but only about how individuals or religious persons perceive them to be (Cox 1996, 147). Within this perspective, Muslims look at the world not as a machine or scientific paradigm, but as a living reality or lively cosmos.

Ontologically, there are hierarchically ordered levels of reality or manifold worlds such as the world of spirits (*'ālam ar-rūḥ*), the world of angels (*'ālam al-mlā'ka*), the world of *jinn* (*'ālam al-jinn*),[26] the world of human beings (*'ālam al-ins*), and the other world (*'ālam al-ākhira*) including eschatology (*'ālam al-barzakh*) and the Day of Judgment. All entities and creatures, unseen and seen, including humans, angels, and *jinn* as well as the visible world of nature with its heavens, sun, moon, stars, and earth are created, maintained, and balanced by Allah. The Sunni and Shi'a Muslims I interviewed in Egypt, Bahrain, and the Emirates believe that heaven is an infinitely inhabited place in which God, the Creator, along with created entities such angels and bearers of the Throne (*ḥamalat al-'arsh*) exist, but belong to the invisible and incomprehensible world (*'ālam al-ghaib*). Paradise and hell are located both within and beyond the heavens. The belief in "inhabiting the world" is not confined to a specific territory; rather it extends to include this entirety.

Except for humans who have the choice to be or not to be Muslim, the entire physical world or universe surrenders to and praises God, a feature rendering it from Muslims' perspectives an *Islamic* entity. Muslims view the Ka'ba, in Mecca,[27] as the key feature that symbolically, ritually, and substantially makes the entire cosmos *Muslim* because of the physical, spiritual, and human dimensions it entails. The Ka'ba is an inseparable component of Muslims' ontological and existential worldviews and is a symbol of the real unity of all Muslim communities. It is considered the focal point for Muslims dispersed all over the world. The Ka'ba is known as the House of God (*Bait Allah*) or sanctuary toward which Muslims turn in prayer five times every day, and around which they circulate during the pilgrimage (*hajj*). Muslims often refer to the "divinely inhabited house" (*al-bait al-ma'mūr*), an invisible cosmic center located above the Ka'ba. In this sacred cosmic house, such unseen entities and forces as angels, spirits, and divine grace (*baraka*) are believed to exist (figure 1.2).

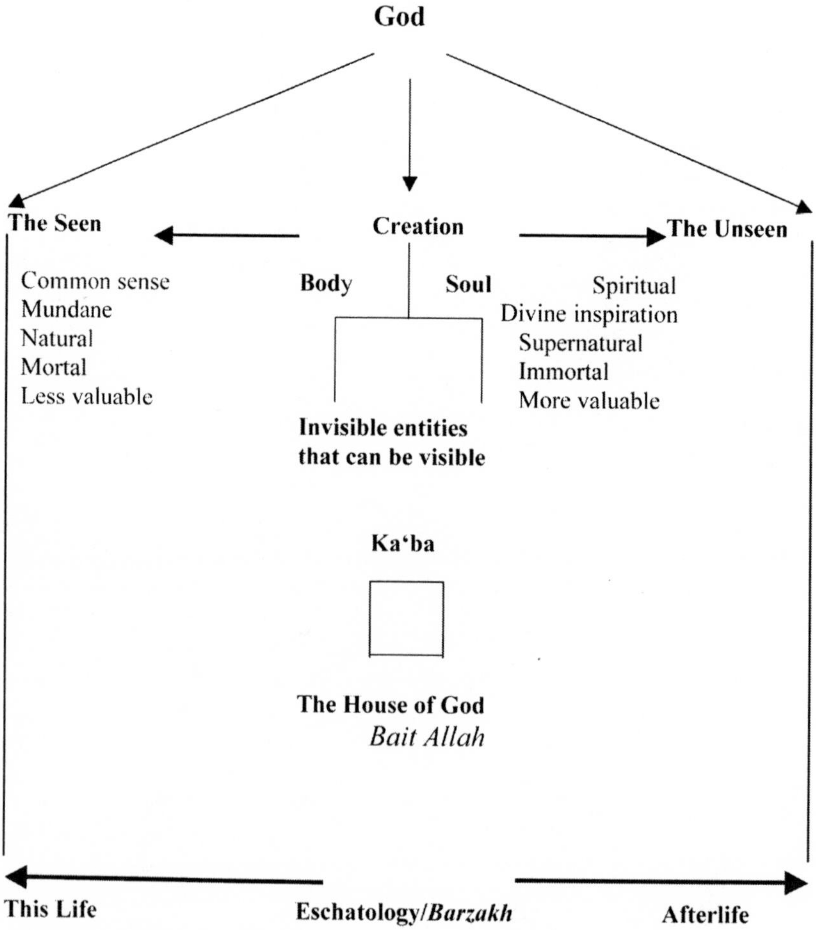

Figure 1.2. Muslims' ontology or worldview with its seen and unseen domains.

The universe encompasses positive and negative features related to specific unseen beings and forces. Positive attributes, for example, are associated with angels, grace or blessing (*baraka*), cosmic sustenance or livelihood (*ar-rizq*), and wonders (*karāmāt*) made by those who are believed to possess hidden-constructive knowledge (religion), while negative attributes are associated with devils, envy (*ḥasad*), and hidden-destructive knowledge, magic (*siḥr*).[28] These positive and negative attributes of cosmic forces are not separate or detached from Muslims' everyday lives.

Muslims, in various countries including Egypt, the UAE, and Bahrain, for instance, are concerned with the notion of social, economic, and divine cover (*as-satr*) as related to the scheme of the cosmological paradigm of livelihood or source of revenue (*ar-rizq*), which belongs to the unseen world (*'ālam al-ghaib*) and through which the occurrences of unexpected fortunes can be explained. It is not uncommon to hear a person saying "this matter belongs to the realm of the unknown" (*fī 'ilm al-ghaib*) to express his belief that the continuity of his economic resources is determined by a higher power or God. This cosmic potential asserts the assumption that a livelihood is fundamental to cosmic structure. This statement, however, is not fatalistic, but rather signifies the existence of a divine omnipotent power that dominates the universe through mercy (*raḥmah*) and goes beyond human understanding. One argues here that heavenly or divine coverage or shelter might not have a place in the paradigm of globalism and secularism, but it occupies a central position in the Muslim worldview.

This feature of invisibility is applicable to humans as reflected in the Shi'i worldview of disappearance or occultation (*ghaiba*) and expected reappearance of Imam al-Mahdi, a cosmic figure believed to be alive though unseen, which is not merely a belief, but rather an ontological entity linked to the structure of the universe.[29] However, the manipulation of the concept of invisibility (*ghaib*) differs from culture to culture. In Malaysia, for example, people show interest in the invisible world. They seek to become invisible through special training called *silat ghaib*, involving the manipulation of *jinn* and the souls of the dead.[30]

The beliefs in the vital spiritual essence associated with all beings (*semangat*) including humans and spirits (*hantu*) in rural Malay society are part of belief systems derived from indigenous, animistic, Hindu, and Muslim worldviews. However, in fulfilling the pragmatic needs of everyday life, these beliefs and related practices, especially in folk healing, are often framed in Islamic terms so as to be convincingly accepted (bin Osman 1972, 220–22). Unlike *semangat*, embodied in humans, spirits (*hantu*) are disembodied beings capable of crossing the boundaries between the material and supernatural worlds. These two categories of spirits, embodied and disembodied, reflect inside/outside, interior/exterior, and social/spatial divides (Ong 1988, 30).

Despite the multiplicity of Muslim worldviews, the most common perspective Muslims have is that which perceives the universe as a place of visible and invisible spheres. These domains entail two kinds of knowledge. One is associated with the knowledge of this world (*dunyā*) or everyday observation (*ash-shahādah*) and directly related to mundane and secular activities concerning what is apparent (*ẓāhir*) or visible (*manẓūr*); the other, with the knowledge of the inner esoteric realm (*bāṭin* or *mastūr*) or divine invisible world (*'ālam al-ghaib*). Though the visible and invisible compose two different worlds and are associated with different worldviews, they form a unity, which is the universe itself. This is clearly expressed by Muslims, ordinary and scholars, in their statement that Islam is concerned simultaneously with the visible and the invisible, or *dunyā wa dīn*, respectively, mundane/secular and sacred/religious lives.[31]

However, within this hierarchical unity the invisible that encompasses sacred reality is the most significant, bestowing meaning to the visible or secular world. The invisible, open to all possibilities, is not confined to social or political borders but, rather, transcendent of them. Allah is the ultimate *Ghaib*, invisible, unseen and unknowable divinity, bestowing unity to seemingly diversified worlds as expressed in the Qur'anic verse, "Say: O Allah the Creator of the heavens and the earth, who has the knowledge of the invisible and the visible!" (*'ālim al-ghaib wa ash-shahādah*) (Qur'an 39:46).[32]

THE SPATIAL PARADIGM

Behind the level of empirical, spatial, or geographical reality is cultural reality, and behind that is worldview. Cultures organize themselves spatially (Bonnemaison 2005, 83) wherein there exists a continuous dialectic between geographical settings and worldviews. For Muslims, the universe is conceptually ordered in spatial and temporal terms and imbued with values of superiority and inferiority, the sacred and profane, and benevolence and malevolence. Certain significant aspects of worldviews are bound to certain geographies, landscapes, or places. The spatial or geographic paradigm is rendered extremely powerful in unifying Muslims when their sacred territories or countries are occupied, abused, or humiliated by aggressive policies or foreign forces.

For all Muslims, there are certain sacred and universally unifying places on earth. Mecca, the city in which the Ka'ba (*qibla*), the sacred sanctuary and pilgrimage shrine of Muslims, is located, is considered the holiest place on earth. More specifically, the Ka'ba is surrounded by the courtyard of al-Masjid al-Ḥarām, the greatest and most sacred of mosques. All Muslims, wherever they are on earth, pray five times a day in the direction of the Ka'ba. During the Muslim month of Dhu al-Hijja a pilgrimage to Mecca or Ka'ba, one of the Five Pillars of the faith, is required of every Muslim who can afford it.[33] On their way to the Ka'ba, from near or far, pilgrims are in the sacred state of *iḥrām*, a necessary spiritual and physical condition for their pilgrimage and *'umrah* (the visitation or minor pilgrimage). Pilgrims from various communities are apt to return with containers full of the blessed water of *zamzam* to be given as gifts to those they love. Also, some Muslims preserve containers of *zamzam* water to be used for the washing of their corpse when they die. *Zamzam* water, believed to be divinely blessed, is an indexical substance referring to the consecrated place associated with sacred history and sanctified narration.

Medina (Yathrib), to which Muhammad migrated when he was forced to depart Mecca, is known as the City of the Prophet and is considered the second-holiest site in Islam. Both Mecca and Medina are located in the desert of the Arabian Peninsula. Muslims have developed a conceptual distinction that attributes a higher value to the desert in spite of the fact that it is economically less significant than the fertile land. The desert, associated with sanctity, is a place believed to be invested with invisible, powerful beings and forces. The Arabic word used to describe this view of the desert is *al-jabal* (the mountain), which encompasses meanings of highness, strength, toughness, masculinity, and steadfastness. Desert attributes of dryness, cleanliness, and openness fit the image Muslims have about sacred places (sanctified by Qur'anic verses),[34] devoid of mundane and material attraction.

The third-most sacred city for Muslims is Jerusalem (Al-Quds), which was the first place *(qibla)* toward which Muslims turned for prayer before the Ka'ba in Mecca. The two most important Muslim sites in Jerusalem are the Dome of the Rock (Qubbat aṣ-Ṣakhrah) and the Al-Aqsa Mosque.

According to the sacred Muslim narration of the Nocturnal Journey and Ascent of the Prophet *(al-Isrā' wa al-mi'rāj)*,[35] on the night of the twenty-seventh of the Arabic month of Rajab (before the Hijra, or the Prophet's migration from Mecca to Medina, which occurred in the first year of the Muslim calendar), the Prophet Muhammad mounted *al-burāq*[36] and miraculously traveled from al-Masjid al-Ḥarām, the sacred mosque in Mecca, to the Al-Aqsa Mosque, the farthest mosque in Jerusalem, where he led all prophets in collective prayer. Then, accompanied by the archangel Jibril (Gabriel), he ascended to the highest point of the seventh heaven, passing through all the heavens, and then turned back to his place in Mecca. Only the Prophet was allowed to reach this highest point known as *sidrat al-muntaha*, close to the Gardens of the Abode *(jannat al-ma'wa)*. During this heavenly journey, God assigned the five daily prayers to all Muslims. Some Muslim commentators interpret the Prophet's ascension to heaven (the *mi'rāj*) literally, while others view it as a vision (Ibn Hisham 1978, 3–9; Ibn Kathir 1937, 2–24; Younis 1967, 5–9). The sanctified narrative, accentuating the cosmic significance of the Prophet, indicates that the sacred geography eradicates what apparently seems to be divided geography. The Prophet's miraculous travel, suspending the natural laws of time and space, from Mecca to Jerusalem and back, spatially horizontal in nature, linked two sacred places, while his ascension to the heavens, spatially vertical, mediated between natural and spiritual or celestial worlds. By passing with his soul and body through the divine and lucid levels of heaven, the Prophet was assured that heaven and earth are undivided geography. Noteworthy is the fact that the Prophet died and was buried in Medina (figure 1.3).

In a discussion with the head of the Sufi Order of Ahmadiyya (Badwiyya) in Egypt,[37] he asserted that the Sufis' conviction that they can travel to different places simultaneously is impacted by the Prophet's night journey. Such a belief is found in various Muslim countries, such as Indonesia.[38] The location of the blessed and highly revered Sufis is often linked with their spiritual capacity to empower themselves. The appearances of the venerated Sufis in tangible places or specific geographies are important elements in reconstructing and redefining these places in terms of religiosity and sanctity.

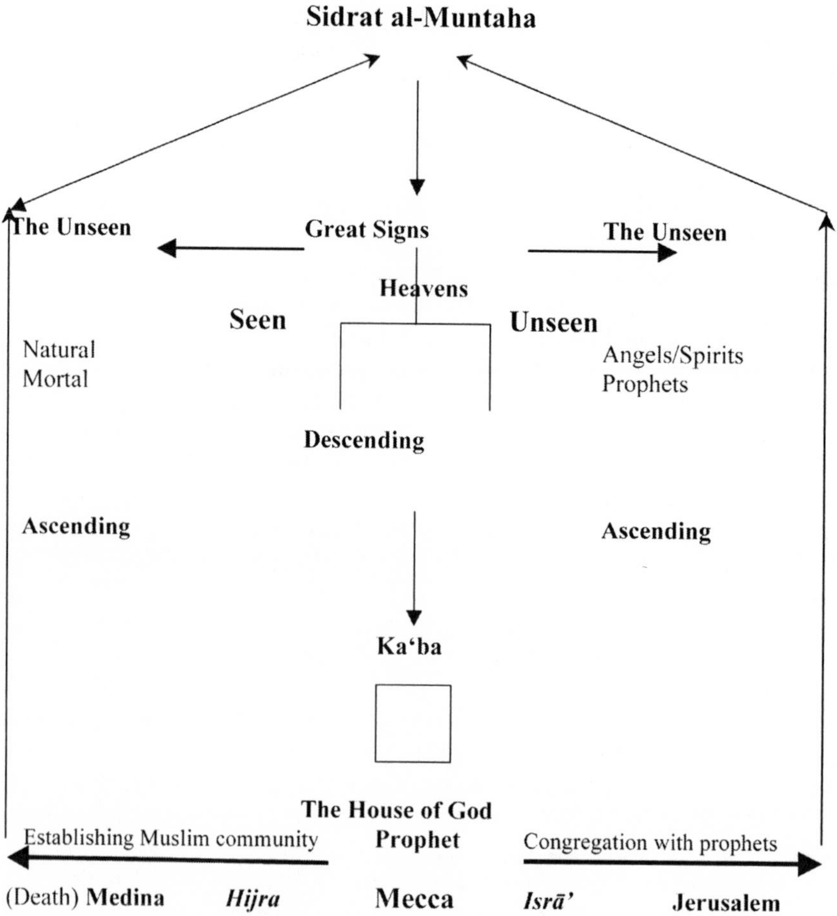

Figure 1.3. Hijra and Nocturnal Journey and Ascent of the Prophet to the heavens.

There are numerous sacred places and shrine cities associated with Sufi orders and Shi'i communities, among others, dispersed throughout the Muslim world. In an interview with Shi'i individuals from Bahrain, they referred to both Najaf (or al-Najaf al-Ashraf) and Karbala in Iraq as the most highly revered places with shrines that attract Shi'i pilgrims from all over the world.[39] Najaf is the place of the holy shrine (*marqad*) of Imam 'Ali ibn Abi Talib, while Karbala is the home of the shrine of Husain, the third Shi'i Imam and son of 'Ali. It is also the place of the shrine of al-'Abbas, the sibling of Husain. Karbala is religiously and historically significant because of the martyrdom of Husain and his companions. If the Shi'i pilgrims to Mecca bring *zamzam* water with them, the pilgrims to Karbala bring small pieces of dried clay or stone made of the earth of Karbala (*at-turba al-ḥusainiyya*) as well as prayer beads (*sibḥa*), made of the same clay, as tokens of blessing. It is believed that the earth of Karbala is mixed with the blood of Husain, hence *at-turba al-ḥusainiyya*, whose color is a mixture of red and brown, is an indexical or referential sign of the martyrdom of Husain as well as of the sacred land in which he was buried. I was given a square-shaped piece of *at-turba al-ḥusainiyya* from a Shi'i friend who made a visit to the sacred shrines in Karbala. He informed me that the Shi'a place their forehead on such pieces while prostrating in prayer. In a Shi'i mosque I saw a person who accidentally stepped on a piece of *at-turba al-ḥusainiyya* lift it from the floor, kiss it, and put it back.

A site of religious learning and scholarship such as al-Azhar Mosque in Egypt,[40] Qum in Iran,[41] or Jabal 'Amil in Lebanon is utilized to sanctify a larger geographic place. For instance, a Lebanese Shi'i person states, "The Lebanese Shi'ites were from Jabal 'Amil, and the 'Amili scholars had brought Shi'ism to Iran" (Shaery-Eisenlohr 2009, 547). Other persons argue that Jabal 'Amil is sacred because it is connected to Jerusalem. They also claim that a companion of the Prophet Muhammad introduced Shi'ism to Jabal 'Amil (Shaery-Eisenlohr 2009, 556).

Muslims are concerned with the purification (*ṭahārah*) of the body and the place, as well as the heart, as a way to ensure good faith, theoretically and practically. As opposed to sacred and pure places that entice angels and benevolent spirits, polluted and impure places are believed to attract malevolent unseen creatures. In Egypt, for instance, there is a belief that devils and other evil spirits, called *sukkān al-makān* or *ahl al-arḍ* (the inhabitants of the place or earth), occupy deserted places, cemeteries, and the underworld and are able to move rapidly within different locations on the earth and beyond. Unclean areas such as ruins, lavatories, and graveyards attract evil spirits. In Malaysia, spirits are usually associated with special objects or sites marking the boundary between human and natural spaces. These include the burial grounds of aboriginal and animal spirits and strangely shaped rocks and hills. Also, the places occupied by evil spirits are unpopulated territories like swamps and jungles (Ong 1988, 31–33).

THE TEMPORAL PARADIGM

Muslim worldviews are structured not only in spatial and ontological terms, but also in temporal paradigms. For instance, the sacred time of prayers intersects with the sacred place, the Ka'ba, toward which Muslims turn in prayer. The "temporal forms and spatial structures structure not only the group's representation of the world but the group itself, which orders itself in accordance with this representation" (Bourdieu 1977, 163). The belief of ordinary Muslims is understood in the context of their views concerning the cosmos or universe as a whole. Muslims rely on a rich set of Islamic temporal visions to locate themselves in cosmological time and social space. The temporal paradigm that unifies Muslims encompasses two inseparable and entwined components, one theoretical or doctrinal, the other practical. The theoretical component refers to the overarching cosmic dimension of time that includes three worlds: this world, the other world, and the world of *barzakh* (the transitional time between them). This cosmic dimension encompasses a future-oriented worldview that can be depicted as transitional, not linear, repetitive, or cyclical. The practical component refers to core rituals such as prayer, fasting during Ramadan, and pilgrimage, among other practices.

Without getting into the detail of the etymological implications of Arabic terminologies, both of the Arabic words *zaman* (or *zamān*) and *waqt* refer to time, but they are used differently, depending on the context. *Zamān* denotes either a long period of time such as epoch or century (*qarn*), or a short period of time such as one hour (*sā'a min az-zaman*). *Zamān* is also often used metaphorically to mean an external force such as destiny or fate (*qadar*) affecting people's lives. The word *waqt*, however, is used to refer to a certain period or interval of time, such as a specific minute or hour determined or measured for certain activities, including, for instance, time for prayer (*waqt aṣ-ṣalāh*), time for work (*waqt al-'amal*), or time for rest (*waqt al-rāḥah*).

The most common intervals or divisions of time among Muslims worldwide are those regulating the rhythm of Muslims' daily prayers. Muslims around the globe, publicly and privately, perform their prayers, *ṣalawāt* (sing. *ṣalāh* or *ṣalāt*), five times a day, every day, starting at dawn and ending at nighttime. In addition to commercial broadcasts, microphones hanging on the minarets of mosques are used loudly, assertively, and regularly to alert men and women in their public and private zones to hear and respond to their call.

The cosmological scheme, especially related to this worldly life, determines the appropriate time and place in which people conduct certain practices and rituals. For example, rural Egyptians have different concepts and attitudes toward different periods of time. On the one hand, they relate what is blessed, resplendent, and fruitful to the period that extends from dawn to noon. On the other, they associate what is austere, ominous, and less fruitful with the periods of noon, sunset, and midnight, at which time certain kinds of illness, especially spirit possession caused by alien or evil spirits or *jinn* could take place.[42] The times in which *jinn*, *'afārīt*, and other spirits are believed to be active are carefully noted. People are advised to reduce their activities and movement at night as well as at noon because of the potential danger of these invisible creatures. However, both men and women share the common belief, found among Muslims in general, that all *jinn*, *'afārīt*, and evil spirits are shackled during the holy month of Ramadan. In this month no spirit possession of any sort takes place, and no spirit exorcisms or *zār* cults are performed. The "imaginary is the birthplace of all beliefs, and at the same time the origin of the distinction between the sacred and the profane" (Godelier 1999, 27).

Sacred time is associated not only with sacred places, but also with sacred historical events and holy persons. Muslims celebrate certain blessed (*mubāraka*) days such as *'īd al-Fiṭr* (the feast following the fast of Ramadan, locally called *al-'īd aṣ-ṣaghīr* or the Small Feast), *'īd al-Aḍha* (the Feast of Sacrifice, locally called *al-'īd al-kabīr*), the Prophet's birthday, the Night of Power (*lailat al-Qadr*), mid-Sha'ban, and the Nocturnal Journey and Ascent of the Prophet, or *al-Isrā' wa al-mi'rāj* (twenty-seventh of Rajab).

Egyptian Muslims, like many Muslims throughout the world, have a firm belief in the Night of Power (*lailat al-Qadr*), the celebrated night of the twenty-seventh of Ramadan in which the Qur'an was revealed to the Prophet Muhammad. However, the Shi'a of Bahrain celebrate the Night of Power on the twenty-first of Ramadan. This night is associated with Muslims' beliefs concerning what the Egyptians call *tāqat lailat al-gadr*, meaning the opening that appears in the center of the heaven. Those who witness this opening are fortunate enough to be granted the fulfillment of their wishes. For the majority of Muslim scholars, such a belief is unacceptable. Sunni Muslims celebrate the middle (*al-niṣf*) of Sha'ban (the eighth Islamic month) because it is the night in which the direction (*qibla*) toward which people pray was changed from Al-Aqsa Mosque to the sacred mosque surrounding the Ka'ba. It also is believed that it is the night in which people's good deeds are blessed and raised to Allah. For the Shi'a, the night of mid-Sha'ban is celebrated because it was the night on which Imam Mahdi was born.

The attitudes toward time among the Muslims of the society of Kabyle (in Algeria), to give another example, are expressed in terms of submission and indifference to events that they cannot control, a concept that implies event time similar to the notion of *zamān* as an external force, fate, or destiny that people cannot change. As Bourdieu explained, such fatalistic time is a consequence of economic hardship and limited resources. When negative economic conditions changed for the better, the attitudes toward time also changed. The transition from event time to clock time or from a culture of fatalism to one of control occurred when the people of Kabyle were given the opportunity to work in factories with good income (Bourdieu 1963).

Various Muslim societies have developed different notions of time.[43] For example, the Javanese, in addition to their attitudes toward cardinal points or direction, use numerological divination called *petungan* or "counting" (Geertz 1960, 29) to determine the good or preferred time for doing certain things or moving to certain places. The Javanese adopt two-week systems, one Islamic (consisting of seven days), the other native (divided into five days related to certain colors and cardinal directions).[44] Each "day has a number (*neptu*): Monday 4, Sunday 5, Tuesday 3, Wednesday 7, Thursday 8, Friday 6, Saturday 9; *Legi* 5, *Paing* 9, *Pong* 7, *Wagé* 4, *Kliwon* 8" (Geertz 1960, 31). These two-week systems occur concurrently. For example, Saturday (Saptu) has the number 9, while Wagé has the number 4, constituting together Saptu-Wagé and producing the number 13. However, Geertz states, whether a specific number is good or not is dependent upon the direction toward which a person is moving. If a person is moving from south to north in a specific year on the Saptu-Wagé cycle with the number 13, the action or choice might be right.

CONCLUSION

This chapter has discussed five formal and popular paradigms representing the unity and diversity of Muslim worldviews and practices. There are varying scales of differences represented in the worldviews of Sunni, Shi'i, and Sufi adherents. However, these differences operate within the unifying religion of Islam. This, in turn, emphasizes the fact that there is one Islam with multiple worldviews and traditions. This is an essential conclusion because, on the one hand, it reflects the way Muslim people define not only themselves but also the world in which they live, and, on the other, it emphasizes the unity of Islam that encompasses various worldviews and traditions, not just, as some scholars suggest, "Islams" and "local Islams," which are terms that do not exist in Muslims' everyday vocabulary.

Muslims share common worldviews contingent on shared paradigms; however, they interpret and employ the entailments of these paradigms in diverse manners. These paradigms are structured through mediation and interaction between humanity and divinity. There has been a consistent mediation between the visible and invisible, between this world and the other world, between matter and spirit, and between the perceptible and the imperceptible. The mediation takes different forms, from angels such as Gabriel dictating the Qur'an—the Word of God—to the Prophet, the Ka'ba connecting the heavens with the earth, the eschatological world *barzakh* linking this life with the other life, and the light linking the celestial world with the mundane world. It is important, then, to stress that the concept of mediation implies transition and not cycle or linearity, through which Muslims perceive the world only as a transit for corporeal man to the perpetual or transcendental world in the hereafter. However, it must be emphasized that mediation here does not mean that there is a person or agency that mediates or even claims to mediate between Muslims and God in any form. Islam stresses the direct relationship between the faithful and God through their worship, notwithstanding the use of intercession by some adherents within certain contexts.

If contemporary Muslim worldviews are characterized by cultural, ethnic, and regional diversity, this diversity strengthens and enriches the underlying unity of Muslim worldviews. Although there are local variations concerning certain worldviews and practices, certain reinterpretations are made so as to provide Islamic meanings to these local worldviews. It is also possible that local worldviews and practices continue to prevail as folk or popular worldviews, satisfying people's certain pragmatic and social needs, along with the core tenets of formal religion serving more spiritual and transcendental aspirations.

2

The Worldview of the Sunni

Applying ethnographic and cross-cultural approaches, this chapter highlights the underlying worldviews and popular outlooks of Muslims as understood and enacted by Egyptian and Emirati people. Ethnographic studies were conducted in both rural and urban communities in Egypt and the Emirates. In Egypt, I collected ethnographic material from Tanta, the capital city of Gharbiyya governorate in the Middle Delta, and the villages of Shibshir al-Hissa and al-Rajdiyya that administratively belong to Tanta.[1] Tanta is famous for the shrine and mosque of the Sufi leader and *Sidi* (saint) al-Sayyid Ahmad al-Badawi. In the Emirates, ethnographic data were collected from al-Ain, the second largest city in the Emirate of Abu Dhabi and the birthplace of Shaikh Zayed bin Sultan Al Nahyan (the first president of the United Arab Emirates), and the village of Umm Ghafa, located fifteen miles east of al-Ain.[2]

Muslim worldviews are drawn from the Qur'an and the Prophet's tradition (Sunnah). Therefore, the discussion focuses on Sunni Muslims as they represent the majority of the overall indigenous population in both countries.[3] This discussion focuses on Emirati Muslim nationals and not the expatriate population residing and working in the United Arab Emirates.[4] Through addressing historical, economic, cultural, demographic, and geographical factors, this chapter further aims to show how the Sunni worldview shapes people's understandings of their identity and daily activity.

THE SETTINGS

The geography of both Egypt and the United Arab Emirates represents unique cases (figures 2.1 and 2.2). The strategic location of Egypt places it in the heart

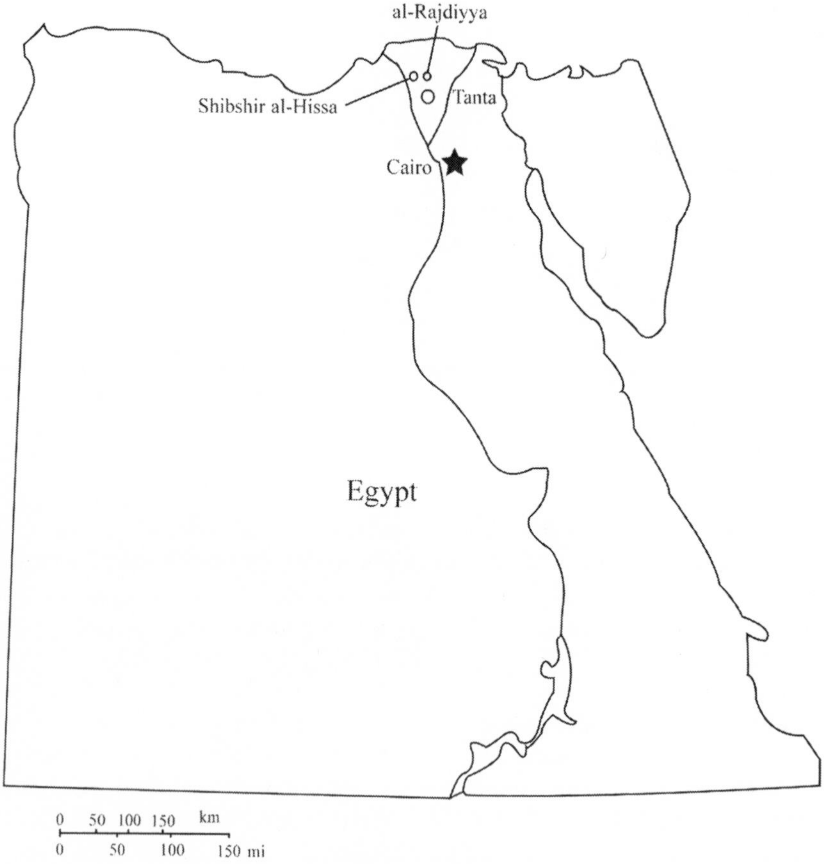

Figure 2.1. Egypt.

of the Middle East, linking it to the continents of Africa, Asia, and Europe. Likewise, the location of the UAE forms a strategic link between traditional Eastern (for example, Iranian and Indian) and Arab countries, rendering it exposed to and impacted by differing historical and cultural elements.[5]

Further, though the Muslim societies of both Egypt and the United Arab Emirates share cultural commonalities, such as language, religion, and folk heritage, they show profound differences in such aspects as demography, economy, and political systems. For example, though Egypt is highly populated (81,405,174 in January 2012),[6] its people are homogeneous when compared with those of the Emirates, which is known for the plurality and complexity of its demographic structure and where the number of expatriates (mostly non-Muslims from various countries) exceeds that of the nationals or locals. According to the National Bureau of Statistics of the United Arab Emirates, the population of the UAE

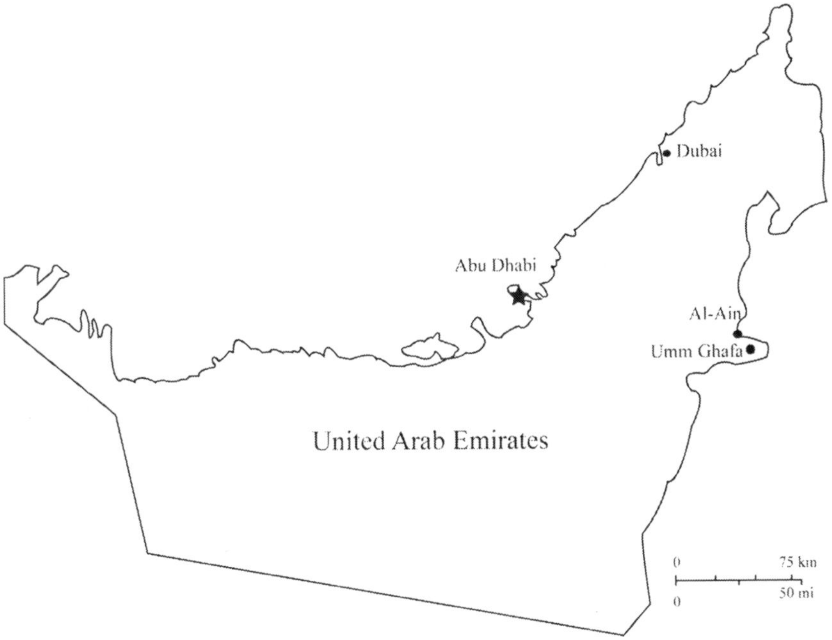

Figure 2.2. United Arab Emirates.

(national and non-national) in 2005 was 4,106,427. The estimate of the total population in 2010 was 8,264,070. Of the total population in 2010, Emirati nationals numbered 947,997, or 11.7 percent of the total population.[7]

The people of the Emirates, though they identify themselves with Islam, tend to define each other more on the basis of tribal identity and nationality, as presented in the dichotomous criteria of national (*muwāṭin*) versus non-national (*ghair muwāṭin*) or local versus nonlocal, than on any other criteria (el-Aswad 2011d, 2011e). Dichotomies such as these, where there is not a similar influx of expatriate workers to support a burgeoning economy, do not occur in Egypt.

Economically Egypt is considered a country with a lower-middle income. The estimated GNI per capita was $1,801 in 2009.[8] The UAE, conversely, is considered one of the most affluent. In 2009, the estimated GNI per capita in the UAE was $54,000, making it one of the wealthiest countries in the world.[9]

Politically, the systems of the two countries vary dramatically. While it is acceptable to maintain the family dynasty as a form of political legitimacy within Arab monarchies such as that of the United Arab Emirates, it is illegitimate to inherit the presidency (*tawrīth*) of a republic state such as that of Egypt, where people oppose such a nondemocratic notion. As was recently witnessed in Egypt, the Liberation (Tahrir) Square revolt that demolished Hosni Mubarak's regime on February 11, 2011, was not only prodemocracy but also against the notion that Gamal Mubarak, son of Mubarak, was being groomed to succeed his father (el-Aswad 2011a). In terms of differentiation, there is an accepted hierarchy in the Emirates not only between tribes but also between individuals within a tribe, whereas in Egypt, there is class differentiation based on economic, educational, and political factors.

ECONOMY AND SOCIAL COSMOLOGY

Worldview or cosmology is a rich source of imagery and discourse in which individuals and groups can creatively participate as they search for explanations and justification for their activities. Both economic resources and economic activities are assessed, viewed, and manipulated within cosmological paradigms. Since the mid-1970s, both Egypt and the Emirates have experienced profound changes in economic and political domains that have resulted in deep transformations of significant aspects of their worldviews.

In 1974, Egypt initiated its' *infitāḥ*, or free market (open-door), policy, emphasizing a change from socialism to capitalism and encouraging the private sector, or privatization, to replace the public sector dominated by the state.[10] Meanwhile, the oil boom in Abu Dhabi motivated its former ruler, the late Shaikh Zayed Ben Sultan Al Nahyan, to establish in 1971 a confederation of seven emirates oriented toward a free market and tax-free capitalism.[11] The UAE has effectively utilized the geographic position of the seven emirates to establish a significant geopolitical marketplace, with vast reservoirs of oil, in the Arab Gulf.

Within this capitalist or semicapitalist orientation, religion and kinship, more specifically family, have been rendered extremely visible, especially in presidential public discourses. In Egypt, for instance, then president Anwar al-Sadat enjoyed being referred to as "the pious president" (*ar-ra'īs al-mu'min*) and "the father of the family" (*rabb al-'ā'ila*), while in the Emirates the title used with reference to the president was the patriarch or the father[12] (*al-wālid* or *ash-shaikh*).[13] The term *shaikh* (fem. *shaikha*), as used in the Emirates, has political meaning and designates a member of the ruling family. Religion and family have continued to be highly influential forces as well as among the most common cultural and social features of these Arab societies, especially when the "father," called "shepherd" (*rā'in*) or ruler, is perceived as being on the side of or in support of the people.[14]

Economically, the implementation of the open-door policy or free market with its global dimensions has caused different consequences influencing crucial components of the worldviews of the people of these two societies. In Egypt, the open-door policy and privatization, in addition to the invasion of Western material values, have caused social inequality as evidenced by the uneven distribution of wealth and have widened the gap between the rich and the poor. Through hard work, however, the poor anticipate or hope that one day their misery will be replaced by economic relief (*farag* or *faraj*) (el-Aswad 2003a), as it has in other societies such as the Arab Gulf countries.

Less than three years after the initiation of the open-door policy, the Egyptian political system was severely disturbed by an uprising that occurred in January 1977 in Cairo and other cities in response to the state's attempt to raise prices of basic food items, such as bread, violating the subsistence economy of the poor. The poverty of Egypt as viewed by Egyptians cannot be explained or justified in terms of a deficiency of natural resources. On the contrary, Egypt is rich in both natural resources and manpower, but the problem is basically a sociopolitical one where corruption (*fasād*), favoritism (*maḥsūbiyya*), and a stagnant bureaucracy and officialdom have been blamed for an unjust and unequal distribution of wealth. This does not simply mean that Egyptians accept the world as it is. From January 25 to February 11, 2011, they forced a change in their society when they revolted in street protests against the corrupt regime of Mubarak, forcing him to step down from his position as president.

The revolution, however, was not religiously organized, but rather politically motivated.[15] It started with young people, using cybernetworking and Facebook, and later was joined by various political parties and other groups, including the Muslim Brotherhood and Salafism, or Salafiyya, groups. This means that what are so-called political Islam and Islamist groups were not the core factors that triggered the revolution. Simply, the revolution was against authoritarian and non-democratic regimes. However, this statement does not mean that the overarching Muslim worldview was absent; rather, it inspired people. Muslims follow the tradition of the Prophet when he said, "Whoever amongst you sees anything objectionable, let him change it with his hand, if he is not able, then with his tongue, and if he is not even able to do so, then with his heart, and the latter is the weakest form of faith."[16] Therefore, they felt within their right to pursue change, especially in the face of what was deemed objectionable.

Equity, justice, democracy, and pluralism have become main concerns of intellectuals and ordinary people not only in Egypt but also in the entire Islamic world. The phenomenon is known as the Arab Spring, where uprisings and revolts in Tunisia, Egypt, Yemen, Bahrain, Libya, and Syria erupted in the first quarter of 2011. The awareness of the need for democracy has become a demand of Muslims in their relationships with their governments.

Religious worldviews are recognized as vehicles for the meanings and values that individuals are willing to implement in their daily interactions. They have common or shared values and meanings that render the universe and their lives meaningful. According to Muslim worldviews, the universe is well ordered and organized. The order of the universe, however, is not to be described merely in material or physical terms, but also, and more importantly, in transcendental or religious and moral concepts. Natural resources are given to humans by God, and people, therefore, are responsible for using them equally and rationally (el-Aswad

2002). Corruption in the universe is a consequence of the injustice people exercise on each other. In Egypt, the January 25 revolution was triggered to eliminate corruption and restore equity and justice for all members of the society.

In the bread uprising of January 18–19, 1977, falsely depicted by Anwar Sadat as "the uprising of thieves" (*intifāḍat ḥaramiyya*), Egyptians, especially the poor, were interested in securing the "bread of their livelihood" (*luqmat al-'aysh*), while in the revolt on January 25, 2011, they showed profound interest in both bread and freedom. The Arabic word *'aysh* means both "bread" and "life" or "living." These two inseparable meanings have made the phrase "life of freedom" (*'aysh al-ḥuriyya*) an apropos term crafted, engraved, and offered by young Egyptians in Tahrir Square opening a new chapter of Egyptian history.

During the revolution in Tahrir Square, it was not surprising to hear people shout forcefully, "Thieves, thieves, thieves" (*ḥaramiyya*), directing their chants to the government and its businessmen. They had also written a phrase in huge letters on the ground that read, "Catch a thief" (*imsik ḥarāmy*). Such phrases resonate and reverberate in the Egyptian folk saying, "Its guard is its thief" (*ḥāmīha ḥarāmīha*), with reference to a plundering and deceitful governor.

The relationship between Egypt's grassroots and elites has been affected by the political and economic transformations from feudalist, to socialist, to capitalist systems that have occurred in Egypt's modern history. The majority of businessmen or new elites, allied to prominent statesmen, were power-oriented brokers who gained wealth in the short time during the initial period of the open-door policy and were depicted as "fat cats" (*al-qṭṭaṭ al-sumān*). The term "shark" (*samak al-qirsh*) has been used to refer to those who are greedy and obsessed with money. The whale (*al-ḥūt*) has also been used with reference to the big person who swallows smaller ones. I heard that there had been a "sugar whale" (*ḥūt al-sukkar*) monopolizing the sugar market in Egypt for decades. Such symbolic phrases reflect Egyptians' worldview of the negative and corrupt sides of the social cosmology.

The economic open-door policy has turned out to be an "open-door policy of corruption" (*infitāḥ al-fasād*). Individuals I interviewed emphasized the concept of devil (*shaiṭān*) embodied in both humans and the cosmos when talking about the corruption that has occurred in recent decades. Some interviewees recounted that those who lack ethical and religious principles are unable to experience or take pleasure in the beauty of the more sublime dimensions of life; rather, they enjoy possessing material matter such as luxuries, big houses, fancy cars, and expensive food. The experience of possessing and consuming is oriented toward the material or tangible and associated with self-centeredness. Other interviewees, however, stated that there is no problem in possessing material things; the problem lies in the unethical methods of gaining them, especially at the expense of others.

The manipulative elites or "fat cats" have taken advantage of both the state and its people. As recounted by the folk, they have never acted mercifully or with loyalty toward the people; rather, they abused them and "sold the country" (*bā'u al-balad*) through privatization. As for being linked to globalization, the privatization policy that has given the private sector unprecedented priority over the public sector has had a grievous impact on the educational, social, and health services offered to poor Egyptians.

During the recent period of corruption, the majority of Egyptians suffered from poverty while a few elites possessed billions of dollars, a situation unprecedented in Egyptian history. Inflation skyrocketed and the Egyptian pound lost its economic significance or "respect" (*iḥtrāmahu*), as Nagy, an Egyptian accountant, recounted. The government changed the one pound bill ($0.17 in February 2010) to such a cheap metal coin that Egyptians call it the *dirham* (with reference to the Emirati currency [$0.27]). The irony is that the Emirati *dirham* has exceeded the Egyptian pound in value (where one *dirham* is equivalent to 1.60 EGP). Therefore, the Egyptians have named the pound "small change" (*fakkah*).

Throughout this corrupt period, ethics and social values reached low levels in Egypt. It has not been uncommon to hear people say, "Feed the mouth to make the eye [people] shy so as to control them" (*iṭ'am al-famm titsiḥī al-'ain*) and "Bribe to get healthy" (*irshū tashfū*), indicating and encouraging bribery. In his response to a question I addressed regarding a solution to the problem of corruption, Shaykh Hamid asserted that "there is no *iṣlāḥ* [social, economic, and political reform] without 'righteousness' [*ṣalāḥ*]," where people establish the inner moral resources that help them to make appropriate choices. The solution thus lies in the people's capacity to make moral choices. It is evident in all these examples that ethics is not treated in isolation and that what is right and wrong is seen in the light of a wider cosmic vision (Smart 1995, 117).

Consequently, two crucial interrelated phenomena have developed in Egypt: migration to the Arab Gulf (for wealth) and migration to God (*al-hijra ilā Allah*) or faith. Islam encourages travel in search of knowledge and other material and nonmaterial benefits. On the one hand, many Egyptians have migrated in waves to the oil-producing countries, including the Emirates, seeking job opportunities. They have either left their families behind or have taken them to new and different social milieus, stirring up unprecedented and unforeseen social issues. On the other hand, a call for the return to Islamic values and practices has dramatically increased as refracted in two different social mediums: one politically oriented, seeking change by force or violence as represented in the actions of Islamist militants in the 1980s and 1990s,[17] and the other socially motivated, as mirrored in moderate or ordinary Muslims seeking social change through peaceful means. At this popular or moderate level, Islamic revivalism has been reflected as follows:

1. In response to corruption and social mystification, there has been an increasing tendency among Egyptians toward employing scriptural tradition including the Holy Qur'an, the Sunnah (the tradition of the Prophet Muhammad), and Muslim interpretations. This trend is mostly reflected in Muslim Brotherhood and Salafiyya religious groups.[18]

2. In response to inadequate services offered by the government, there have been active movements of civil society organized by Muslim associations (*jam'iyyāt islāmiyya*), charitable associations (*jam'iyyāt khayriyya*), and private voluntary organizations aiming to serve local communities.
3. Peaceful means of reform and social awakening were represented in the January 25 revolution triggered by almost all Egyptians from different economic, social, and educational levels.
4. Sufi orders with their annual celebrations have been successful in attracting people of different economic, social, and educational levels, providing them with both social and transsocial experiences represented in moral, spiritual, psychological, and economic support.[19]

A common feature within these has been the individuals' imminent concern with maintaining and preserving their Muslim identity. In Egypt most Muslims have "continued to believe in the ideal of religious hegemony over everyday life and politics" (Flores 1993, 33).[20]

The picture is different in the Emirates. Almost forty years ago the Emirates was a poor, sparsely populated, nomadic society. Since the 1970s the country has witnessed a profound and unexpected change from a subsistence economy dependent on traditional, pastoral, rural, and small trade activities into an economy of oil revenues and entrepreneurial enterprises. But, unlike Egypt, in which economic inequality and corruption caused by official elites were prevalent, the UAE has been economically stable and developed because of fair allocation and distribution of oil revenues among nationals. In brief, core factors that have enabled the UAE, in general, and Abu Dhabi, in particular, to be one of the most impressively vibrant economies in the Arab world include immense oil wealth, Sheikh Zayed's leadership, the establishment of a federation after British withdrawal from the region, generous distributions of the wealth to nationals, the removal of all forms of taxation, placing key representatives of loyal powerful families and clans in government and private companies, artful diplomacy, and the adoption of novel sectors. These sectors comprise high technology, heavy industries, a pioneering renewable energy plan, aerospace industry, shipping industry, various military manufacturers, extensive real estate projects, tourism, green industries, and other areas of non-oil diversification (Davidson 2009).

Emirati rulers, observing both Muslim and tribal ethics, have been key factors in solidifying the relationship between the traditional social structure and the newly established state. Among various economic services offered to Emiratis by the government is the Marriage Fund, established by Federal Law No. 47 of 1992, allowing UAE national male grooms of at least twenty-one years of age to apply for a 70,000 AED ($19,058) marriage grant so as to marry a female UAE national of at least eighteen years of age (el-Aswad 2011d).[21]

Nevertheless, with the advent of prosperity and wealth, Emirati nationals have changed their views concerning certain kinds of work. Manual work is rendered unacceptable and even unimaginable among Emirati locals who used to undertake traditional labor in agriculture, herding, and fishing. Rarely today do Emirati men work manually as farmers, fishermen, carpenters, plumbers, shoemakers, or taxi drivers. Emirati people, especially those who lived in the oases, used to cultivate land, but now they hire non-Emirati laborers from Arab countries and Southeast Asia to do the work.

Despite rapid and globalized economic change, the people of the Emirates have shown a sincere concern about preserving their religion or Islamic identity as well as their local heritage. As mentioned, the majority of indigenous people of the Emirates are Sunni. However, unlike Egyptians who venerate saints and Sufis (*awliyā'*, sing. *walī*), Emiratis do not celebrate sainthood, and there is not a certain place or shrine of a specific saint or Sufi. A grand and magnificent mosque (figure 2.3) has recently been built in Abu Dhabi in memory of the late Shaikh Zayed, but it does not represent the notion of Sufism or mysticism found in Egypt.

This might be attributed to the influence of the Wahhabi worldview (Wahhabism) in the early nineteenth century (el-Aswad 2005d).[22] However, presently, Emiratis are not extremely affected by the Wahhabi worldview, and people, especially women, enjoy freedom in both socioeconomic activities and religious practices. I hasten to say here that women in both Egypt and the Emirates are involved in both public, or government, and private sectors. They own property, make economic (bank) transactions, and make decisions related to their private lives.

Figure 2.3. Zayed's Mosque, Emirates.

The Emirates are guided by the tradition of the Prophet Muhammad in their secular or mundane domains of physical purification, hygiene, hospitality, and social relationships. Perfumes and dyes are used by both men and women in ritualistic ways almost every day, and more specifically on Fridays, to avoid contamination, to bring blessing to the house, and to maintain pleasant and harmonious relationships with other people (el-Aswad 1995, 1996b, 2001b, 2005e). However, some new dimensions of Emiratis' worldview have been constructed since the establishment of the state in 1971 and the Gulf Cooperation Council in 1981[23] and are related to the increase in affluent lifestyles.

In the Emirates there has been a clear-cut split between outward modern economic activities and inward traditional or authentic culture that clusters around "Emirati-ness" or pan-Emirates and pan-Gulf, notwithstanding the identification with Islam. Preserved local customs, including social gatherings (*majlis*), table manners, and costume,[24] are used as symbolic vehicles conveying the Emirates' authentic (distinctive) identity not merely as Arab, but (more importantly) as people of the "Gulf" (*Khalījī* or *ahl al-Khalīj*). Friedman notes, "Where difference can be attributed to demarcated populations we have culture or cultures" and "it is easy enough to convert difference into essence, race, text, code, structure" (Friedman 1995, 80). Also, local costume becomes an icon that symbolizes these new dimensions of identity, indicating affluence, power, distinction,

Figure 2.4. Male *majlis* in the UAE.

and difference from nonlocals. This sense of difference, power, and control is reflected in a statement made by a dignitary tribesman, who asserted that all business enterprises and economic projects, big or small, have to be sponsored either by the state or by indigenous persons.

In the built environment of both urban and rural communities in the Emirates, one observes that though locals live in new and futuristic houses full of electronic appliances representing modernity, they are still attached to their traditional worldview (el-Aswad 1996a) in the social and customary arrangements of domestic activities, where, for instance, there is a reception room (*majlis* or *maylis*) for men and another for women, emphasizing gender segregation (figure 2.4). This segregation, however, is viewed through both social and religious lenses. In addition, though the locals own very expensive Western furniture and kitchen utensils, they still prefer to sit on mats or carpets and eat their food with their right hands in a specified manner, without the use of spoons or forks (el-Aswad 2003a, 2003b, 2009, 2010).

THE DYNAMICS OF SUNNI WORLDVIEWS

The economic disparity between Egypt and the UAE is mirrored in the dissimilarity of some significant constituents of their worldviews as presented in the different interpretations offered by their citizens. The unanticipated economic affluence of the Emirates has been interpreted differently by locals. Some interviewees, basically of the older generation, pointed out that their wealth has been bestowed upon them as a blessing (*ni'mah*) or goodness (*khair*) by Allah after the harsh and difficult economic conditions that they and their ancestors had endured for a long period of time.

It is interesting to observe that the concept of goodness (*khair*) is so powerful among people of the Emirates that they call their late president Shaikh Zayed "*al-khair*," meaning that prosperity or goodness became available during his lifetime. According to this viewpoint, the Emirates has transformed from a society that used to be characterized by the image of "limited good," using Foster's term (1965), to a society with the image of "unlimited good" (*khair wide*),[25] or from a tribal, closed, static, deprived, and stagnant society to a modern, open, dynamic, entrepreneurial, and changing society. Their wealth, generating a fluent social cosmology, is sanctified and rationalized in religious terms. The image of the "unlimited good" is profoundly related to the religious concept of "livelihood" (*al-rizq*) that belongs to the divine invisible reality (*'ālam al-ghaib*), encompassing the notion of possibility, according to which what is potential can be substantially made real through God's will. Metaphorically, *al-rizq* is akin to the rain, locally called *raḥmah*, which means mercy bestowed by Allah. *Al-rizq*, like rain, comes unexpectedly and revives the desert without the intervention of humans. This powerful metaphor, prevalent in both Bedouin and rural communities, is used to explain other resources of livelihood available to humans, as in the case of oil from the Arab Gulf countries. As Salim, an elderly Bedouin, put it, "the divine power [*al-qudra al-ilahiyya*] renders the dry wet, the desert green, and the poor rich." The new worldview of the Emiratis implies the cosmology of empowerment and is contingent on the concept of "substantiation," meaning that what was possible or potential (unexpected economic relief, *faray* or *faraj*) has become real or actual prosperity.

Most young interviewees, especially university students, however, do not fully accept the interpretation offered by the elderly, arguing that oil fields, among other significant natural resources, are found in other regions that do not belong exclusively to the Muslim world. Yet instead of stressing the fact that their country depends on nonlocal manpower, they confirm that their society is blessed because of the wealth that attracts many expatriates from different parts of the world who come to serve them. The features of wealth and the need to use skilled external manpower necessary for implementing public and private projects intensify or deify the young nationals' sense of identity, which, in turn, sharpens the distinction between them and the non-nationals who are there to work. Inauspicious features of personality such as superiority, self-importance, and arrogance have become prevalent among them, notwithstanding a fear of dissolving into the other. This feeling is mostly generated by the locals' image of themselves as being a "minority" in their homeland despite the fact that the federation or state has accentuated the identity of *muwāṭin*, or "national," of the individuals to be identified with the Emirates as a nation and not with its fragmented tribes. Within this context, though wealth is absolutely desired and fought for, it is viewed by the old generation as a source of danger that threatens the youth and the whole society.

Young generations of Emiratis have expressed their crisis as a feeling of being torn apart between their local culture, impacted by a Muslim worldview, and modern, global, or secular ways of life, impacted by a Western worldview. They speak Arabic with Emirati dialects, eat indigenous food, use incense, and wear traditional costumes (including veils for women) so as to symbolically identify themselves with their society, but at the same time they speak English and employ symbols signifying Western (global) modernity, such as using computers, networking through cybercirculation (including the Internet and Facebook), eating Western fast food, wearing expensive perfumes, and driving extravagant front-wheel-drive cars (el-Aswad 1996d, 2010e).[26] However, it can be assumed that symbols of modernity do not "have deep impact on people's beliefs, values, or behavior. In principle, an individual could wear jeans and running shoes, eat hamburgers, even watch a Disney cartoon, and remain fully embedded in this or that traditional culture" (Berger 2002, 7). Meanwhile, one argues, to take another example, that although some families and the younger generations of both Egyptian and Emirati societies deal with new global phenomena such as eating out in one of the global chains of fast-food restaurants, it does not mean that they follow the same modes of behavior prevalent in Western or American culture. What happens is the emergence of a localized phenomenon where fast-food restaurants become new centers for social gatherings, relaxation, and gossip, bearing little, if any, resemblance to the society that created fast food (figure 2.5).

If life for the people of the Emirates is affluent and beautiful (*zain*), for Egyptians, it is economically "shrinking," "restrained" (*ḍīq*), "opaque," or "foggy" (*ḍabāb*). Such a dwindling economy has generated a practical logic of everyday necessity that is expressed through folk sayings such as "Whatever is needed for the house is not permitted to the mosque" (*illy yaḥtāgahu al-bait yaḥram 'alā al-gāma'*) and "Each person knows, through reason, what is good for his safety" (*Kull wāḥid fī rāsuh ya'raf khalāṣuh*).

The world as created and maintained by God is perfect; however, life as administered by humans is corrupt. Whatever income people acquire, it never satisfies their basic needs. "Her [Egypt's] goodness is not for her [her people] but for the other"(*khairhā li ghairhā*) is a popular saying I heard from a schoolteacher who was blaming external global forces and their domestic representatives (the fat cats) for robbing and stealing people's wealth. He indicated that the world as made by Allah is rich and nurturing, yet powerful and corrupt people unjustly redistribute its wealth and take the lion's share. Such a statement is echoed in devastating economic surroundings such as insignificant income, inflation,

Figure 2.5. Young people in a shopping mall and modern restaurant in the UAE.

increasing taxation, growing demands of dependents, sickness, and the shortage of savings necessary for coping with unexpected misfortunes, to mention some of the challenging elements that have had a negative impact on people's overall well-being. This negative image is reflected in the ongoing daily conversations between individuals who convey to each other their dissatisfaction with the economic conditions. A simple way of expressing this "tight but covered" worldview or outlook is revealed when they answer the question: "How are you doing?" The answer, representing the most common feature of Egyptian qualities as being humorous in the most devastating conditions, varies from "okay" (*māshī*), "half and half" (*nuṣṣ wa nuṣṣ*), "mediocre" (*ya'ny*), "alive" (*'āyyish*), or "it would be fixed one day" (*tit'addil*) to "the goodness might be found in another chance" (*Khairhā fī ghairhā*), "covered" or "secured" (*mastūra*). Such a statement implies the notion of possibility or potentiality; something might or might not happen, as a yet latent possibility, contrary to the concept of "substantiation" characterizing Emiratis' worldviews. However, whether the world is viewed as "affluent" and "substantiated" or economically "tight" and whether there are good or corrupt human elements in it, people tend to view it in terms of their Muslim worldviews.

Most of the key concepts of Islamic worldviews are explicitly and implicitly embodied and enacted in the discourse of the Muslims being studied in both Egypt and the Emirates. However, it is interesting to note that only a few of the individuals interviewed mentioned the classic Islamic view of the world as being divided into two domains known as "the abode of peace or Islam" (*dār al-Salām*) and "the abode of war" (*dār al-Ḥarb*); rather, most pointed to the coexistence of multiple worlds. Though the world is viewed through multiple and overlapping perspectives, the most dominant outlook views the world as a place of seen or present (*ash-shahādah*) and unseen or absent (*al-ghaib*) domains. People "come to imagine transcendent cosmic order in terms of the rules that govern their everyday lives and vice versa" (Beyer 1994, 83). The religious domain of *al-ghaib*, the unseen or unknowable, implies optimism and hope for a good life as well as high expectations for a promising future (*al-yusr ba'd al-'usr*) or prosperity after hardship (*al-rizq wa al-khalaf*). All worlds, visible and invisible, this life and the afterlife, are expressions of the same divine cosmological order in the sense that they are created and encompassed by the Ultimate One (*Allah al-Wāḥid*). To authenticate this belief, Muslims tend to utter the phrase "a cosmos ordered by its Owner" (*kaun wa munaẓẓamu ṣāḥbu*).

The invisible, represented in its highest form in the conviction of "Allah's will" (*mashī'a*), empowers and allows for possibility, a pivotal notion in Muslims' thought, and renders the whole world a dynamic structure. Anything is possible because there is always room for the invisible to work. An unexpected fortune or great success can be comprehended within this logic. The phrase "when God wills," frequently used by individuals in their daily interactions when they desire, anticipate, or promise some action or thing, offers people a sense of strength and hope for a better future, imaginative or real, that the state or government fails to grant. This explains their dynamic, open, and flexible viewpoint and attentiveness for any possible event, peculiar or normal, to occur.

Hidden and invisible spheres are not to be deemed illogical or contradictory symptoms that indicate an outdated or archaic standpoint; rather, they form generative and dynamic elements in an imaginary cosmological order shaping and being shaped by Muslim tradition and the experiences of both individuals and collectivities. Without the invisible domain, the visible or mundane world would be devoid of meaning. Muslims of the two communities under study quoted verses of the Qur'an in which Allah is described as "the Visible and the Invisible" (*aẓ-ẓāhir wa al-bāṭin*).[27] One meaning of globalization indicates that people are aware that they are part of something bigger. "Of course this might as well be God or the Absolute Spirit, as the world of human kind" (Friedman 1995, 70). As the authoritative aspect of a comprehensive worldview, religion is bound to be involved in debate about the direction of globalization (Robertson 1992). This particular sense of globalization resembles that of Muslim cosmology.

The belief implying that Allah determines the sustenance and provisions of man and aids individuals in achieving certain goals is deeply reflected in people's thought and action. For both Egyptians and Emiratis, achievement in economic enterprise and other aspects of life is an effect of both man's effort and the blessings of divine order. What people really want from work and other daily activities is "moral covering" (*as-satr*), being morally, socially, and economically secured. In their mundane or economic activities, Muslims work industriously to maximize their interests and incomes so as to enhance their social positions. Their activities, however, are validated by the scheme of the cosmological notion of divine livelihood (*al-rizq*), which belongs to the invisible or unknowable world (*'ālam al-ghaib*).

Despite the growing attitude toward material possessions, Muslims still assert that it is not the material accumulation, but the blessing (*baraka*) of what they have that matters. A little but blessed capital might be better than a large but envied or unblessed capital. In many contexts, however, the belief in "livelihood dominated by God" (*rizq*) is emotionally interpreted. One Egyptian interviewee, a high-ranking officer of the interior ministry, recounted with great passion that one day he desperately needed money. He went to the bank to withdraw all of his money, knowing that the quantity would not be enough. Yet immediately after withdrawing his money and while he was turning to go home, a person approached him, telling him that he had dropped some money. The officer, who was sure that he put his money in his wallet, looked down and found a handful of Egyptian pounds. He quietly and thankfully took them from the floor, knowing that it was not his money. The officer said, "Nobody was there in the hall except me and that person and of course the agent behind the window. I took the money and put it in my pocket and thanked the man. Then I looked around again to see if there was anyone who might have lost the money, but I did not find anybody. I went to my car and counted the money. It was five hundred Egyptian pounds, the exact amount of money I needed in addition to the money I had just withdrawn. Allah covered me [*satarnī*], thanks to Allah." When I asked him why he accepted money that did not belong to him, he confirmed that Allah sent this *rizq* (money) to him because he never abused his power to make fortunes (as other corrupt officers do) and he was praying to God to assist him in his unexpected financial crisis. I was surprised and touched to see tears in his eyes.

Like Egyptians, the people of the UAE, despite their affluence, are also concerned with the concept of "divine covering" (*as-satr*) as related to the cosmological scheme of "livelihood" or source of revenue (*rizq*), which belongs to the unseen and unknowable world (*al-ghaib*). Salim, a high-ranking official in the Emirati government, recounted that people are assured of their sources of living (*rizq*) by God. This sense of a divine world necessitates that the world is possible, and if a world is possible, then it is real or actual (Gangadean 1998, 139). Though *al-rizq* falls in the unseen divine realm, it cannot be attained without action or movement (*haraka*) and involvement in mundane activities (*ma'āsh*). This principle is firmly unified with the virtue of endurance or patience (*ṣabr*) and refers to the ability to undertake and tirelessly endure arduous activities without complaining as well as the ability to willingly and actively avoid what is unacceptable or forbidden (*ḥarām*) (el-Aswad 2002).[28] Consequently, patience is identified as the half of faith (*niṣf al-imān*). Patience, a focal point of "self-control," is metaphorically depicted as sweet and beautiful as well as a "key"(*muftāḥ*) that opens closed doors.

Another example of the dynamism of Muslim cosmologies is the *hijra* or migration, where people tend to travel seeking various opportunities notwithstanding their preference to reside in their local communities among their kin and people (*ahlī wa nāsī*), where life is secured and sociable. Religious beliefs and practices have induced Egyptians, thinking of their livelihood (*ar-rizq*) and economic gain, to journey abroad to Arab Gulf countries, including the Emirates, whose proximity to the birthplace of Islam has bestowed meaning to the migration as being motivated not only by material interest but also by the Islamic perception of *hijra*, or migration to sacred places or to God.[29] The personal and cultural pride, as expressed by the Egyptians I interviewed, accentuated their positive self-image as being industrious workers who have participated in building major projects and even cities, not only in Egypt but also in the Arab world. A similar positive attitude had also been expressed by the elderly of the Emirates who, in the 1960s, before the oil boom, used to work abroad in other oil-rich Arab countries such as Saudi Arabia, Kuwait, and Bahrain. Recently, however, and because of their reliance on foreign or expatriate manpower, especially of maids or servants working inside domestic zones or houses, this positive image has changed, and a negative impact on the self-image of many natives has been observed. An elderly person from the Emirates metaphorically criticized the young generation as being idle and dependent on the other, saying, "The youth of today are sleepy" (*shabāb al-yaum ma al-naum*). In addition, a considerable number of

Emirati nationals question the expatriates' intentions and moral behaviors, which may conflict with Islamic principles.

For most of the Egyptian immigrants, people of the Emirates were very friendly and kind in their social life, but in the domain of business or work they were strict, pragmatic, and relatively manipulative. A returning Egyptian immigrant indicated that he was really confused and stressed because of the biased and unfair treatment he received in the peaceful Muslim country where the salary of the native or national (*muwāṭin*) was triple that of his, though he did most of the work. Expatriates are hired cheaply in order to reduce costs. When I discussed such a view with individuals of the Emirates, they agreed but expressed some reservations. They pointed to the saying, "Wealth or goodness is for the natives of the country" (*al-khair li ahl al-balad*), with reference to the fairness of taking care of the locals toward whom economic and other activities and services were being directed. But this, they maintained, did not mean that an unskilled or uneducated national received the same salary as a highly educated or skilled and professional expatriate. What is unique in the migration and labor experience is that it has broadened communication and interaction among people from various ethnic groups and cultural backgrounds, viewed by the individuals being studied as a blessing that should be maintained. But there is a difference between the two cases of Egypt and the Emirates. For Egyptians, it is through ongoing travel within and without national borders, while for Emiratis, it is through receiving or hosting the other, Muslim or non-Muslim (el-Aswad 2003a). Accepting the other, the foreigner, has become a significant sign of dynamic change in both Egyptian and Emirati cultural outlooks. Also, exposure or social networking via the Internet, Facebook, and other forms of electronic circulation is another example of change.

Muslim worldviews work as a resisting force against the penetration of global and secular monoculture. Family and kin relationships are religiously and socially highly emphasized in Arab societies. For example, kinship relationship is sanctified by Islam through the principle of kin connectivity (*ṣilat ar-raḥim*), accentuating the importance of keeping blood and affinal relationships well maintained in a rapidly changing society. Another related important belief is anchored in the assumption that man is the trustee of God's resources on earth. This concept is explicitly reflected in the notion of the "inhabitation" of the universe (*ta'mīr al-kaun*) that certifies people's attitudes toward producing offspring regardless of their economic differences. For example, among individuals of both Egyptian and Emirati societies, the main objective of both building a house and establishing a family is to inhabit the universe (*y'ammar al-kaun*). This means that the house as a whole is sanctified or seen as a sanctuary (*ḥaram*) that is to be blessed by God's mercy. This logic of divine mercy explains people's attitudes toward having a large number of children. These attitudes, however, are found in both the Emirates, whose government financially supports and encourages locals to have more children, as well as in Egypt, despite its government's ongoing campaigns for birth control.[30] Therefore, the debate between the Egyptian government and the folk concerning the relationship between the size of the family and its economic resources mirrors two different outlooks. Each outlook attempts to explain the logic of economic activity. For individuals, a newborn infant is by divine mercy assured of his/her own livelihood (*rizq*) apart from the actual economic condition it might confront. Such a view gives little attention to global organizations attempting to augment people's awareness of the danger of overpopulation.

Social and secular worldviews are rendered sanctified, morally acceptable, and justifiable through association with sacred or religious propositions. Modes of secular behavior and entrepreneurial spirit are materialized and found even among the traditional Bedouins of the Emirates, who have become, beyond Ibn Khaldun's theory of historical cycles,[31] entrepreneurs or businessmen, dealers, brokers, and technocrats. The growing increase of materialism and consumerism as shown in the building of skyscrapers and the spread of grand malls or shopping centers, designed and built according to Western style, are viewed as examples of the impact of globalization on local culture as well as of the growing trends of the secular orientation among people. Global flows of goods, ideas, and practices have been facilitated by the agency of indigenous actors. In other words, the native entrepreneurs, with tremendous sources of privileges, have gained wealth and power through their involvement in the global market. However, they have succeeded in assimilating outside influences without deserting their authenticity and social connectivity. In short, the Egyptians and Emiratis interviewed show a great concern for the domination of covetousness and greed in people's social relationships. They complain of the growing materialistic attitudes at the expense of spirituality and religiosity that might result in the annihilation of the world.[32]

CONCLUSION

The thesis of this chapter is that Muslims in such geographically, demographically, economically, and politically different societies as Egypt and the Emirates are deeply influenced by an overarching Muslim worldview, a holistic view maintained by both men of religious learning and the common people. These societies, in brief, show confidence in a graceful cosmology created, sustained, and blessed by God. Such a worldview is not entirely ordered by instrumental logic or material/practical reason, as is the case of a secular worldview. Muslim worldviews as cognized and enacted by common people are tied neither to government regimes nor to Islamist militants or Muslim groups motivated by political schemes.

I have argued that Islamic sacred postulates have tremendous power in maintaining Muslim worldviews in such a way that it seems difficult to understand the secular and visible aspects of life without reference to the sacred and invisible domains. For both Egyptian and Emirati individuals, the sacred has not been detached from the world where economic and material gains have been perceived in religious terms. They depend upon assistance from divine sources. It is not surprising that earthly power should be seen as a way of expressing and strengthening Allah's dominion (Smart 1995, 113).

The belief in the divine realm of the unseen or unknowable (*al-ghaib*) brings about an imaginary world of possibilities generating hope in a good life as well as breeding high expectations of a promising and prosperous future. Muslim worldview functions as a spiritual shield protecting people against the disintegrating factors embedded in the extreme forms of globalism and secularism. However, spirituality or religiosity does not dismiss mundane and secular engagement with reality insofar as there is a connection with the imperceptible, benevolent reality.

3

The Esoteric Worldview of the Shi'a

The worldviews and practices of the Shi'a, especially in Bahrain, have lacked ethnographic study yet are profoundly rich and extremely complex and, therefore, require special attention and consideration. This chapter demonstrates the impact of the imagined worldview, with its visible and invisible realms, on the daily practices of the Shi'a in Bahrain. It implies that the hidden dimensions of Shi'i esoteric cosmology (*kaun*) promote social aspects reflecting their conceptualizations. It further evinces how the Shi'a manipulate observable ways of creatively enacting and embodying their esoteric and hidden beliefs as represented in various forms of daily life including iconography, art displays, folk dramas, consecrated geographies, religious discourses, and calendrical rites together with their annual liturgies of Muharram, the Islamic month in which Imam Husain, grandson of the Prophet, was martyred.

The connection between systems of meaning and action is not clearly delineated in much of symbolic-interpretive anthropology, where more attention is given to textual and ethical dimensions than to historical, social, and political contexts (Roseberry 1989, 24–28). In its emphasis on the society as the sole model of universal categories, classification, and religion, Durkheimian sociology explains bodily symbolism and ritual as representations and residues of social structures (Bloch 1977; Kaspin 1996). The argument that the body is the existential ground of culture and self (Csordas 1994) accentuates one aspect, the seen or bodily, at the expense of the other, the unseen or esoteric.

The cosmology of Bahraini Shi'a, imaginary and lived, represents a uniquely ordered synthesis of multiple differing views influenced by cultural and religious elements represented in the tradition of the Imamate and related esoteric beliefs and practices concerning occultation (*al-ghaiba*). The Shi'i communities see themselves as observing not only the doctrine of the Imamate, but also ritual performances and related emotions devoted to the Prophet Muhammad's family and the Twelve Imams.

ETHNOGRAPHY AND PHENOMENOLOGY OF THE ESOTERIC WORLD

This discussion applies the heuristic tools of ethnography and interpretive-phenomenological anthropology to mystical concepts of the unseen, esoteric world, as enacted within the communities of the Bahraini Shi'a. Phenomenological anthropology is concerned and combined with ethnographic fieldwork methodology to comprehend people's inner and experiential views. Phenomenology is "the analysis of what kind of constituents there are in our thoughts and lives (whether these be valid or invalid being aside from the question)" (Roseberry 1989, 103).

For the Shi'i worldview, the term "esoteric" means inner or inwardness and has to do with doctrinal concepts that are highly theoretical. It also refers to invisible, mystic, hidden, secretive, and private domains (Amir-Moezzi 1994, 29–31). Nevertheless, several scholars have approached Muslim worldviews within a scheme of binary oppositions such as seen/unseen (*ẓāhir/bāṭin*), corporeal/spiritual, apparent/hidden, exterior/interior, and esoteric/exoteric (Geertz 1960; Gilsenan 1982). Such a dualism has been criticized and denounced as designating a Western dichotomous legacy (el-Aswad 2002; Viveiros de Castro 1998). My point here is that these categories are inseparable or are fused together and are represented in people's everyday experiences rather than in abstract and rigid binary oppositions. These categories can be better understood through scrutinizing hierarchical relations within and among cosmological and conceptual orders in their integrated wholeness as well as through relating their relevance to social and historical conditions.

Related to esotericism, the concept of invisibility encompasses conceptual and social dimensions. Conceptually, invisibility indicates what is existentially absent, unseen, hidden, internal, and spiritual (el-Aswad 2002). A Shi'i person can speak about the hidden Imam, hidden knowledge, hidden meaning, hidden sentiments, and hidden worlds. Socially, invisibility designates certain underprivileged social categories such as minorities, immigrants, suppressed religious sects, the unemployed, children, women, and marginalized groups whose social and economic status has deteriorated as a consequence of local and global sociopolitical causes. Such groups strive to unearth possible alternatives to both reinstate meaning or visibility to their lives and reduce the eroding forces of their identities (el-Aswad 2010b).

To demarcate the relationship between esoteric beliefs and related practices in different urban and rural communities, I conducted extensive ethnographic studies in Manama, the capital city of Bahrain,[1] and four villages: 'Arad, al-Duraz, ad-Dayh, and Blad al-Qadim.[2] The ethnographic material of this chapter was obtained through several fieldwork projects of varying intervals conducted between 2004 and 2007. The complicated topic of the Shi'i hidden cosmology or worldview required a lengthy period to understand and assimilate in terms of both its underlying principles and content. In these locations, I conducted in-depth interviews with forty Shi'i and fifteen Sunni persons from diverse socioeconomic and educational backgrounds and nine prominent Shi'i religious leaders. I observed and participated in several activities and gatherings such as 'Ashura mourning rituals,[3] art exhibitions, folk theater, and religious discourses that took place in mosques, *ma'tams*, and *ḥusainiyyas*.[4] I also visited the shrines of several local Shi'i saints. In the process, I discovered that there are no Sunni saints commemorated in shrines in Bahrain. In addition to the aforementioned locations, I chose certain villages with Shi'a majorities such as Bani Jamrah, Karzakkan, Sar, and Sitra to observe different forms of 'Ashura ritual, art, and folk performance.

THE SHI'A OF BAHRAIN

The Kingdom of Bahrain, a group of connected islands, is the smallest country in the Arab Gulf region, with a total land area of nearly 240 square miles (figure 3.1). Unlike the other Arab Gulf states, Bahrain has a Shi'a majority, locally known as "Baharna," reaching as high as 70 percent among Bahraini nationals (Bahry 2000, 132). In 2008, the population of Bahrain was 1,050,000. Muslims (Sunni and Shi'a) constituted 99 percent; the rest were Hindus, Christians, Jews, and Bahais. Ethnic groups were as follows: Bahraini Arabs 63 percent, Asians 19 percent, other Arabs 10 percent, and Iranians (*'Ajam*) 8 percent (Kazim 2009, 17). Despite the fact that Bahrain has experienced rapid changes in urbanization, modernity, advanced technology, and economic liberalization, the majority of Bahraini people continue to live in rural, peripheral areas. Shi'a are economically and politically marginalized, inhabiting the least developed areas in both rural and urban communities (Khury 1981, 26).

Shi'ism has been followed by Bahraini Arabs since the early history of the schism in Islam (Bahry 2000, 132). Bahraini Shi'a, following Imam 'Ali bin Abi Talib (600–661), the Prophet Muhammad's cousin and son-in-law and the fourth of the "Rightly Guided Sunni Caliphs," believe in the Twelve Imams and thus are called "Twelvers" (*ithna 'ashariyya*).[5] Like other Shi'a, they believe that Imam 'Ali ibn Abi Talib should have been the first Imam, or successor of the Prophet Muhammad. The martyrdom of Imam Husain (680)[6] who was the son of Imam 'Ali, grandson of the prophet Muhammad, and the third Imam of the Shi'a, and his companions is considered the exemplary model of sacrifice and the cornerstone of Shi'a culture.[7]

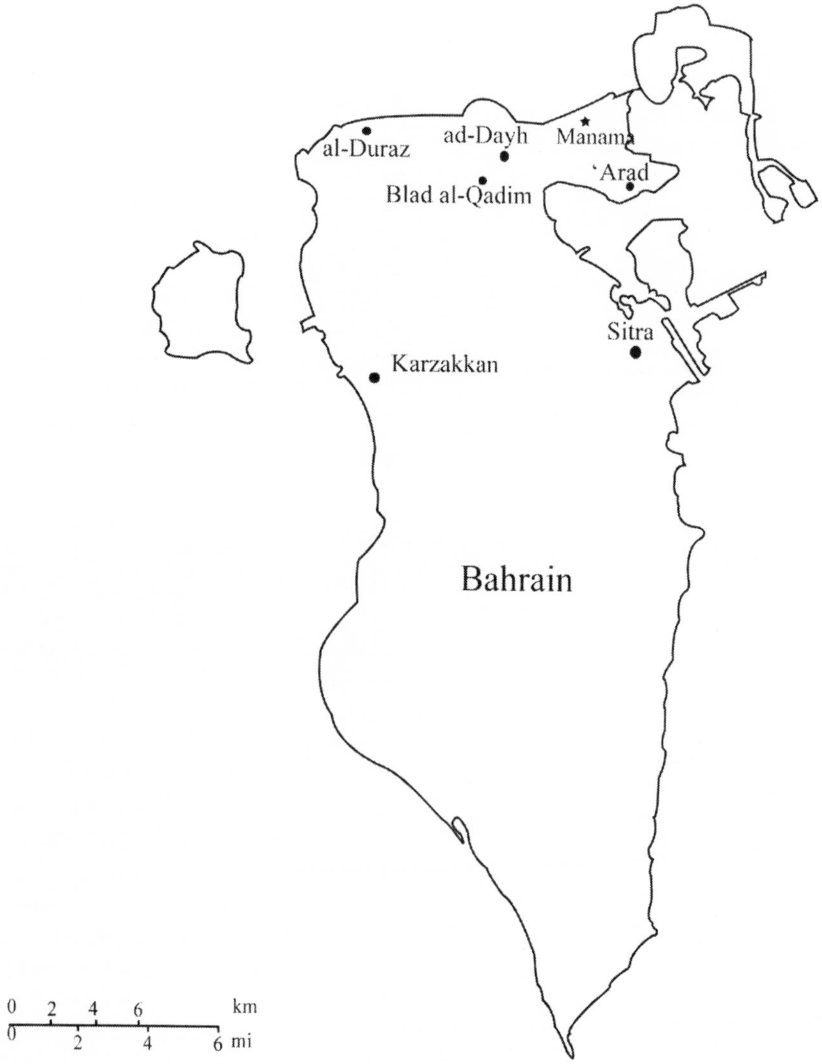

Figure 3.1. Bahrain.

The Arab population of Bahrain was Shi'a centuries before the country was captured in 1783 by the ruling Sunni family, which deprived them of political power (Louër 2008a, 16; Holes 2005, 145). In the eighteenth century, Bahrain Shi'a changed from Usulism, deeply associated with Safavid Iran and which could be easily suspected of being a vector of Iranian influence, to Akhbarism, which was compromising toward the established Sunni orders. Akhbari scholars rejected Usuli principles of deductive reasoning and consensus (*ijmā'*) and independent reasoning (*ijtihād*) as sources of distortion of Islamic doctrine (Louër 2008a, 18, 19; Cole 2002, 54).

Bahraini Shi'a, through embracing Akhbarism, has acted compromisingly toward the established orders. Akhbari scholars considered the Qur'an and the reports from the Prophet and Imams sufficient sources to establish, promote, and practice Islamic law. According to Akhbarism, no ruler can be legitimate during the absence of the Imam, "but conversely none is more illegitimate than another provided that the ruler enforces the minimum Islamic ethic" (Louër 2008a, 16). Akhbarism appeared as a suitable credo for Baharna.[8] I heard a Shi'i person saying that the Akhbaris were very similar to the Sunnis in following the Prophet's tradition. Presently, however, the Usulis are dominant in Bahrain. Alhough not dominant, the Akhbari Shi'i communities are still found in Bahrain as well as in other countries such as Iraq, India, Pakistan, and Saudi Arabia (Cole 2002, 50–57).

The Shi'a, especially those following the Usulis, practice what is known as *taqlid* (imitation), where Muslims who are not certified in religious knowledge seek guidance in religious matters. However, the *'ulama* of Bahraini Shi'a, through dissimulation (*taqiyya*) and diplomacy, have played a conciliatory role. The Shi'a observe *taqiyya*, a concept connoting extreme caution through which people are rendered socially and politically invisible (through abstinence, withdrawal, avoidance, or reservation) when their belief is questioned or life jeopardized. *Taqiyya* involves passive resistance, emphasizing diplomacy and artful forms of resistance instead of direct confrontation with opposing power.

The geographic location of Bahrain renders it sensitive to conflicting views. Its proximity to Iran is recognized in the Shi'i community, just as the proximity to Saudi Arabia is felt in Sunni religious domains (Shehadeh 2004, 26–41). Despite this tension caused by its strategic location, Bahrain is known for its moderation and religious tolerance (Bahry 2000, 131). While the Shi'a have "never revolted against the Sunni rulers, resentment was high against those they considered alien conquerors" (Louër 2008b, 38). Such a conflict "had little to do with sectarian antagonism" (Louër 2008a, 11). Therefore, it is not violent confrontation between Shi'a and Sunni, but rather notions of injustice (*ẓulm*) that have generated members of two different groups in one geographic location, one subordinated (Shi'a) to the other (tribal ruler) through historical and political disparity. Noteworthy also is that Shi'i people along with moderate Sunni follow a strategy of cross-ethnic and largely secular political alliances. Lower-class Sunnis are less happy with their social and economic position. They show great sympathy to Shi'a efforts to reform the existing political and social order (Fuller and Francke 1999, 142).

THE INVISIBLE IN THE SHI'I IMAGINATION

Through the plastic power of imagination, people have free access to the large realm of essential possibilities. Imagination allows for the creation of images and symbols through which people venerate eminent visible and invisible beings and forces. "Imagination shows both the *distinction* of man and his *place* in the universe" (Kaufmann and Heider 1947, 370) and, as such, plays an essential role in the construction of esoteric cosmologies. Cosmology, embodied in the practices and discourses of large groups of common people, indicates inner meaning systems made of distinct points of view or assumptions and images in accordance with which the universe, including society and person, is constructed (Viveiros de Castro 1989, 469; el-Aswad 2002, 2; Smart 1995, 5). Social cosmology or "social imaginary" denotes "the ways people imagine their social existence, how they fit together with others, how things go on between them and their fellows, the expectations that are morally met, and the deeper normative notions and images that underlie these expectations" (Taylor 2004, 23).

Two notions encompass esoteric Bahraini cosmology, one applicable generally to Islam and the other particular to Bahraini Shi'ism. The general notion of the unseen goes beyond a specific Muslim sect and is associated with overarching Muslim worldviews. It encompasses the invisible (*al-ghaib*) or what is simultaneously absent, unknowable, imperceptible, spiritual, and existent (el-Aswad 1994).

In the study of worldviews the focus is on people's beliefs and actions or practices as well as their views of time and space (Boulding 1956; Jones 1972; Kearney 1984; Redfield 1968). The core concepts of the worldview or cosmology of Bahraini Shi'ism more specifically can be illustrated through focusing on four paradigms showing the connection between the unseen/doctrinal and the seen/social levels. First is the doctrinal paradigm, where Shi'i people, both *'ulama* and ordinary individuals, show immense concern for mystical realms of the universe as represented in their belief in and actions toward the occultation of the Hidden Imam. Second is the spatial paradigm, where unseen forces and entities are physically and geographically validated. Third is the temporal or calendrical paradigm that includes discursive actions (such as *ḥusainiyya* discourses)[9] and nondiscursive actions, including collective performances, rituals (more specifically 'Ashura), public processions, and bodily symbolism. Fourth are the visual paradigms, including iconography, art exhibitions, and folk theater, that are socially recognized ways for revealing and negotiating hidden aspects of the cosmos and society.

In dealing with these paradigms, this chapter, applying semiotic analysis, follows Peirce's triple classification of signs, mainly icon, index, and symbol. For Peirce, the relationship between signs, their objects, and their meanings or mental representations (interpretants) is fundamental in semiotic analysis. All representations involve signs. There are three kinds of relations a sign might have to what it signifies. Resemblance is necessary for the icon. A sign is considered iconic, such as a photo or image, when it resembles what it refers to. Contiguity turns a sign into an index, such as knocking on a door. An index demonstrates the existence of its object. Finally, a sign becomes a symbol when nothing but convention determines its relationship with what it stands for (Peirce 1931–1958).

THE DOCTRINAL PARADIGM

The Qur'an contains apparent (exoteric) and hidden (esoteric) meanings. This, in turn, implies the existence of two religious ways of knowledge; one is acquired (*kasbī*), represented in the *shari'a*, seeking to worship God, and the other is spiritual or internal (*bāṭin*), reflected in the truth (*ḥaqīqa*), aimed at knowing God. The inner or mystic dimension is emphasized by Sufism, dominantly Sunni, as well as by Shi'ism (el-Aswad 2006).[10]

Although the meaning of a specific religious doctrine can be elaborated within the consciousness of both Shi'i religious scholars (*'ulama*) and the common people, the *'ulama* prefer esoteric interpretations of the Qur'an and the traditions of the Prophet and Imams over exoteric interpretations. For the Shi'a, the doctrine of the Imamate (*Imamah* or spiritual leadership), a fundamental element in their religious orientation, is based on the belief that God would bequeath guidance to the Muslim community after the Prophet Muhammad's death (Amir-Moezzi 1994, 75; Fuller and Francke 1999, 12–13). There is a serious attempt by the Shi'i religious scholars to reflect on the doctrine of Imamate, in general, and the exegesis of the current but hidden and awaited Imam, al-Mahdi al-Muntazar, in particular.[11] Although the doctrine of al-Mahdi is common to both Sunni and Shia Muslims, the Shi'i religious scholars mediate between the Hidden Imam and the common Shi'a who, in turn, seek guidance from the *marja'* (source of emulation) or *'ulama*.

For Bahraini Shi'a, the relationship between the al-Mahdi and Shi'i esoteric worldview can be realized by concentrating on the hierarchically complementary relationship between the part and the whole, or the world (Dumont 1986). Shi'i worldview or cosmology is contingent on an eschatological construct founded on a messianic figure, the Hidden Imam, who is considered to be present and alive.[12] As a living cosmic figure, al-Mahdi is not confined to the cycle of life and death of ordinary people; rather, he encompasses certain events belonging to the past, present, and future.

The mystical attribute of al-Mahdi is set in a time altogether different from historical time. Whereas the stories of the first eleven Imams are historical in nature, the history of the Twelfth Imam is esoteric and mystical. For the Shi'a, the Awaited Imam disappeared by divine command as a five-year-old child on the day his father, the eleventh Imam, Hasan 'Askari (who because of political persecution lived in dissimulation), died in 873.[13] For the Shi'a, al-Mahdi, a cosmological icon, is expected to return as the divinely guided ruler to end the cycle of injustice (*ẓulm*) as well as to establish a reign of justice (*'adl*) at the end of time (*ākhir az-zamān*), hence he is called the Master of Time (*ṣāḥib az-Zamān*).[14] Until then, the religious scholars (*'ulama* or *marja'*) are general agents of, and serve as the link to, the Awaited Imam. Within this context, the notion of invisibility provides the *possibility* of a more complete sociopolitical, cultural, and religious experience (figure 3.2).

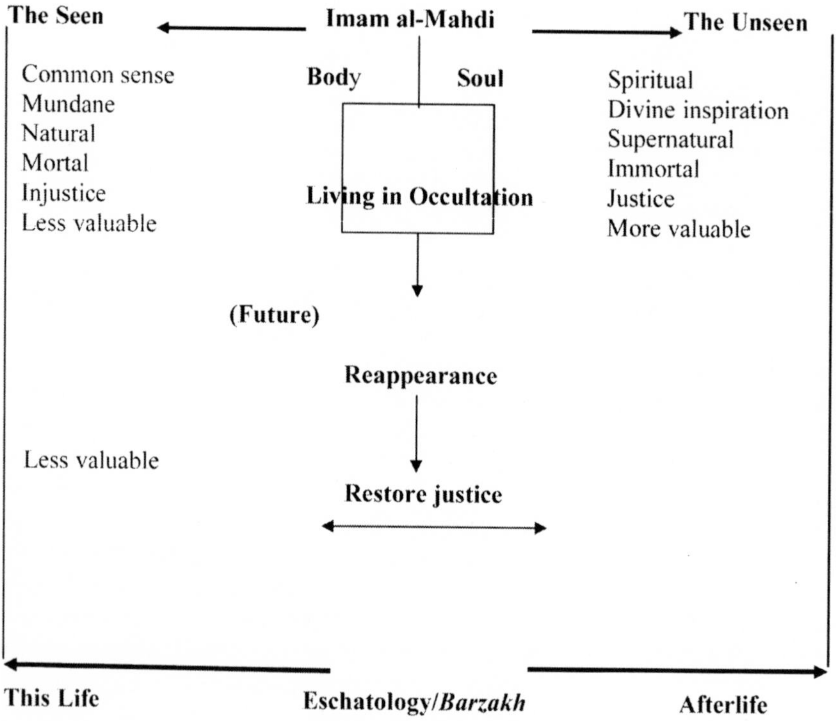

Figure 3.2. Al-Mahdi in the Shi'i worldview with its seen and unseen domains.

The doctrine of the Imamate implies certain interpretations and activities indicating happy and poignant events. This doctrine, through the theme of justice, explains how the commemoration of Imam al-Mahdi's birth, a happy event, can be connected with the mourning commemoration of Imam Husain. In other words, the theme of justice, a core principle in Shi'i cosmology and sociopolitical outlook, links the martyrdom of Imam Husain, who sacrificed life defending it, with the birth of the current but hidden Imam al-Mahdi, who is believed to be alive and expected to reappear in future to restore justice. Thus, the suffering of Husain, caused by discrimination and injustice, has brought about a solemn yearning to establish justice in society. The unseen world, taking precedence over the seen reality, confirms the notion that "justice will inevitably be attained by a higher power" (el-Aswad 2002, 90).

SPATIAL PARADIGM: INDEXICALITY OF THE UNSEEN AND THE DISCOURSE OF SPIRITUALITY

The concept of cosmology refers to assumptions concerning the structure of the universe and is extended here to include geography, "ecology and society as well as human and nonhuman beings and forces, both perceptible and imperceptible, as constituting integrated parts of that universe" (el-Aswad 2002, 2). Places are constructed in people's memories and affections by repeated encounters and complex associations through which a sense of place involves a sense of being (Butz and Eyles 1997).

For Bahraini Shi'a, certain places are believed to be associated with the miraculous wonders of al-Mahdi and other spiritual figures. Such places are known as *al-Qadam*, literally meaning "foot," or *Qadam al-Mahdi* (also called *Waṭiya*), in which footmarks of Imam al-Mahdi are believed to be imprinted. As the index that indicates the existence of its object, the footprint similarly signifies a miraculous walking that, in turn, refers to a wandering living person. The *Qadam al-Mahdi* is a cubic building a few meters in height, width, and length crowned with a green dome (*qubbah*)[15] encasing each of the engraved footprints (figure 3.3).

There are several sites in which various forms of *Qadam al-Mahdi* are found, including villages such as al-Duraz, al-Qadam, Blad al-Qadim, al-Jufair, Sar, and Shahrakkan, among others. These sites, serving as indexical relations between the Shi'a, Imam al-Mahdi, and the earth, are in locations where the unseen is

Figure 3.3. Qadam al-Mahdi, Bahrain.

conceived to be felt most fervently and where people share social values and sentiments with others. Apart from calendrical rituals, discussed subsequently, certain offerings are presented to the local shrine of al-Mahdi as part of the fulfillment of a vow (*nadr*) or a plea to Allah. I saw Shi'i people place colorful pieces of cloth on al-Mahdi's footmark for the purpose of transmitting blessing (*baraka*) to themselves. Shi'i women use green strips to make knots (*rabt*) and tie them to the shrines' windows or doors accompanied with supplications for marriage, pregnancy, recovery from illness, and the like. When their prayers are answered, they return to untie the knots and confirm their vows (figure 3.4).

These locations of *al-Qadam* as well as shrines of al-Mahdi and other local saints are operating indexically, referring to esoteric and unseen realms of the cosmos that render geography sacred. Visitations (*ziyāra*) are made to the shrines and graves of Imams and saints for the sake of *baraka* and mystical intercession (*shafā'a*).[16] Such indexically sanctified sites and shared symbolism allow the Shi'a to converse about the esoteric dimensions of reality, creating a real and profound experience.

There are other places, such as the *ma'tam* or *ḥusainiyya*, that reaffirm spiritual existence. The *ma'tam*, a large hall used for religious, social, and political gatherings as well as for special events such as funeral rituals and marriage ceremonies, is considered a public place in which speakers and listeners, or hosts and guests, observe common social and cultural codes. Buildings, such as *ma'tams* and

Figure 3.4. Shi'i woman knotting green thread in a shrine, Bahrain.

mosques, function to substantiate beliefs (Rappaport 1999, 145). The discourses of the *ḥusainiyya* allow communication between unseen (hidden Imams and martyrs) and seen realities. The esoteric cosmology and spirituality that exist in the minds and hearts of the Shi'i people are substantiated in the discourses of the *ḥusainiyya*.

Moral pedagogy, especially the willingness to learn and teach about the ethics of the Karbala events, is a critical constituent of the *ma'tam*. Interestingly, in the *ma'tams*, I observed people praying in prostration on *at-turba al-ḥusainiyya*, a small piece of dried clay brought from the earth of Karbala, or using prayer beads (*sibḥah*) also made of the same clay (figure 3.5). Sunni Muslims do not observe these practices.

I attended several *ma'tams*, including *ma'tam* Ben Rajab, *ma'tam* Ben Salloum, *ma'tam* al-Gassab, *ma'tam* Samamik, *ma'tam* Haj 'Abbass, *ma'tam al-'ajam* (built by Bahraini Shi'a from Iranian descent, and *ma'tam al-Qal'a* (see figure 3.6) in Manama and its surrounding villages where nationally and regionally reputable *shaikhs* (*faqīh*) lectured about various relevant, contemporary aspects of people's daily lives, including, for instance, social and political reform, democracy, freedom, equality, tolerance, and acceptance of the other. Also, the *shaikhs* addressed what they called the ethics of Husain (*al-adab al-Husainī*), indicating exemplary distinctive qualities such as courtesy, propriety, integrity, honesty, patience, justice, bravery, modesty, generosity, nobility, and moral equality. Some Sunni Muslims willingly attended the *ma'tam*.

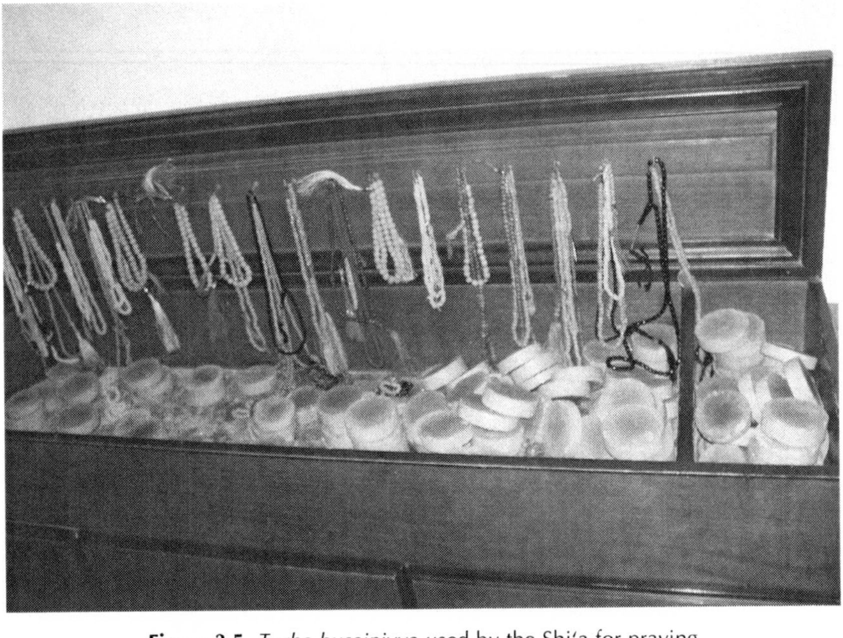

Figure 3.5. *Turba ḥusainiyya* used by the Shi'a for praying.

Figure 3.6. *Ma'tam* in Bahrain.

Essentially, the *shaikhs* were invited in these *ma'tams* to conduct *ḥusainiyya* recitations commemorating the martyrdom of Imam Husain. Shi'i Muslims congregated to recite verses of the Qur'an, collectively read poems praising the Prophet and his family (*ahl al-bait*), and narrate mournful elegies (*ta'ziyas*). On one occasion, following a Qur'anic reciter (*qāri'*), the *shaikh* (*faqīh*), began to deliver his sermon. "We are in the presence of the Imam Husain, the infallible Imams and Imam al-Mahdi," the *shaikh* proclaimed. "May Allah praise Muhammad and his family" (*allahuma ṣalī 'ala Mohammad wa āl Muhammad*) was loudly and collectively resonated three times by the audience following the leader's mention of each Imam and member of *ahl al-bait*. Such verses and phrases were uttered to get the attendees to chant in unison as well as to transport them from the material world into a more spiritual realm. This unique atmosphere of spirituality deepens communication between participants who assert that blessing (*baraka*) exists when people pray, work, and eat together. The Shi'i participants believe that the spirits of saints and Imams, including al-Husain and al-Mahdi, descend to participate in collective gatherings. I heard Shi'i persons say, with reference to al-Mahdi, "When will you appear, O, son of al-Husain." Both the *shaikh* and attendants respond with passion to a past, invisible, historical event that is rendered present, visible, and alive through ritual narration.

In the *ma'tam*, the shaikh passionately reiterated the dreadful episodes of the battle of al-Taff (near Karbala, in which Imam Husain was martyred) and created an emotional atmosphere for the participants. He narrated publicly that when the decapitated head of Husain was brought in a pot to 'Ubaydallah ibn Ziyad, the governor of Kufa, a child tugged the robe of the sultan and told him that the eyes of the severed head were moving. In the same sermon the *shaikh* relayed that ibn Ziyad inserted a stick in the head's mouth, bared its teeth, and consequently further dehumanized the martyr.[17] In yet another version the head spoke with wisdom, much like the head of Yahya ibn Zakariyya (John the Baptist). Such narration reinvents the tradition and renders this remote history of martyrdom real, recent, and perceptible. Further, bereavement, concealed in people's heart, is rendered visible in the *ma'tam*. Tears are understood as an embodiment of participants' spiritual states and inner or hidden emotions of sadness and sorrow. Such hidden modes of sorrow are expressed in religious rituals performed, for example, in other Shi'i communities in Iran and Iraq.[18]

It is within this cosmic and social imagery imbued with divine wonders also that al-Khiḍr, the invisible-cosmic saint[19] known as the "Pious Slave" (*al-'abd aṣ-ṣāliḥ*) upon whom Allah has bestowed divine hidden knowledge, is believed to be present (and sometimes visible) among those who recall his name.[20] Such discursive acts and related symbols constitute a reality for the Shi'a.

TEMPORAL PARADIGM: CALENDRICAL CYCLES AND SHI'I COSMOLOGICAL ORDER

Different copies of the Shi'i calendar (*ruznāmah*) were given to me by several Shi'i friends and informants to help me achieve a better understanding of their rituals and ceremonies. Baqir, a Shi'i volunteer who was organizing the celebration, gave me one of these calendars on the night of the mid-Sha'ban (the eighth Islamic month) where the Shi'a were celebrating the birthday of Imam al-Mahdi. When I thanked him, saying "*shukran*," he said, "People here do not say 'thank you or *shukran*,' rather 'may Allah reward you [*ma'jūr*] or may Allah have mercy on your parents" (*Allah yarḥam wālidaik*). On giving me the calendar, Baqir said, "We venerate al-Mahdi, the Master of the Present and Time" (*ṣāhib al-'aṣr wa az-zamān*), accentuating the permeability of the esoteric cosmology. All of the calendars I received were divided into various little squares, most of which indicated certain important days during which significant events for the Shi'a occurred. The formulation of social-historical events as components of social cosmology relies on calendrical rituals that are not restricted to the liturgies of Muharram or 'Ashura. The calendrical rituals divide the year into contrasting periods differentiating sad and tragic events from happy events.

Shi'i calendrical rituals manipulate social-cosmological cycles marking the beginning and the end of certain historical events that reproduce the Shi'i cosmological order. Each rite is ordered according to its place in the calendrical cycle of rituals. For example, the annual burning of tents (*ḥarq ṣafar*) that occurs at the end of the month of Safar (the second Islamic month) is a significant element of the Shi'i local rituals that demarcates the end of sorrowful memories related to the tragic events that occurred in the Islamic months of Muharram and Safar. Like Muharram, Safar is the month in which unfortunate events, such as the deaths of the Prophet Muhammad and Imam Hasan as well as the arrival of Imam Husain's captive relatives to Yazid's palace at Syria, happened. On the last Wednesday of the month of Safar, Bahraini Shi'a ritualistically burn a number of tents, signaling the end of the period of mourning and the beginning of the period of delight.

The Shi'a maintain major calendrical mourning rituals starting with the Islamic month of Muharram and ending at the last day of Safar, or, more specifically, at the birthday of the Prophet Muhammad (in Rabi' al-Awwal, the third month in the Islamic calendar).[21] In mid-February 2005, I had the chance to attend the Muharram rituals in Manama and the villages. Also, I was invited by separate Shi'i friends to participate in various ritual activities in such villages as 'Arad, Bani Jamrah, ad-Dayh, al-Duraz, and Karzakkan. Though I knew much theoretically about 'Ashura mourning rituals, these invitations provided me with a unique opportunity to see and participate in rituals I had never experienced. During 2006, my choices to participate were more selective and focused. For example, I focused on certain nights such as those of the "Seventh" (*al-sābi'*), commemorating al-'Abbas, the martyred sibling of Husain, the "Eighth" (*al-thāmin*), commemorating al-Qasim, the son of Imam Hasan and nephew of Imam Husain, the "Ninth" (*al-tāsi'*), commemorating 'Ali al-Akbar, the martyred son of Husain, and the "Tenth" (*al-'Ashir*), the night of 'Ashura. Each night's ritualistic processions varied in degree of intensity; however, the events that culminated in the night of 'Ashura were the most intense (figure 3.7).

The 'Ashura mourning rituals and processions (*mawkab al-'azā'*) that I observed in the villages, especially those of al-Duraz, 'Arad, and Bani Jamrah, commenced nearly one hour after sunset. Each village commemorated Muharram and carried out its own rituals honoring historical and religious personalities in *ma'tams*. Then, the participants, wearing black or dark clothes, organized themselves in processions and walked through the villages' main streets. Large communal feasts of mainly meat and rice accompanied by fruits and beverages were publicly arranged both inside and outside *ma'tams*. Young and old men from different economic and educational backgrounds, including doctors, engineers, lawyers, workers, and college students, among others, volunteered in both the preparation and serving of the food. "For the sake of al-Husain and *ahl al-bait*, we love," was a phrase I heard many times while men offered the food to the guests, audience, or those walking by (figure 3.8). On asking a Shi'i person to give me a cup of water, I heard him utter, "Drink water and curse Yazid" (*ishrab maiy wa il'an Yazid*). When I asked him about the meaning of that phrase, he

Figure 3.7. 'Ashura rituals in Manama, Bahrain.

Figure 3.8. 'Ashura commemoration inside the *ma'tam*.

recounted that most Shi'i people say such a phrase to condemn Yazid for cutting off the water and showing no mercy to Imam Husain and his companions who suffered from thirst before their martyrdom. Such a phrase renders past and historical events present and sensible. Thus, the sharing of food is considered a collective practice substantiating the Shi'i conviction that the spirits of Imam Husain and other Imams are witnessing or participating in such devout occasions.[22]

At around 10 p.m., most participants left their villages and went to Manama to further participate in the grand processions until dawn, symbolizing Shi'i unity and visibility. The tenth of Muharram ('Ashura) is considered the major day for rituals, where various Shi'i communities performed emotionally laden mourning rituals. Symbols, iconic images, and replicas (*tashbīhāt*) of characters and events of the battle of Karbala were depicted in the processions as well as in displays on street corners and sidewalks, accentuating the participants' religious views. Different ethnic groups, including, for example, Pakistanis, Iranians, Bengalis, and Indians, among others, participated in the 'Ashura rituals, bestowing a sense of unity on all participants.

In each procession, accompanied by drummers and singers (*radūd*) with microphones carried on wooden posts, men marched in two rows shouting the phrase "*Yā Husain.*" Each procession had its own banner, slogan, and style of performance that included mild to more severe forms of self-flagellation (*nadbah* or *laṭmah*). The mild forms included the *laṭmah* or beating of the left side of the chest with the right hand and right side of the chest with the left hand. Some used only the right hand to beat the left side of the chest.[23] These bodily actions display that the Shi'a are guilt ridden. I heard a man, while beating his chest, say, "Karbala is my land [soil] and 'Ashura is my time" (*Karbalā' arḍī wa 'ashurā' zamānī*). Severe forms included scourging of the back (*zangīl*),[24] or piercing of the head (*taṭbīr*) until bleeding. Many South Asian Muslims practice flagellation during Muharram in various forms (Hyder 2006). A significant aspect of these performances was the dramatic way of making hidden feelings and intense passions visible.

Through the manipulation of the body (el-Aswad 2005c), the Shi'a confirmed that the martyrdom in Karbala holds, presently and in the future, powerful ethical and political symbolism for the oppressed and marginalized. Such rituals and physical displays not only symbolize the struggle against injustice but also act to change any ideological or materialistic power that precludes individuals from their rights. The Shi'i cosmic views of time, represented in both religious beliefs and calendrical rituals, indicate that the past and the present are in the future. "While the Balinese in their ritual communication live in a timeless present, that is in a phenomenological representation of time where the present and the past are so fused that the present is a mere manifestation of the past" (Bloch 1977, 288), Bahraini Shi'a live in a seamless temporal paradigm through which both past and present lead to or predict the future where justice will be established.

VISUAL PARADIGM: ICONOGRAPHY, ART EXHIBITION, AND FOLK THEATER

The visual paradigm reflects all other paradigms discussed in previous sections. This section focuses on the role played by iconography, art exhibitions, and folk theater in revealing certain significant dimensions of the esoteric cosmology of Bahraini Shi'a. Physical display of emotions and beliefs is substantiated not only through bodily symbolism but also through iconography or works of art. Art, in all its forms, helps people visualize, relive, and personalize events. The most effective ways of expressing people's thought and feeling are those implementing visible means, including symbols of the visual art (Langer 1953). Signs and pictorial symbolism, mediating between the external world of objects and the internal world of ideas, express the most basic ideas, emotions, and judgments of people simultaneously (Austin 1977; Chelkowski 1985).

Both Shi'i artists and laymen engage themselves in creating iconographical images so as to comprehend the mystery and permeability of their esoteric cosmology. The suggestive power of the artistic way of representation makes it an easy task to translate what people perceive and understand into perfectly clear figures of imagination (Kaufmann and Heider 1947, 132). At the beginning of Muharram, the Shi'a hang black flags, banners, and posters on houses, mosques, *ma'tams*, and wooden stands in the streets. Colorful forms of calligraphy, iconography, replicas (*tashbīhāt*), and visual representations are presented and shown in exhibitions in the streets of Manama as well as in most of the villages with Shi'i majorities. The value of thinking and acting through icons and replicas is central to the imagination of the Shi'a in their pursuits of religiosity. In the Shi'i tradition, icons are generally images depicting holy beings, such as Imams, and events or objects (real or imaginative) that are painted on wood, printed on paper or metal, or embroidered on cloth or flat panels and hung on walls as well as on the façades of buildings. These replicas or images, acts of imagination seeking to make the unseen seen, blend in artistically with other replicas and images held by those who participate in 'Ashura processions.

Despite the fact that the Sunnis have great respect for 'Ashura, they do not follow the artistic and ritualistic fashions for commemorating religiously significant events in the same manner as the Shi'a (el-Aswad 2003a, 2008b). Shi'i culture manipulates images and replicas, particularly in religious art, as far as they are based on mere imaginary resemblances (rather than full identification) and function as symbolic devices to depict Imams and holy persons.

Art symbolism is extensively epitomized in 'Ashura processions as well as in the Husaini art gallery (*al-marsam al-ḥusainī*). For instance, artistic depictions included the following: a big turban (symbolizing the head of al-Husain), a white horse (marked with red spots reminiscent of the blood of Husain), coffins (representing the martyrdom of Husain), cradles (representing Abdulla, the slaughtered son of Husain), posts elevating the hands of al-'Abbas (Husain's brother),[25] a green ship (signifying the notion of salvation), a replica of the Imam ʻAli, and the veiled face of al-Mahdi (figure 3.9).

Individuals and interviewees I conversed with emphasized that these drawings and visual replicas of holy persons are not objects for prayer, but rather are perceived as means of memories as well as of intercession (*shafā'a*) through which *baraka* and peace are transmitted to people. Further, these tokens are visible, collective, and public signs evincing not only the Shi'i hidden sorrowful feelings associated with the historical events of Imam Husain at Karbala, but also their anticipation for a future full of justice.

Discursive and nondiscursive actions are fused together through art and bodily movement. This was clearly displayed when I saw the Shi'a saluting the Hidden Imam through bodily displays on hearing his name (al-Mahdi or al-Hujjah) or seeing his green-robed image with his face concealed by white paint. Postures of salutation, such as lowering the head, lightly patting the forehead with the right hand, closing the eyes, uttering invocations to Allah to bring about the speedy reappearance of the Hidden Imam, and the like, are substantiated, self-referential messages rendering the unseen seen and the spiritual indexical. As Rappaport has observed, "Corporeal representation gives weight to the incorporeal and gives visible substance to aspects of existence which are themselves impalpable, but of great importance in the ordering of social life" (Rappaport 1999, 141).

Figure 3.9. Replica representing the head of al-Husain.

Another form of art that renders the invisible visible is the social drama (Turner 1982) or "folk or living theater" in which the core themes enacted are shared and relived by both actors and spectators (Chelkowski 1979, 1985). Social drama or folk theater here refers to gatherings in which Shiʿi men volunteered to perform certain episodes of the tragic events of Karbala. Despite the difference between rituals and dramas, they are related as far as they refer to performative actions or "things done" (Rappaport 1999, 135).[26] Basically, drama is an enactment of a certain narrative story or myth and rests on its ability to move or persuade people. In the Shiʿa case, the performance evokes strong emotion and sympathy by enlivening the historical event, making it more recent or present than remote or past, encouraging people to react emotionally and intellectually to it. The significance of the contents of such performances derives not from the experience and interpretation of the performers but from their role in giving voice to precepts having their origin outside or beyond the individual (Brenneis 1987, 242), that is, within the Shiʿi heritage.

A segment of history is made present through folk theater. In March 2005, I attended folk plays in the villages of Bani Jamrah and ʿArad. Although the audience in Bani Jamrah, totaling approximately 1,000, outnumbered those of ʿArad by one third, I noticed that except for the assigned space for the performers, there were no physical borders between the actors and the audience. In the two locations the plays were performed in an open, rectangular-shaped area in the middle of which were the performers. The borders were divided into two lines, each L-shaped, enabling the male and female audiences to view the performances separately.

In the village of Bani Jamrah, fifteen kilometers west of Manama, there was a play commemorating the Fortieth (*al-Arbaʿīn*, referring to the forty days that follow the day of ʿAshura). Tents were set up in two separate camps representing those of Husain's family (wearing green garments, and viewed as defensive) and those of Yazid ibn Muʿawiya's army (wearing red garments, and viewed as offensive). In the middle, the effigy of the headless corpse of Imam Husain lay on the ground. Six of the enemy soldiers, riding back and forth between the two camps on horses, stomped on the replica, further depicting its mutilation and humiliation. While the figure lay on the ground, heads of Husain and his male relatives were erected on spears. A white horse, symbolizing the sainthood and bravery of the fallen Imam, walked riderless back toward the tents of Husain's family. Toward the end of the drama, the tents of the Imam Husain and his family were burned to the ground.

Another play, called *After Zaynab* (*mā baʿd Zaynab*),[27] took place in the village of ʿArad, about six miles east of Manama. The play was held on the evening of Friday, the twenty-first of Safar (1426 AH), or March 31, 2005, and, as in the other villages, portrayed the martyrdom of Husain. Enacted in an open area, an actor playing the role of Husain asked the enemy to provide some water to his toddler, ʿAbd Allah. The enemy responded by hitting the child in the throat and killing him. There was subsequent weeping and mourning by the audience. The play further illustrated Husain fighting alone after he lost his brother, al-'Abbas (known as the water fetcher [*al-saqqay*] and the protector of children), his nephew al-Qasim, and his other male relatives in battle. Imam Husain was hit in the face by a stone and fell from his horse. Shamar, a vicious enemy, came and severed the head of Husain from his body. At this point, both men and women in the audience were crying heavily, and one man, affected by the intense emotion, fainted and fell down to the ground. Two people carried him from the scene and offered him assistance. Back at the play, the horse of Husain walked alone toward the tent where the women, including Zaynab, recognized that Husain had been martyred. There ensued the crying and mourning of Sukayna and Zaynab who, along with other women, were later taken captive by the enemy. The replica of Husain's corpse lay on the ground, where Zaynab, putting her hands underneath it, uttered, "May Allah accept this body as a sacrifice" (*qurbān*). Toward the end, an actor narrated the following poem:

Your blood, Husain	O martyred thirsty
A cry in the sky of Karbala	awakening the universe from its apathy
With the sword of truth	
and green banner of justice,	Al-Qā'm, al-Mahdi, is coming with victory

CONCLUSION

The point of departure for this chapter is fundamentally cosmological insofar as cosmology or worldview encompasses a totality of the universe, society, and person. The connection between the unseen/doctrinal and the seen/social levels is addressed through highlighting four paradigms: the doctrinal/ritual, the spatial, the temporal, and the visual. My research has focused on the social side of the esoteric cosmology illustrating the impact of religious practices on the visible sociopolitical lives of Bahraini Shi'a. Central to all of these practices is the notion of revealing hidden truth and justice.

The Bahraini Shi'a accentuate the permeability of their esoteric cosmology benefiting from daily discourses (including poetry) and, to a still higher degree, from those of art and, above all, ritual representations of history. Through reproducing historical events, art, folk theater, and 'Ashura rituals give physicality to the living but esoteric or unseen cosmology.

The esoteric cosmology, embodied in narratives of Shi'i Imams (more specifically the Hidden Imam) and 'Ashura rituals, reconstructs Shi'i tradition and initiates possible worlds awash with anticipation for a better life. The sociopolitical invisibility of Bahraini Shi'a is rendered visible and active through religious discursive and nondiscursive actions certifying their mundane aspirations.

Theoretically, the chapter shows that the binary of visible/invisible can be articulated as "in/visible" because what is "visible" indicates, is encompassed by, or is a product of what is "invisible." Put differently, what is unimaginable, esoteric, or invisible, absent, and incomprehensible becomes, through recitations, rituals, art displays, and folk dramas, imaginable, visible, present, and comprehensible.

Bahraini Shi'a keep their future in perspective (in their imagination) by placing the past in the present in preparation or anticipation of the future. They envision the future through the commonly shared anticipation of the emergence of the Hidden Imam, who, it is believed, will reinstate justice locally, regionally, and globally.

The particularity of Bahraini Shi'ism is situated in the cosmological and social contexts within which the issues of occultation, concealment, dissimulation, and hidden mystery can be comprehended. The permeability of the esoteric cosmology of Bahrain Shi'a is embedded in its ability to construct a sense of identity that is fortified not only by participating in the imaginary cosmology, but also by acting out the inner views related to past and future events of particular religious and social significance.

4

The Mystic Worldview of Sufism

Mystic worldviews in Islam are manifested in Sufism (*tṣawwuf*) and, though differently, in other forms of esoteric worldviews of the Imamate Shi'a.[1] As Sells notes, "Islamic mysticism is one of the most extensive traditions of spirituality in the history of religions" (Sells 1996, 1). Sufism highlights the spirituality and deep religiosity of Muslims and is treated here as an integral part of Muslim worldviews.[2] This chapter, based on ethnographic material,[3] considers the core features of the mystic worldviews of Sufis as represented in various Sufi orders. The discussion deals with the regional and Egyptian Sufi orders (*ṭuruq*, sing. *ṭarīqa*) of Ahmadiyya (known also as Badawiyya and/or Sutūḥiyya),[4] founded in Tanta by the Sufi leader Sidi al-Sayyid Ahmad al-Badawi[5] in the thirteenth century, and Shinnawiyya that stemmed from Ahmadiyya/Badawiyya. Special focus is given to the Sufi order of Shinnawiyya, which has been given less scholarly attention than the larger, predominant Sufi order of Ahmadiyya.

The Shinnawiyya Sufi order was established in the thirteenth century by Shaikh 'Umar al-Shinnawi (1215–1251), a spiritual disciple of the grand saint Ahmad al-Badawi. For centuries, members of the Shinnawiyya Sufi order have grown in number and have spread among various local Muslim communities located in proximity to the shrine of al-Badawi in Tanta, Egypt (el-Aswad 2006a). The current head of the Shinnawiyya Sufi order is Shaikh Said al-Shinnawi, son of Shaikh Hasan al-Shinnawi (1926–2008), the former patron head of the order and former president of the Supreme Council of Sufi Orders in Egypt (1997–2008) (figure 4.1).[6]

Participation in Sufi orders and related saint veneration are organized and practiced in local, regional, and global contexts through both traditional modes of communication and the extensive use of cybernetworking. This chapter

Figure 4.1. Shaikh Hasan al-Shinnawi, former head of the Supreme Council of Sufi Orders in Egypt. Courtesy of Shaikh Said el-Shinnawi, the head of the Shinnawiyya Sufi order in Tanta, Egypt.

gives special attention to the phenomenological and semantic scopes of mystic worldviews through focusing on allegorical-symbolic forms of mystic reality as expressed in wide-ranging discursive and nondiscursive contexts.

Studies of Islamic mysticism that have treated Sufism and sainthood either as peripheral aspects of religion or as polytheistic phenomena (Goldziher 1971, 259) or have depicted Sufism as being practiced by backward people holding incongruous beliefs (Arberry 1950 and Nicholson 2002, among others)[7] have been criticized as stemming from an Orientalist perspective. Although mystic and spiritual realities are not situated in the scientific paradigm of modern culture, they nevertheless play a momentous role in the everyday lives of Muslims, traditional or modern, intellectual and ordinary alike. In other words, the experiences of the sacred have been an imperative aspect of mystic worldviews, and they should be included in objective social scientific inquires (Swenson 1999). It has been argued that great Muslim thinkers such as Abu Hamid al-Ghazālī,[8] ʻAbd al-Ḥalīm Maḥmud, the former Grand Imam or Shaikh al-Azhar,[9] and Abu al-Wafa al-Taftazānī, former vice rector of Cairo University,[10] among others, are exemplars of religious scholars who have contributed intellectually to Sufism (el-Aswad 2006a).[11] Sufism has attracted both the literate and illiterate as well as the elite and the folk.

The mystic worldview, relying on intuitive understanding, concerns inexplicable issues such as the meaning of life, death, life after death, destiny of human beings, esoteric forces affecting people's lives, purification of the self, perfection of the world, realization of transcendent reality, and achieving unity with the divinity. In brief, the crux of mystic worldview is that God is the sole and real beloved Being with whom all mystics aspire to be in touch.[12] If the central occupation of the mystic is the effort to know God experientially, all other human activity is subordinated to this central goal (Renard 2004). Mystic experiences are inseparable from imaginative, creative, visionary, illuminative, and sanctified domains.

Faith, trust, and humility are central tenets of both Ahmadiyya and Shinnawiyya Sufi orders. These principles are carefully incorporated into the ritual initiation ceremony of the covenant (*al-'ahd*) for each new Sufi disciple. Also, compassion and emotional intimacy are closely related underlying values of the order. Members consider their Sufi order as a kind of communally oriented circle anchored on a commitment to shared sacred tenets and values. As Salim, a middle-age Sufi who has been a member of the Shinnawiyya for fifteen years, recounted, "When a Sufi says, 'follow your heart' or 'consult you heart' [*istaftī qalbak*], he is fully aware that he acts not only as an individual but also as a member who complies with the ethics of his Sufi order." The order's identity becomes part of each adherent's own individual identity as being a Sufi belonging to a specific order (Ahmadiyya [Badawiyya] or Shinnawiyya, for example). However, Sufis conform to the order without losing their individuality. A member of the order can gain knowledge of his real self, learning the desirable characteristics to which he aspires and the defective attributes against which he must protect.

Sufis seek both to suppress the idea of aggressive materialism confined to this transitory world and to elevate the spiritual quality inherent in people. This spiritual higher consciousness enables people to be aware of higher dimensions of being as well as the hidden secret that can be transmitted through faith. In their gatherings, Sufis feel secure to express and expose, emotionally and spiritually, what they consider as pure and true. They see themselves on a path of self-discovery, a path of growth, which they hope will lead to spiritual empowerment and ability to love and share. To varying degrees, they see the possibility of making a better world, starting with their immediate personal relationships with members of the order, friends, family members, and others within the broader society.

There is a dominant belief among Muslims, which is supported by the Qur'an and Islamic tradition, that nobody, visible or invisible, alive or dead, can know the future or what is unseen and absent (*al-ghaib*) except Allah. Nevertheless, in their everyday lives people show great curiosity about the unknown (*al-majhūl*) and the future (*al-mustaqbal*), particularly in times of crises. Generally speaking, what is unknown, unseen, or hidden is either feared or revered, or both. This awesome and distressing preoccupation with secret, mysterious or mystic and concealed matters is patterned in a widely repeated saying, "We seek our Lord's protection against the concealed (*al-mikhabbī*) when it appears and reveals itself (*ẓahar wa bān*)."

Sufi adherents are aware that secrets of the unseen or unknowable (*asrār al-ghaib*) are beyond their capacities but never stop aspiring to have glimpse them either through *mujāhda* and meditation or through the mediation of their patron *shaikh*. A Sufi leader affirms that through performing specific rituals, praying and reciting certain sacred verses of the Qur'an, or uttering the divine names of God (*dhikr*), he, by God's will (*mashī'at Allah*), will be given signs (*ishārāt*), markers (*'alāmāt*) revealing aspects of the hidden reality. Clearly, these rituals, prayers, and utterances reveal the belief that behind one world or reality lies another. In this context, Sufi adherents seek to attach themselves to a Sufi leader or *shaikh* so as to experience the spiritual dimensions of religious lives as well as to attain blessing by being close to the Prophet and God.

DIALOGUE, *DHIKR*, AND MYSTIC ATTRACTION

Shaikh Hasan, the former patron of the Shinnawiyya Sufi order, discussed in an interview what he described as the balance of dialogues.[13] According to his narrative, there are three inseparable types of dialogues related to the self, God, and society. There are dialogues with the self, dialogues with Allah, and dialogues with others that are required to facilitate mystic harmony and spiritual balance. Through achieving the balance of dialogues as well as living in harmony with sacred principles, Sufis hope to reach a state of grace and spirituality of which few may be aware.

The dialogue with the self indicates self-awareness of unlimited spiritual energy that is needed for achieving self-liberation and balance between the esoteric and exoteric worlds. The serious effort a person expends toward knowing and controlling his/her inner life is perceived as a spiritual or holy struggle (*jihād*). The objective of *jihād*, then, is to attain salvation or liberation through one's own efforts. In this sense, *jihād* is not restricted to the popular meaning of a religiously and politically externalized and mobilized war. "Allah looks at the hearts of people," is a phrase I heard from Shaikh Hasan, who continued, saying, "To be with Allah is to remember and see Him in everything you do or observe, believing that if you do not see Him, He definitely sees you."[14]

The dialogue with God refers to the invocation or remembrance of Allah (*dhikr*, locally pronounced *zikr*) that is believed to form an inner, spiritual connection with God. Saints are known as "friends of God" (*awliyā' Allah*). The Qur'anic verse, "Behold! verily on the friends of Allah there is no fear, Nor shall they grieve" (10:62), is frequently used by Sufi leaders and common Muslims to certify their belief in those who have achieved the merit of spiritual experience and the honored status of being close to Allah. God bestows spiritual enlightenment on those who enact their faith in their daily life, and people should do their best to draw closer to Allah. Sufi *shaikhs* are hierarchically demarcated based on their powers of blessing. Only a few are known for their *baraka* or extraordinary ability to manipulate mystic knowledge for the welfare of the community. In this context, the wonders (*karāmāt*) made by Sufi *shaikhs* or saints are rendered intelligible. Wonders are signs of grace, blessing, and mercy. In terms of mystic reciprocity, one of the Sufis explained these exceptional wonders by quoting a Hadith Qudsi: "Insofar as the slave [*'abd*] continues to be near to Me through good deeds of charity, I will love him. If I love him I will be the ear by which he hears; the eye (sight) by which he sees; the hand by which he strikes; and the legs by which he walks. If he asks me anything, I will give him and if he seeks my protection, I would will grant it."[15] It is the *divine will* that explains the Sufi mystics' extraordinary actions, blessings, and wonders.

The dialogue with others or members of the small community or larger society must be guided within the ethics of Muslim brothers.[16] For the Sufis, the concept of unity of existence indicates not only a firm belief in one God but also unity of all Muslim believers as being brothers (*ukhwa fī l-Islam*). This means that brotherhood is based on spiritual ties of Islam, not of blood. Sufi brotherhood, Shaikh Hasan maintained, in its spiritual aspect, frees humans from blood and tribal affiliation and satisfies spiritual-social needs in a spiritually barren and dry world. It constitutes a unique tie, transcending egoistic desires by involving individuals in charitable deeds (*a' māl khayriyya*) of the Muslim community. A good Muslim is one who uses dialogue to convince others, Muslims or non-Muslims, of his/her views, showing tolerance toward the differing perspectives of other people.[17] This means that the Sufis go further to state that Muslims accept adherents of other religions (of the Book, *ahl al-kitāb*) that believe in one God and the Day of Judgment.

Put simply, a significant dimension of the Sufis' mysticism is found in the symbolic importance given to the concept of "brotherhood." In addition to the patron relationship of father/son where the leader of the order is considered both supporter (*sanad*) and commander of the disciple (*murīd*), brotherhood signifies the equal relationship between members of the order. Ideally, brotherhood serves as a leveling mechanism that goes beyond the recognized ranks of the Sufi members to include all Muslims in one unified community, notwithstanding the competitions among them.

The triple dialogue can be demonstrated in both individual or private and collective or public experiences. There are patterns of mystic worldviews dealing with the Ultimate based on inner and subjective experience known as spiritual states (*ḥāl* or *aḥwāl*) attained by means of spiritual guidance, meditation, remembrance of God (*dhikr*), intuition, dreams, and visions. This worldly life is depicted by Sufis as deceptive and full of contradictions and illusions hindering the genuine understanding of *ḥaqīqa* or what is real and hidden that underlies the surface of phenomena. Sufis believe life has only one ultimate source or truth (*Ḥaqq*), God, rendering the entire world a unity notwithstanding the apparent differences. To know the truth, *ḥaqīqa*, Sufis rely on the "disclosure" or "unveiling" (*al-kashf*) of what is hidden or veiled.

Though mystic worldview is not necessarily based on ecstatic experience, it does not reject or negate such an experience when it occurs. I attended various Sufi gatherings (*ḥaḍra*) led by Shaikh Hasan al-Shinnawi. In the *ḥaḍra*, Sufi participants organized themselves in a "circle for the collective remembrance of God" (*ḥalaqat dhikr*). After reciting some verses of Qur'an, praying, and reading poems praising God, the Prophet, and saints, the participants stood to collectively perform the bodily *dhikr*. While moving their bodies toward the right, they said, "Allah"; toward the left, they said, "Alive." They spent almost one hour solemnly repeating the phrase "God is alive" (Allah *ḥayy*) in the same fashion. Now and then, the leader, standing in the middle of the circle, was uttering, in a deep voice, the word "He" (*huwa*), with reference to God. The *shaikh* asked the participants to "remember God" (*udhkur* Allah). They responded collectively, "There is no God but Allah." Then, he said, "confirm the oneness of God" (*waḥḥid* Allah) and the attendants responded, also collectively, using the same phrase, "There is no God but Allah."

While chanting the *dhikr* and other religious songs praising the Prophet and Muslim saints (*madīḥ*), it happened that a man entered into a trance, uttering repeatedly and rapidly the name of Allah as he frothed at the mouth. He also made some barely audible ecstatic utterances (*shaṭaḥāt*) such as: "I am walking by the light of God" (*māshī bi nūr* Allah), "I am longing for the light of God" (*'āshiq nūr Allah*), and "I am walking through the light of God" (*māshī fī nūr Allah*). Such a person was described as being "mystically attracted" (*majzūb* or *majdhūb*). Mystic experience, subjective and emotional, can be neither literally expressed nor conveyed in regular words. In this context, the *dhikr*, empowered with the inner force, has become not just a discursive action but a dynamic bodily agent permeating a new state of existence or consciousness. The ecstatic utterances (*shaṭaḥāt*) themselves are metaphors structured by projections contingent on the human body and perceptual-sensory experience, a process known as "phenomenological embodiment" (Lakoff and Johnson, 1999, 36). In an immediate reaction to the *majzūb*'s ecstatic utterance and behavior, the other participants, involved in the collective *dhikr*, shouted, "Support us, O Prophet" (*madad yā nabī*), "Support us, O Prophet's family" (*madad yā āl al-bait*), and "Support us, O Badawi" (*madad yā Badawi*), among other phrases, displaying feelings of excitement, urgency, bewilderment, and hope for divine intervention and support.

Commenting on the *majzūb*'s behavior, members of the Shinnawiyya Sufi order recounted that the *majzūb* was in a distinct state superior to daily experience. He entered another state of being and was taken there by Allah's sublime glory (*al-jalālah*).[18] The *majzūb* is metaphorically depicted as the person for whom the veil that hides the unseen world is removed (*makshūf 'anhu al-ḥijāb*). As one of the *dhikr* participants described, "the *majzūb* belongs to 'people of God' (*ahl Allah*)." In the *dhikr*, it is a great honor for a *majzūb* to enter into a trance, during which time he is pulled toward or attracted to Allah and leaves, temporarily, this inferior or seen realm and enters the mystic domain of the unseen world. In other words, the *majzūb* experiences a beatific and timeless state that is described by Sufi adherents as "being taken over by divine gravity." This transformation of Sufi behavior is thought of as a manifestation of spiritual states (*aḥwāl rūḥāniyya*). In the mystical experience, the Eternal somehow lies within people, and the mystic cannot know God and other mysteries unless he finds them in himself (Smart 1995, 67, Nicholson 2002, 60).

The *majzūb* is believed to have an inner force that connects him directly with Allah. The perception of the ultimate reality, however, varies from person to person as well as from *shaikh* to *shaikh*. Ecstatic utterances (*shaṭaḥāt*) and unfamiliar words voiced by the mystically attracted (*majzūb*) are interpreted by participants as revealing and disclosing the secrets of the unseen world. If people do not understand these words, they expect that certain events will occur in the future to clarify the incomprehensible utterances. For the *majzūb*, the cosmos is an open book. The transition from the private invisibility of the mystic (Sufi) into the social visibility of the order is brought into being. In this transformation the secret is exposed. It is interesting to note that such behavior is not interpreted by the order as abnormal. Even when some members think that such a behavior is unusual, they never criticize it; rather, they show enthusiasm and wonderment. The Sufis' statement "being enticed by divine gravity" denotes a sublime engagement with the sacred.

THE COSMIC DIMENSION OF THE MYSTIC WORLDVIEW

The mystic worldview of both Sunni and Shi'a Muslims is infused with deeply significant cosmic dimensions according to which there exists, beyond the material reality of nature, another reality that is viewed as even more real and more authentic.[19] As mentioned, the universe is constructed of visible and invisible components depicted, respectively, in terms of perceptible and imperceptible or natural and divine worlds. The visible world is surrounded and penetrated by invisible forces and beings. These categories of unseen forces and entities are dispersed throughout the universe, including humans. I heard in various religious and social contexts the phrase, "Muhammad is the master of the two worlds" (*Sayyid al-kaunain*).

The prophet Muhammad is venerated by Sufis as an exemplary model for the true Sufi due to his meditation and contemplation in the cave on the mount (*Ghār* of Hirā'). Although inner insights and meditations are important aspects of mystic worldviews, divine knowledge (*ladunnī* or *rabbānī*), bestowed directly by God to the faithful, is viewed by mystics as the highest form of mysticism. Hierarchically, highly revered and holy persons such as prophets and friends of God (*awliyā' Allah*) have powerful souls or spirits enabling them to receive such divine knowledge as well as to demonstrate miracles and wonders.[20] This section addresses the impact of the most influential holy persons, namely the Prophet

Muhammad, the Evergreen holy man (al-Khiḍr), the cosmic Pole (*Quṭb*),[21] and the Hidden Imam, in the development of the cosmic dimension of Muslims' mystic worldviews.

Hearing and attending to the Qur'an formally and informally, privately and publicly, is a significant part of the daily socialization process in Muslim-majority societies.[22] Shaikh Yasin, a leading member of the Ahmadiyya (Badawiyya) Sufi order, recounted that the Qur'an, containing divine "secrets" (*asrār*, sing. *sir*), sanctifies the spiritual dimensions of both the universe and human being.[23] He asserted that it is through the recitation of the Qur'an that Sufis and regular Muslims alike experience unique spiritual dimensions of reality.[24] In the Qur'an the Prophet is described as having both exoteric and esoteric (*'ilm ladunnī*) knowledge. Shaikh Yasin recited two verses of the Qur'an indicating the divine mystical knowledge bestowed on the Prophet: "Thus do We relate to thee some stories of what happened before: for We have sent thee a Message from Our own Presence [*Laduna*]" (20:99), and "As to thee, the Qur'an is bestowed upon thee from the Presence of One [*Ladun*] Who is wise and all-knowing" (27:6).[25] All mystic doctrines refer essentially to Muhammad's esoteric reality (*al-ḥaqiqa al-muḥamadiyya*) as present in both Sufism and Shi'ism (Nasr 1988).

Shaikh Yasin stated that, without going into a complex and detailed exegesis of Sufi experience, the mystic knowledge (*m'arifa*) is based on divine principles of mercy (*raḥma*), patience (*ṣabr*), truth (*ḥaqq*), and justice (*'adl*), leading to peace (*salām*) and love (*ḥub*). A highly revered Sufi is depicted as the person who is acquainted with God (*'ārif bi-Allah*). "What all of us [Sufis] have in common," Shaikh Yasin recounted, "is the hope of the mercy of Allah." According to Shaikh Yasin, every Sufi aspires to know and love God with all of his heart (*qalb*), but it is God's mercy that allows such love. With tearful eyes, Shaikh Yasin recited, "Our Lord, Let not our hearts deviate after Thou hast guided us, and grant us mercy from Thine own Presence [*ladunka*]; for Thou art the Grantor of bounties without measure." He also related, "Our model is the Prophet, who is depicted in the Qur'an as a 'mercy' for all creatures" (*raḥmatan lil 'ālamīn*) (21:107).[26] Mercy (*raḥma*) is a divine cosmic principle applied from God to the Prophet as well as to all entities, including people. God has inscribed for Himself the rule of mercy. He describes His mercy as extending to all things.[27] The Book, the Qur'an (Word of God), is also a "mercy," "For We had certainly sent unto them a Book, based on knowledge, which We explained in detail—a guide and a Mercy to all who believe" (7:52).[28]

Shaikh Yasin emphasized that the cosmic Nocturnal Journey and Ascent of the Prophet (*al-Isrā' wa al-mi'rāj*) is a prototype of the mystic experience.[29] Referring to the luminous quality of the Prophet Muhammad (*al-nūr al-Muhammadī*), who is believed to have existed before the creation of the universe, he emphasized that only radiating light can penetrate the universe in such a short period of time. Additionally, the Prophet's family is viewed as a light-giving tree that enlightens the cosmos. Shaikh Yasin recited some verses of the Qur'an affirming that the Prophet, in that journey, went beyond the visible universe and saw the greatest signs of his Lord.[30] Such a miracle shows the Prophet's intimate relationship with God. Among ordinary Muslims the devotion to the Prophet, as their exemplary model, is so great that I heard people frequently recount: "Praising the Prophet is my capital and profit" (*ṣalāt an-nabī rāsmālī wa maksabī*). They hold in veneration and with highest aspiration God, the Prophet, and his family.

Holy persons are depicted as cosmic navigators who know the geography and traffic of the universe. They are known for their ability to be in more than one place at once. In the southern Philippines, for instance, Muslims of the Sama community describe *Tuan Awliya* as men who possess mystical knowledge because they know God. God has blessed them and given them the powers of *barakat*, enabling *Tuan Awliya* to walk on water, become invisible, and travel far distances at the blink of an eye (Horvatich 1994, 813). These attributes and images Sunni Muslims have of the *Walīy* (being near to Allah) and the spiritual Pole (*Quṭb*) of Sufism seem to have much in common with the Shi'ite concept of Imam (Geoffroy 2010; Nasr 1988). The *Quṭb* is endowed with divine power to manage the affairs of both the terrestrial universe and Muslim community. Just as in Sufism each *shaikh* or master is in contact with the Pole (*Quṭb*) of his age, in Shi'ism all spiritual functions in every age are inwardly connected with the Imam. In brief, the idea of the Imam as the Pole of the universe and the concept of the *Quṭb* in Sufism are nearly identical (Nasr 1988). However, there are differences between these concepts that will be discussed subsequently.

Patience (*ṣabr*) is a core conditional principle for achieving mystic experience. For Muslims, patience is "half of faith" (*niṣf al-imān*).[31] The Arabic word *ṣabr* implies two intertwined meanings—one material, the other ideational. The material meaning refers to the aloe plant as well as to the bitter laxative drug or medicine made of the juice of aloe leaves, generating powerful metaphors that elaborate the ideational meaning.[32] Ideationally, *ṣabr* means patience, steadfastness, endurance, and self-control. It also implies the values of clemency, kindness, tranquility, and serenity. Patience means dealing with affairs, mundane or spiritual, not in hastiness, but through thoughtfulness. Further, patience is frequently equated with silence (*ṣamṭ*), the ability to keep silent (*kitmān* or *katūm*), and managing one's wrath or rage (*katm al-ghayẓ*). Using a proverb to express the values of self-control and endurance, a Sufi said, "to be patient with myself is much better than asking people to be patient with me." Patience heals but necessitates time. And anticipation necessitates patience (*ṭūl al-'umr tiballagh al-'amal*).

The notions of patience, mercy, and divine or hidden knowledge are intertwined and inseparable from the overall mystic tradition of Islam.[33] This is clearly evident in the mystical story of al-Khiḍr and Moses.[34] Al-Khiḍr, the evergreen but invisible *Walīy*, believed to be alive and attentive to whoever mentions his name, is known as the "Pious Slave" (*al-'abd aṣ-ṣāliḥ*), upon whom Allah has bestowed divine mercy (*raḥma*) and hidden knowledge (*'ilm ladunnī*)[35] and whom Moses met at a place where two seas conjunct. Al-Khiḍr explained to the prophet Moses, through three exemplary events, the hidden or unseen but real dimension of life. In the story, al-Khiḍr expressed his fear that Moses would not be patient with or able to understand his seemingly illogical deeds. If Moses could not show patience, trust, and understanding, al-Khiḍr would depart from him. The events were that al-Khiḍr scuttled a fishing boat owned by some poor fishermen, killed a young man, and then fixed and restored the fallen wall of a city known for its corruption. Moses, overwhelmed and confused, questioned al-Khiḍr, who, before his departure, explained what he did. He scuttled the boat in order to save it from an unjust ruler who wished to confiscate the good boats in the city. The young man was killed because he was not good to his pious parents and intended to commit a crime that would disgrace them. Finally, al-Khiḍr restored the fallen wall because there was a treasure buried under it. That treasure belonged to two orphans who would suffer economic hardship in losing it. The underlying message of this narrative is that beside the commonsense knowledge that depends on the logic of daily experience and observation, there is spiritual, hidden knowledge guided by inner insight and revelation.

At the literal and visible level, al-Khiḍr's actions seem to be illogical and evil, but at the deep, symbolic, and hidden level they are not. In this context, al-Khiḍr represents a spiritual archetype or model of hidden knowledge, surpassing the normal, as well as a model for holy mystic persons. Some scholars, however, provide some explanation of this spiritual experience by suggesting that it is based on what they call the imaginative empathic projection of people's embodied mind. According to this view, a significant function of the embodied mind is empathic, involving a form of emulation. As Lakoff and Johnson (1999, 565, italics in original) have stated, "This most common of experiences is a form of 'transcendence,' a form of *being in the other*. Imaginative empathic projection is a major part of what has always been called spiritual experience. Meditative traditions have, for millennia, developed techniques for cultivating it."

THE CORPOREAL AND THE SPIRITUAL

People's corporeality is part of the corporeality of the world, but "the mind is not merely corporeal but also passionate, desiring, and social. It has a culture and cannot exist culture-free" (Lakoff and Johnson 1999, 565). The statement that, among the Egyptian Sufis, the emphasis is on the biological or "physical descent" as a means of receiving the prophetic light (Hoffman-Ladd 1992, 630) is debatable. It is true that because of the devotion to the Prophet's family (*ahl al-bait*), it is not surprising to find well-known *shaikhs* and saints sanctify their descent by tracing their roots or kin relationships, real or imaginative, to the line of the Prophet.[36] However, in my study of both Ahmadiyya (Badawiyya) and Shinnawiyya Sufi orders in the Nile Delta, I observe that the Arabic words for genealogy (*nasab*) and heritage or inheritance (*wirātha*) are metaphorically and interchangeably used in Sufi discourses to indicate meanings going beyond mere corporeal or blood relationships.[37] This, in turn, implies that there is a transformation from relationships based on blood or tribal (kin) affiliation, vertical in nature, to that based on broader spiritual and brotherly ties, horizontal in nature. Biological genealogy (*nasab ad-dam*) represents the visible (*ẓāhir*) aspect of kin or human relationship, while spiritual genealogy (*nasab rūḥī*) signifies the soulful and hidden (*bāṭin*) dimension of that relationship.

Important abstract concepts, from love to causation to morality, are conceptualized through multiple complex metaphors without which these concepts would be devoid of meanings (Lakoff and Johnson 1999, 73). Connections between descent terminology, Sufi metaphors, and the language of spirituality are significant here. In interviewing members of the two Sufi orders, they bestowed more value to the concept of spiritual genealogy than to corporeal or biological genealogy. Yet they reiterated the phrase "the son of the Shaikh is a Shaikh," seemingly emphasizing the hereditary nature of sainthood. When I questioned them referring to the fact that not all descendants of a saint are saints, most interviewees, including leading figures of the two orders, offered insightful exegeses. For instance, Shaikh Said, the patron of the Shinnawiyya Sufi order, recounted that although the genealogy of the Pole (*Quṭb*) al-Badawi goes back to 'Ali ibn Abi Talib, cousin and son-in-law of the Prophet Muhammad, he was never married and consequently had no biological offspring. But al-Badawi, the patron maintains, has been a spiritual father of numerous prominent Sufi saints.

To confirm his idea, Shaikh Hasan recounted that despite the fact that the biological genealogy of Sidi 'Umar (the founder of the Shinnawiyya Sufi order) has been traced to prominent Sufi figures such as Shihab al-Din al-Suhrawardi[38] and Abu Yazid al-Bistami,[39] leading Sufi figures, the spiritual genealogy, and Sufi experience of Sidi 'Umar are directly related to the grand saint al-Badawi. It has been a custom that on the night of the last day of the celebration (*mawlid*) of al-Badawi,[40] members of al-Shinnawiyya order perform rituals for honoring certain saints, some of whom are spiritually, not biologically, related to both the grand saint al-Badawi and the Shinnawi family.

Other members, however, state, without mentioning blood ties, that all Muslims are descendants of the primordial light of Muhammad, especially those who maintain religious piety. People, especially mystics, seek the divine not outside but within themselves. They also seek the divine not in physical or material (blood) forms but in spiritual and soulful entities. "We are brothers and sisters because we are descendants of one soul" was another phrase I heard accentuating the spiritual principle. The terms "brother" and "father" are used metaphorically in Islamic discourse: however, Sufi leaders move from their strict "biological" meanings to focus on their spiritual and social connotations as further reflected in ideas of fraternity and companionship.

The concept of spiritual genealogy is further elaborated by the patron of the Shinnawiyya Sufi order, who allegorically made a distinction between "the son of the mud" (*walad aṭ-ṭīn*), signifying the kinship blood bond, and "the son of religion" (*walad ad-dīn*), conveying the spiritual bond. He went on to say that "the son of the religion follows [you as] a religious leader, while the son of mud may kill his parents." To support his view he quoted the Qur'an (46:14): "Among your wives and children (some are) enemies to yourselves: hence beware of them." Other members of the Shinnawiyya mentioned Qur'anic verses indicating biological sons who were not faithful to their pious fathers (prophets), such as the son of Noah (Qur'an 11:46) and the son who was killed by al-Khiḍr (Qur'an 10:80), the saint known for his divine knowledge (*'ilm ladunnī*).

I heard other narratives from Shaikh Wajdy, a leading Shaikh of the Ahmadiyya (Badawiyya) Sufi order. He differentiated between what he metaphorically called the "rope of God" (*ḥabl* Allah) and the "rope of people" (*ḥabl an-nās*). The rope of God, he recounted, is the spiritual relation between people and God that must be maintained through observing and preserving the Qur'an, which is the actual rope holding Muslims together. To corroborate his idea, Shaikh Wajdy recited a verse of the Qur'an (103:3), "And hold fast, all together, by the rope which Allah (stretches out for you), and be not divided among yourselves; and remember with gratitude Allah's favor on you." By the "rope of people" he meant both biological and social relationships between individuals that imply material, practical, political, and economic interests.

Apart from the biological lineage of a certain saint, the religious identity of brotherly disciples is derived from their connection with a chain of Sufi saints (Werbner 1996). The emphasis here is not just on the biological aspect per se, but, and more importantly, on the Sufi ethical chain (*silsila*) and spiritual genealogy. In this context, "*spiritual genealogy* is taken to mean the affiliation and allegiance among members adhering to certain religious or sanctified principles, values, rituals and practices expressed in hereditary, social, and trans-social or spiritual terms" (el-Aswad 2006a, 503). What is stressed here is that mystic or spiritual genealogy goes beyond a specific Sufi order and is associated with overarching Muslim worldviews.

Within the circles of both Ahmadiyya and Shinnawiyya Sufi orders, the respect shown to the *shaikh* is more important than that shown to the biological father, because the *shaikh* leads the follower to the eternal life (or paradise) through mysticism, while the father begets the son in this transitory life (*ad-duniyā*). Thus, "spiritual genealogy is viewed here as if it were part of the biological nature of people that should be nourished by religious or Sufi experience" (el-Aswad 2006a, 504). The perfect successor of the *shaikh* of a Sufi order is one who must have not only inherited the genes of the *shaikh* (genetic reproduction), but also, and most importantly, have absorbed and experienced the ethos (spiritual reproduction or symbolic capital) of the order. However, if the *shaikh* does not have a biological son, then the closest disciple or spiritual son can be a successor. The perfect case, then, is the one in which the *shaikh*'s biological son follows his father's mystic path, without which he will not be a legitimate or acknowledged Sufi. What is needed is piety (*taqwā*) or purity of the soul. This statement highlights the individual awareness of the spiritual and ethical dimension as the core element in the new orientation of the Sufi order that must be implemented not only by its members, but also by all Muslims.

What is presented here is not simply an ideology of spiritual genealogy but an intricate web of cultural codes, social practices, persons, and institutions that generate and fortify a new way of looking at and dealing with people's problems. Spiritual genealogy is socially and economically relevant because it motivates people or, to be more specific, members of the Sufi order to better serve their community.

In sum, there is consensus among interviewees that Sufi or mystic knowledge is based on the Qur'an and Sunnah and is guided by Sufi leaders who show piety (*taqwā*), righteousness (*ṣalāḥ*), patience (*ṣabr*), and humility (*tawāḍu'*) toward Allah and obey Him for the benefit of His mercy and grace. They also emphasize that spiritual genealogy necessitates a certain divine knowledge that goes beyond natural disposition or innate and intellectual gift.

SUFI MYSTICISM AND SHI'I ESOTERICISM

One of the Sufi leaders of the Shinnawiyya order stated that although Sufism cannot be practiced without knowing and applying the principles and the rules (*shari'a*) of Islam, it cannot be achieved through schools or books as such. Rather, Sufism requires three fundamental elements. It requires spiritual guidance and divine knowledge that can be achieved though intimacy and closeness to the *shaikh* or Sufi leader. It entails *mujāhda*, a multiple-meaning concept indicating practice, experience, endurance, and patience in achieving divine and spiritual insights. It also necessitates natural or innate disposition (*fiṭrī*), found in all people, without which all spiritual, intellectual, and practical efforts would be fruitless.

For all mystics, Sunni and Shi'i, the real beloved is Allah.[41] The Prophet Muhammad and his family are highly revered and loved. The sincere devotion Egyptian Sufis have to the Prophet and his family forms a unique aspect of their religious life bearing remarkable parallels to Shi'ism (Hoffman-Ladd 1992, 616). The role of Imam 'Ali in Islamic esotericism is acknowledged by Shi'a and Sunni alike. However, the spiritual eminence of 'Ali appears to Sufism within the Sunni world not as being strictly related to Shi'ism, but as being directly associated with Islamic esotericism in general (Nasr 1988; Geoffroy 2010). Most Sunni Sufis honor all the Prophet's companions (*al-ṣaḥāba*), but they do not share the Shi'i faith that 'Ali was intended by Muhammad to be the first caliph after his death (Hoffman-Ladd 1992, 624).

For the Shi'a, the luminous entities of the Imams as well as the Prophet are crucial in the mystic experience. More specifically, recognizing the Imam as a being of light is central to the mystics seeking closeness to God (Amir-Moezzi 2011, 52, 147; Carney 2005, 720).[42] Further, the Shi'a tend to focus on the biological genealogy of Imams, tracing the line vertically to the Prophet through Fatima and ʻAli, notwithstanding the spiritual notion of the Muhammadan light. Sunni Sufis, however, tend to consider the spiritual genealogy, more horizontally than vertically, as derived from the Muhammadan light in such a way that spiritual genealogy is viewed as if it were biological genealogy. For the Sufi, the *shaikh*'s role is to guide and lead the disciple along a mystic and spiritual path. Then the disciple maintains his efforts (*mujāhadāt*) to achieve his spiritual objective or, as expressed by a Sufi master, "the piety of the heart" (*taqwā al-qalb*). Through the *mujāhadāt*, the disciple might even go beyond his master along the Sufi path. Such a concept is not found among the Shiʻa, who emulate their *shaikh* or *marjaʻ* and consider the Hidden Imam as the final, indisputable, and unquestionable spiritual guide.

It is evident, then, that Sufi mysticism and Shiʻi esotericism differ concerning the resource of hidden knowledge. For the Sunni Sufis, the ultimate resource of the knowledge of hidden mysteries is the Prophet. For instance, among Egyptian Sufis, al-Sayyid al-Badawi, being a Pole (*Quṭb*), is described as the gate of the Prophet (*bāb an-nabī*). For the Shiʻa, however, the Imam, the pole of the two worlds (the earthly and the hidden), is the final source or reference whose function is to disclose the secrets of hidden reality through the interpretation (*taʼwīl*) of the inner meanings of religion (Carney 2005, 726). Also, the Imam is believed by the Shiʻa to be alive and therefore able to guide men toward a religious or spiritual life. A spiritual leader could achieve the rank of the pole of the earthly world through direct relationship with the Imam. This pole, called *nāṭiq* (speaker), is known as the gate of the Hidden Imam (Amir-Moezzi 2011, 52, 470).

For the Shiʻa, God can be known only through His manifestation in the figure of the Imam. It is not merely the teachings of the Imam that direct the believers forward but his very reality as being theophanic and created of light (Amir-Moezzi 2011; Nasr 1988, 2009). Ethnographic material from Bahrain confirms that the Imam is the *hujja Allah*, or the Proof of God. The Shiʻa's belief that Imams are the "Proofs of God" means that they are beings by which God is to be known (Carney 2005, 718). Jaʻfar al-Sadiq, the sixth Imam, who contributed to the development of the doctrine of the Imam's divinity, is known for saying, "He who knows us knows God, and he who knows us not, knows not God," and "Without God, we would not be known, and without us, God would not be known" (Amir-Moezzi 2011, 114).[43]

The notion of infallibility (*maʻṣūmiyya*) of Imams is a key principle in Shiʻi esoteric worldviews, where the Imam is believed to be inerrant as a descendant of the Prophet, inheriting the initiation guidance (*walāyah*) and the knowledge of divine mysteries. Such a notion does not form a core principle in the Sufi mystic worldviews, where the Sufi *shaikhs*, motivated by humility and humbleness, refrain from claiming any sort of infallibility or ability of revealing divine mysteries or even performing extraordinary marvels. However, it is difficult to accept the statement, "Knowledge of the secrets is reserved for the elite (*al-khawāṣṣ*)," not the mass of Sufis or *al-'awāmm* (Hoffman-Ladd 1992, 628). The Sufi *shaikhs* possess information that their followers may neither possess nor fully understand, but both the *shaikh* (the elite) and the ordinary people can reveal hidden matters.

The elite may have the resources to organize and lead Sufi orders, but the spiritual "gift" that humble or ordinary people might have is unquestionable. I heard numerous stories about the ability of some ordinary (even illiterate) people to reveal certain hidden matters. Here is one such story. One day while Shaikh al-Sha'rani, a renowned Egyptian Sufi and scholar who lived in the sixteenth century, was entering a mosque, he observed a humble man with ragged clothes treating palm reeds for agricultural purposes. He ordered the mosque keeper not to permit the filthy man to enter the mosque. Surprised to see the same man in the mosque on the following day, al-Sha'rani questioned the guard, who recounted that the humble man (named Sidi Ali al-Khawwas)[44] was a blessed Sufi or *Walīy* and a man of *baraka*. When al-Sha'rani dismissed the idea that the man was a *Walīy*, the humble man whispered some words that made al-Sha'rani reassess the matter. His words indicated that the man had knowledge of the private life of al-Sha'rani as related to an incident that happened between al-Sha'rani and his wife the previous night. This narrative, then, indicates that people should not be judged based on appearance or social class, and mystic knowledge should be respected and never dismissed (el-Aswad 2006a).

Another common feature shared by Sufism and Shi'ism is the veneration of holy persons and saints.[45] Saintly veneration includes such practices as the visitation (*ziyāra*), the invocation of Allah (*dhikr*), the gathering for religious teaching (*ḥaḍra*), and the pledging of a vow (*nadhr*). Despite the fact that visitations to saintly shrines are contested and disapproved of by scholars, especially those dealing with Islamic jurisprudence, both Sunni and Shi'a still observe them.[46] Specific material and spiritual networks exist around these visitations and related performances, which constitute the cultural vitality of saintly places. As material expressions of spiritual values, visitations to saints' shrines and related practices are clues to the significance of the geography of brotherly saints.

This pattern, showing the connection between spirituality, related to Sufi sainthood, and certain places or geographies, has been documented in other Muslim communities, such as those in India (Buehler 1998; Troll 2003), Persia (Ernst 1993), Bangladesh (Uddin 2006),[47] Pakistan (Werbner and Basu 1998), South Asia (Green 2004, 2006), and the Volga–Ural region in Russia (Frank 1996). The shrine of Nizamuddin Auliya, located in New Delhi, is one of the most popular Muslim shrines in India and attracts thousands of pilgrims and devotees from various religions, including Muslims, Hindus, Sikhs, and Christians. Devotees coming to the Nizamuddin shrine represent almost every stratum of Indian society: rich and poor, powerful and powerless, the crippled, beggars, criminals, politicians, artists, intellectuals, and the common laypersons. Sufi orders reached India by the tenth century and became important centers for learning and for the promulgation of Islam (Saniotis 2004, 399).

Saints are distinguished from ordinary people not only in this life as commanders or religious leaders, but also after death when their shrines are raised and elevated in the cemetery or set apart from it. The property and other economic resources of saints depend on their spiritual as well as social and symbolic capital. In order to attract adherents, religious leaders strive to translate religious understandings and beliefs into social images, cultural symbols, and rituals. Monumental funerary architectures such as mosques and graves or shrines named after saints empower the social position of the *shaikhs* and accentuate the spiritual and spatial position of the saints in their regions. The saint and shrine are central in the religious expression of Muslim societies. For example, among the people of Jhang, a majority Sunni society in the southwest of the Pakistani Punjab, the Sufi is sacralized as the intermediary between man and God (Kamran 2009). In Bahrain there are numerous Shi'i saintly shrines and graves almost in every village. However, except for religious rituals, celebrations, or commemorations that follow the Shi'i calendar (more specifically, Imams and the Prophet's family), there are no birthday celebrations of Shi'i saints.[48]

In Egypt the case is different. There are plenty of shrines of Sunni saints, grand and small, whose birthday celebrations (*mawālid*, sing. *maulid*) are observed. For instance, Tanta alone encompasses a connected chain of Sunni saints and sanctuaries located within the sacred regional network of Sidi al-Badawi that extends beyond the city to include nearby towns and villages.[49] In the anniversary celebration of al-Badawi (buried in a mosque named after him),[50] members of various Sufi orders as well as ordinary people come from various parts of both Egypt and other Muslim countries to celebrate Sidi al-Badawi and recite al-Fatiha (the opening chapter of the Qur'an) on behalf of both the holy saints and the people involved. The devotees touch the rails enclosing al-Badawi's grave with their hands. They put little children on top of the tomb to receive a blessing. They also rub themselves against the wall surrounding the shrine so as to transfer the *baraka* of the saint to themselves. Both men and women participate in these religious festivals. It is interesting to note that Lévy-Bruhl's (1985) principle of "mystical participation," according to which all things in traditional societies are thought to have a mystical participation with each other, is in concordance with the Muslim view that most of the entities of the cosmos or universe participate in the mystic power of *baraka*.

One of the overarching Muslim religious worldviews that explains the significance of graves in general and of saints' shrines in particular is that they are believed to be links between the everyday life and the *sacred* or the world beyond this mundane reality. They inhabit the space and establish an intimate bond between the human body, earth, and celestial universe. Tombs and shrines constitute the *barzakh* (eschatology) linking this world with the other world (el-Aswad 1987).

Within this broader worldview, the focus of the people is on maintaining good relationships with their saints or kin and friends, alive or dead. Inside the shrines visitors are careful to recite al-Fatiha and make the *du'a* or supplication to Allah for the sake of the soul of the dead or saint who can hear and recognize them.[51] Within this socioreligious context, visitation (*ziyāra*) to the shrine of a saint is a way to establish spiritual networks or sanctified ties between the visitors and the saint, on the one hand, and between them and the other people who come to visit, on the other (el-Aswad 2004a).

Such practices, attracting people from different classes and non-Muslims as well, are observed not only in Egypt but also in other Muslim countries. For example, Uddin notes that those who maintain some level of adherence to the Sufi saint tradition in Bangladesh cut across all classes and communal lines. Many Hindus visit Sufi shrines and are welcomed. The Maijbhandaris, who are well known for their *dhikr* (remembrance of God) and music, include many Hindu musicians who "compose songs and sing the praises of these saints" (Uddin 2006, 149).

CONCLUSION

Ethnographically and theoretically, this chapter has demonstrated the complex interplay between various forms of mystic worldviews represented in certain Sunni Sufism and Shi'i esotericism and the overarching Muslim worldviews. In their mystic experience, both Sunni Sufis and Shi'a profoundly focus on knowing and loving God. At the same time, they show great devotion to the Prophet and his family. Also, both Sunni Sufis and Shi'a seek to reach the balance between the exterior (*shari'a*) and interior (*ḥaqīqa*) dimensions of religion in their efforts to know God. Among various causes generating differences between Sunni Sufi mysticism and Shi'i esotericism, the doctrine of Shi'i Imamate is the decisive factor.

Regarding Sufism, Muslim mystic worldviews and practices are presented and enacted in Sufi orders in local as well as broader national and regional contexts. Sufi orders are not asocial ascetic systems set apart from the sociocultural milieu but rather maintain the spiritual power for achieving otherworldly as well as mundane goals. It is the interconnectedness of personal, social, cosmic, and divine spheres that explains the unfathomable and emotional engagement of the members of a Sufi order with their religious leaders, alive or dead, and their saintly places.

It has been evident through Sufi narratives, whether real or imagined, that saints are spiritually and socially involved. For the Sufi mysticism, biological genealogy is imagined but can be transformed into spiritual descent where spiritual descendants share mystical roots with their holy ancestors.

Mystic worldviews, concerned with the knowledge of mysterious forces and unseen entities, have a great influence on Muslims' daily lives. This impact is witnessed in people's invention and reinvention of sanctified social devices and symbolic networks such as the visitation of saintly shrines, the pledging of vows, the distribution of goods (charity) among the needy, and observing birthday celebrations of Sufi saints. Though influenced by the Sufi orders, the saint cult in Muslim societies is associated with broader cultural and social orientations refracted in regional settings.

With reference to the West, some scholars argue that modern people have cut themselves off from the sacred and imaginative realities and live in secular and measurable time. They live in a world described by Max Weber in terms of "disenchantment" (Taylor 2004, 249). However, other scholars, refuting the notions of disenchantment and disembodiment, say, "It is surprising to discover, on the basis of empirical research, that human rationality is not at all what the Western philosophical tradition has held it to be" (Lakoff and Johnson 1999, 4). In Muslim society Sufis and mystics, Sunni and Shi'a alike, are not detached from reality; rather, they live in an "enchanted" world, a world of spirits and forces, which can be described in terms of "embodied spirituality" that requires ethical and aesthetic attitudes to the world that is also central to self-nurturance. Embodied spirituality necessitates an understanding that the world or nature is not inanimate and less than human, but animated and highly significant (Lakoff and Johnson 1999, 566). Divine benevolent forces such as blessing (*baraka*), mercy (*raḥmah*), and wonders (*karāmāt*), dispersed in the universe, are enacted and embodied by those who are believed to possess mystic and hidden knowledge.

Unlike Western society, modernists, technocrats, and professional elites in Muslim world have little impact on the elimination of mystic or Sufi beliefs and practices. In many cases, however, those elites, along with ordinary Muslims, have participated in certain Sufi orders and have been involved in the visitation of saintly places.

The hidden dimensions of the cosmos, society, and person have been demonstrated not in abstract concepts, but rather in outward manifestations, in public discourses, in rituals, in tangible objects, and in bodily symbols. Whether these symbols are presented as bodily parts, such as the hands and eyes, or as bodily behaviors, such as distribution of goods or gift exchange, or as bodily rituals, such as the *dhikr*, or as identities, such as the *shaikhs*, they are capable of converting what is invisible, hidden, abstract, or private, into the visible, concrete, social, or public.

5

❖ ❖

Muslim Worldviews, Imagination, and the Dream World

Dreams and imagination have conventionally been a significant component of Muslims' worldviews and their everyday lives. Though revelation, prophecy, and vision are crucial elements in religion, imagination and dreams play a significant role in substantiating religious beliefs. Some domains of experience and worldview, especially dealing with invisible and esoteric realms that seem difficult for people to comprehend or define, are rendered intelligible by applying imagination. Imagination can translate truth into different systems of images (Lakoff and Johnson 1999; Murray and Cocking 1991).[1]

The religious heritage of Islam shows the significance and power of dream and imagination. Several verses of the Qur'an contain discussions of dreams, and because of the sanctity and centrality of the Qur'an to Islam these verses have become fundamental to all Muslim dream traditions (Bulkeley 2008, 194).[2] Muslims firmly believe that prophets such as Muhammad,[3] Abraham,[4] and Joseph, among others, experienced significant visions and revelatory dreams. More specifically, the prophet Joseph was a divinely gifted dream interpreter, and his interpretation of the dreams of the Egyptian pharaoh as well as of the pharaoh's prisoners is taken by Muslims to be infallible evidence of the existence of the unseen world.[5]

In their inquiries of medieval Muslim culture, scholars such as Chittick (1989), Corbin (1966), Gouda (1991), von Grunebaum (1966), Hughes (2002), Katz (1997), Lecerf (1966), Smith (1980), and Sviri (1999), among others, corroborate that dreams were used by Muslims to explicate theological doctrines, expound eschatological issues, reveal historical events, and employ political actions.[6] Further, by "granting an independent ontological status to imagination and seeing the visionary realm as the self-revelation of God, Islamic philosophy has gone against the mainstream of Western thought" (Chittick 1989, 10).[7] People in several contemporary Muslim societies embrace dreaming in a much higher regard than is generally held anywhere in the West.[8] Recent studies (el-Aswad 2007a, 2010a; Hoffman 1997) assert that religiously significant dreams are a widespread phenomenon in contemporary Egyptian religious life.

This chapter presents the debate among Muslims, Sunni and Shi'a, concerning the reliability of imagination and dreams as a source of information about the unseen world and its symbolic transformations. It is also concerned with the social conditions that bring about moral and social support to certain dreams or imaginary construction. The ethnography of the unseen domains refracted in worldview, imagination, and dream world of the Muslim world, in general, and Arab world, in particular, is scant (el-Aswad 2007a). The study, drawing on ethnographic research conducted in urban and rural communities belonging to Egyptian and Emirati Sunnis and Bahrain Shi'a,[9] presents a phenomenological inquiry, incorporating objective description and subjective interpretation and as such comprises a more constructive-synthetic analysis of meanings rather than a search for determining factors.

Departing from inquiries that focus largely on psychological[10] and/or religious[11] interpretations of dreams, this chapter, applying symbolic-hermeneutic approaches, attempts to explicate the significance of dreams to Muslims within a broad perspective encompassing their relationship to the world with its seen and unseen dimensions. It is inevitable, then, the ethnographic material suggests, to take seriously the triple dimensions of the person, society, and universe or cosmos. In other words, dreams can be interpreted as revealing hidden dimensions of the person, society, and cosmos. Further, the criteria on which the choice of ethnographic material is made are related to Muslims' classifications of dreams: dream vision, ordinary dream, and intentional or predictive dream.

MUSLIM IMAGINATION AND DREAM WORLD

Imagination is not unreal and does not have any significance or value independent of social and material processes individuals experience in their daily lives. Imagination, through generating mental images, provides meaning to experience and understanding to knowledge. Imagination means perceiving the world from a distinct and unique perspective that differs from the ordinary or commonsense experience. Another aspect of imagination refers to the ability to think of possibilities (Thomas 1997, 96). In this chapter, imagination and dreams are addressed within a larger context of Muslim worldviews. This means that dreams are related not only to the dream world, but also to a broader framework encompassing the world of imagination and cultural representation at the level of beliefs, folk narrations, practices, and rituals (Bulkeley 1996; Chidester 2008; Cox Miller 1994; Crapanzano 2004; Ewing 1994; Foster 1973; George 1995; Hollan 1989; Stewart 1997; Tedlock 1992, 2007; Wautscher 1994; Wolf 1994). In "all dreams, a dreamer draws upon the cultural concepts and signs in terms of which he has learned to organize his world" (Ewing 1990, 57). Dreams are crucial in understanding people's perceptions of the world, showing how people classify human and nonhuman entities, components of these entities, natural and supernatural events, and relationships between entities or events. Dreams imply relational processes operating between different kinds of animate and inanimate entities and forces.

According to overarching Muslim worldviews, beyond the scope of the visible and tangible world of experience lies the invisible, imaginary, and unknowable reality (*'ālam al-ghaib*) from which possible realities emerge. As mentioned, there are multiple worlds of which the natural world, including that of human beings, is the only one visible. Other realities, mainly unseen, encompass those of spirits, angels, *jinn*, and eschatology (*barzakh*). Although most of these invisible entities are inaccessible in normal waking life, individuals may see and communicate with them in dreams. It is worth noting that some Muslim scholars interpret the Qur'anic verse (42:51), "No human being can communicate with Allah except through inspiration, or from behind a veil," by suggesting the word "veil" connotes "dream" (al-'Asqalani 1959, 354).

Within the Muslim context, the dream world deals simultaneously with visible and invisible worlds including this world, the eschatological world, and the other world (figure 5.1). These perceived realities, however, are interpenetrating

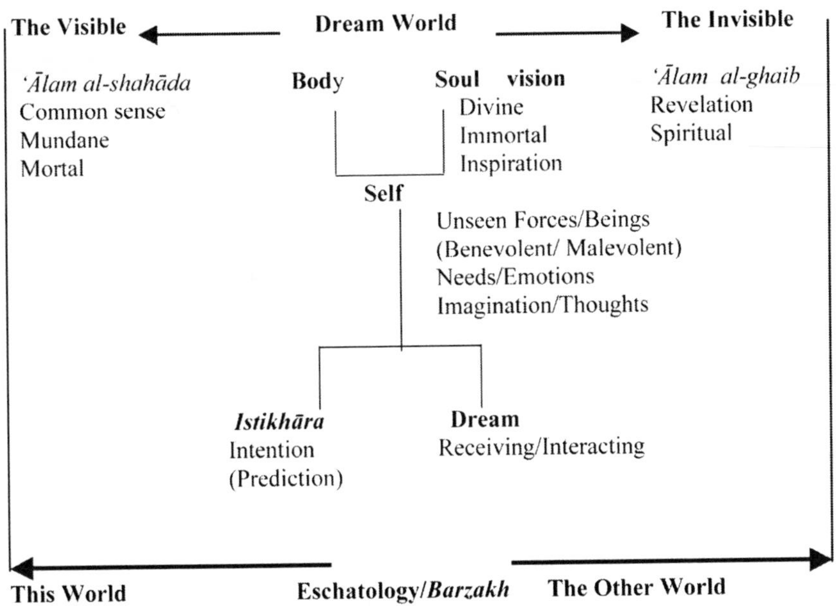

Figure 5.1. Dream world and Muslim imagination.

domains and points of reference correlating with cultural constructs that render different levels of experience, real or imaginary, intelligible. The specific features and contents of their worldviews affect people's dream world or dreaming experience and condition how it is to be communicated. The folk interpretations of dreams are considered here as remarkable works of the imagination relevant to their overarching worldviews.

The dream world epitomizes multidimensional domains and as such serves as a cultural framework for dialoguing with the visible or invisible, constructing and reconstructing reality. While dreams represent personal experiences, they can be socially narrated, discussed, and interpreted as a cosmic entryway into differing domains of reality as well as a symbolic channel of transforming or reconstructing that reality. Another aspect of dreams is that they are complicated and need insights to decode them. They are not perceived or interpreted literally but understood as symbols standing for something else.[12] In the Muslim imagination, dreams can be perceived as messages from divinity, glad tidings, reflections of inner aspirations, self-delusions, threats from menacing creatures, or bad omens.

The argument that dreams are not treated seriously by science because they are not observable or verifiable is questionable. As far as dreams can function as cultural representations like myths or rituals and as far as they are dealt with in relation to people's worldviews, belief systems, and epistemological orientations, they are considered social facts (Basso 1987; Herdt 1992; Kilborne 1981, 1987; Price-Williams 1987; Tedlock 1987, 1992).[13] For example, ethnographic material shows that seeing a camel in a dream is interpreted differently in local Muslim cultures. From the Egyptians' point of view, seeing or talking to a camel in a dream means that a revered saint is revealing himself to the dreamer. For the Emiratis, however, seeing a camel is interpreted negatively, as if encountering a devil, Satan (*shaiṭān*). This interpretation might be related to the way Emiratis perceive the camel as a creature that often retaliates against those who mistreat it. For the Emiratis, the camel is known for having a dreadful temper and a tendency to attack those who abuse it. For Bahraini Shi'a, seeing a camel in a dream is interpreted negatively based not on the specific characteristics of the camel, but rather on the context of the tragic events of Karbala, in which unsaddled camels were used to uncomfortably and humiliatingly carry the children and female relatives of Imam Husain, the martyred, as prisoners.[14]

THE PHENOMENOLOGY OF DREAMING AND THE HIERARCHY OF MEANINGS

The phenomenology of dreaming implies that there are different levels or orders of meaning assigned to dreams by people involved in the interpretation of these dreams in specific social contexts. Dreams relate to multiple meanings and require phenomenological and semiotic analysis. Charles Sanders Peirce

(1931–1958) proposes a tripartite categorization of signs (icon, index, and symbol) based on three categories of relations a sign might have to its object or what it stands for. Resemblance or similarity is necessary for the icon. A sign is considered iconic, such as a photo or image, when it resembles what it refers to. The relationship between a part and a whole, based on contiguity, turns a sign into an index, such as knocking on a door. An index demonstrates the existence of its object. Finally, a sign is rendered a symbol when nothing but convention determines its relationship with what it stands for.[15] The symbol is not literally what it represents. This triple classification of signs entails a hierarchy of meanings and is significantly applied in phenomenological and anthropological literature. Drawing on Peirce's tripartite classification of signs, Roy Rappaport (1999) makes a distinction between three hierarchical levels of meaning. They are high-order meaning, which is grounded in indexicality, identity, participation or unity (as in the identification of self with other), middle-order meaning, which is founded on similarity (as in metaphor), and low-order meaning, which is based on distinction (as in taxonomy).[16]

As the sign or the meaning is hierarchically ordered, so is the world of dreams. A dream indicates a sequence of images, ideas, and emotions that someone experiences during sleep (Casto, Krippner, and Tartz 1999, 45). According to Muslim exegeses, dreams are defined and classified in three hierarchical categories. First is the dream vision (*ru'yā*), which enjoys higher-order meaning and differs from both regular dream and waking vision (*ru'ya*). In their daily discourses and activities, Egyptians, however, use the word *ru'ya* with reference to both dream vision and waking vision. Muslims consider dream visions to be sharper, stronger, more veracious, and higher in dignity than other kinds of dreams.[17] Dream visions are mirrors of the unseen. Though some regular dreams might be contested, dream visions, recounted to me by those whom I interviewed in Egypt, Emirates, and Bahrain, were never doubted. Dream visions are viewed as real as perceptions.

Second are regular dreams that include *manām* (derived from the word *naum*, which means "sleeping"), *ḥulm* [pl. *aḥlām*], colloquially pronounced *ḥilm* in Egypt,[18] and *kābūs*, or nightmares, which are considered demonic or devilish. From a contextual (not textual) point of view, the word *ḥulm* (or *ḥilm*) is used by Egyptians to mean ordinary dream(s) that might be "good" or "bad." They never use the same word, *ḥulm*, to refer to "demonic dreams" as such. They have to modify the word *ḥulm* by adding an adjective that implies good or bad connotations, based on the experience of the dreamer or those who are involved in the dream interpretation. And *kābūs* is used (exclusively) to mean "nightmare" (or devilish impact on the dreamer). Third is the intentional procedure, known as *istikhāra*, or the seeking of God's guidance in making good decisions, the outcomes of which are believed to occur in dreams after voluntarily performing certain invocations and rituals that imply religious significance (el-Aswad 2007a, 2010a).[19]

This classification implicates Muslim theories concerning which components of the person, such as the soul and/or self, among other entities and forces within and without the dreamer, are involved in the dreaming and will be subsequently discussed. Overall, dreams are taken here to indicate simultaneously psychological, social, cosmological, and spiritual realities.[20] Although the soul, which can move freely or independently and communicate with other beings, spirits, and angels, plays a significant role in dreams (especially dream visions), the self (*nafs*) or psyche, inseparable from the body, is the core agency in regular dreams that serve as symbolic ways for expressing individuals' emotions and ideas as well as satisfying their needs. This statement can be illustrated in the following case study I conducted in Tanta, Egypt.[21]

The case study concerns a high-school teacher, Huda, who claimed to have an exceptional gift in interpreting dreams. She indicated that she is familiar with books and manuals of dream interpretation such as those of Ibn Sīrīn, among others, but she relied mostly on her insights and knowledge of social circumstances of the dream teller. She stated that when she has a dream, she experiences a sense or feeling of being aware of persons and events happening to her. Although the feeling of being aware or alert becomes strong the day following the dream, it stays with her for two or three days, sometimes longer. Huda confirmed that the dream becomes true when she is able to relate certain events to it. During the process of relating entities or events of the outside and inside realities together, she asserted, her awareness of her identity becomes intensified.[22] When the images and events seen in the dream are decoded based on real or waking events, she can announce, "The dream has been interpreted" (*al-ḥilm itfassar*). This statement indicates interconnected meanings. First, it implies an anticipation of certain events related to the dream to occur in the sense that the dreamers look for certain symbols in everyday occurrences that can be related to the dream events. Second, it connotes a belief that dreams convey messages that can be recognized or materialized if people take them seriously.

The Egyptians constantly talk about dreams as significant aspects of concern for them. They speak of seeing a dream (*ra'a* or *shāf*) or of being visited by a being (person or supernatural entity) in the dream.[23] Also, they speak of a caller (*hātif*) that might be a spirit, a ghost, or a person.[24] Dreams, however, are subject to different interpretations depending on differing experiences, knowledge, social status, and piety of dreamers and interpreters. They are interpreted metaphorically or iconically, using Peirce's word, where iconic images may be analogous but not identical. Succinctly, dreams can be interpreted through events taking place in people's daily lives (el-Aswad 2010a). This might be a reason, Huda recounted, that some individuals do not convey their good dreams to other persons, except for the trusted, for fear of losing the promised or auspicious signs implicit in them. Such a view is found among Moroccans, who "saw great and potentially dangerous power in the dream. In telling a dream for the first time, they said, the dream transferred its power—evil or good—to his or her audience" (Crapanzano 2004, 21).

Huda elaborated further about the way she listens to people narrating their dreams. For instance, when a relative or friend tells her a dream, she often interjects, saying, "May Allah make it [the dream] good" (*Allahumma ij'alahu khair*), to convey to the dream teller her moral support and encouragement. Additionally, she advises the dream teller to say, before narrating the dream, a protective utterance such as, "Allah bless the Prophet, I have dreamed a dream, its beginning was Muhammad, and its end was 'Ali"[25] (*ḥalamtu ḥilm bi-aṣṣalātu 'ala annabī, awwalahu Muhammad wa ākhirahu 'Ali*). Such an utterance, Huda asserted, is to convey the dreamer's deep concern or hope of having a positive outcome from the dream.

However, Huda insisted that not all dreams can be easily deciphered. Some of these dreams are mere fantasies or illusions caused by evil forces or the adverse side of the self. Pointing out that anything can happen in a dream, she gave an example of her teenage son, who approached her to help him interpret a dream he had. With an ironic gesture she said that her young man dreamed that he saw a lion holding a sword in its mouth and wanted to kill him. She told the dreamer, her son, while laughing, that his "rear was uncovered while asleep," indicating that the dream was nonsense (*aḍghāth aḥlām*). This common phrase, however, indicates that not all dreams are to be taken seriously, especially those related to the notion of wishful thinking reflected in the widely quoted proverb, "A hungry person dreams of a bread market" (*al-ja'ān* [*jau'ān*] *yiḥlam bisūq al-'aish*).

The Shi'a, like other Muslims, treat dreams and dream visions with respect, withstanding those dreams that might seem irrelevant to them. For instance, 'Abdulla al-'Aradi, a Bahraini Shi'i working as a taxi driver, recounted that on having a dream that implies negative or evil connotations, he immediately would go to the lavatory and spit three times, directing his mouth toward his left side. He believed that such negative dreams are "acts of the devil [*a'māl ash-shaiṭān*], the enemy [*'adūw*] of the faithful." He also told me that the dream vision in which the Prophet or Imam appears to the dreamer is true.[26] When I questioned him, stating that the Prophet is the only person that Satan cannot emulate in dreams, he replied, "This is true, but the Imam[27] is Light or from the Prophet's Light and, therefore, Satan cannot imitate Imams appearing in dreams."[28] A young Shi'i woman from the Emirates recounted that dreams are so important that when she does not dream she worries that there is something wrong with her. Describing this phenomenon, she used the phrase "black screen" (*shāsha sūda*). Some other Shi'i persons related that they encounter dreams and dream visions with religious significance more frequently during the periods of Muharram and 'Ashura liturgy than during more mundane times.

DREAMS, IMAGINATION, AND DYNAMICS OF TRANSFORMATION

Dreams highlight the dialectic relationship between processes of "inner," "unseen" subjectivity or spirituality and external forms of narration or presentation. Also, they are transformed into practices. Dreams take place in the individual consciousness, draw from cultural and social circumstances, and are publicly expressed in socially interpretable forms (Graham 1994, 725). Across the polarities of subjective-objective, spiritual-material, and unseen-seen, dreams or dream visions are viewed as vehicles for symbolic transformation of inner or incorporeal and spiritual experiences to outward or corporeal realities, socially or collectively communicated and discussed. People evaluate the validity or worthiness of a particular dream according to how it makes them feel—whether it threatens or affirms their sense of self. It is evident that dream or dream vision is one of the symbolic means that has an impact on transforming or changing how the "self" or "reality" is represented and how the "dreamer" feels about the representation.

Based on the analysis of ethnographic material, I propose two forms of transformations: dream transformation and awakening transformation. Dream transformation means that dreams enable individuals to unveil the hidden and unseen dimensions of the universe and the person transformed into signs or symbols. I take awakening transformation to mean the attempt to change the reality through interpreting dreams and relating them to that reality. Within this context and as far as Muslim worldviews encompass the totality of the self or person, society and universe or cosmos, in the following sections the focus will be on three notions. First, dreams and dream visions cause people to transform themselves or change their inner realities from one state to another. Second, dreams and dream visions cause individuals to transform their social reality through making judicious decisions in dealing with critical incidents. Third, the cosmological dimension of the symbolic transformation is triggered by dreams and dream visions.

DREAMS AND SELF-TRANSFORMATION

A phenomenological inquiry concentrates on cases in which what is experienced as part of the self is symbolically transformed into an aspect of culture, that is, as ideas or beliefs about the meaning of what one is doing (Merten and Schwartz 1982, 797). Regarding self-transformation, the following case study, from Egypt, concerns Shaikh Hamid, an *al-Azhar* (Sunni) graduate who works as a religious leader (imam) of a mosque at Tanta. Ten years ago, he had a dream vision that caused him to become a Sufi. He narrated his dream, saying that he was in the holy mosque of the Prophet, in Medina. After evening prayer he saw, in the dream, a great number of people gathering around a spacious place. They were reciting the Qur'an in a humming, melodic fashion. He walked until he reached a place with a high ceiling, forming a magnificent arch imprinted with Qur'anic calligraphy, from which a huge, splendid, shining, crystal chandelier was hanging. When he drew closer to the congregation he saw the Prophet, whose image was identical to the one he constructed through reading the classic books of al-Bukhārī and Saḥīḥ Muslim among others: the red cheeks on white face, the turban on his head, long eyelashes, and the large mouth. Meanwhile, the Prophet—in the dream—pointed to a fellow sitting close to him who, in turn, offered Shaikh Hamid a cup of water.

Shaikh Hamid interpreted the vision of the Prophet and the cup of water given to him in a broad context or framework encircling what is beyond apparent or physical objects. For Shaikh Hamid, water not only is the key element of life but indicates purity and knowledge, more specifically the mystic knowledge of Sufism. Shaikh Hamid recounted that after the vision he was gradually changed from a mere religious leader serving the Islamic law (*shari'a*) to a mystic or Sufi seeking the hidden truth (*ḥaqīqa*) of life. He became a member of the al-Shinnawiyya Sufi order that originated in Tanta.[29] For the Sufi, dream visions are as real and objective as corporeal matter or daily action. He related the "water" to the story of al-Khiḍr or the "Pious Slave," known for his divine mystic knowledge (*'ilm ladunnī*), imparted to him by Allah.[30] Religion for Shaikh Hamid is allegorically depicted as "clean or pure water" (*mā'un ṭāhūr*) that connotes purity and transparency of heart.

Shaikh Hamid has devoted the rest of his life to charitable deeds and helping the needy. Dream visions, viewed by Shaikh Hamid as belonging to the spiritual realm, provide him with inspiration (*ilhām*) and help him to be receptive to signs coming from the unseen because they free him from fantasies and illusions. He recounted that he sees everything in the world through the eyes of mercy (*raḥma*), which is a divine blessing radiated from Allah, Most Gracious and Most Merciful. Shaikh Hamid, acknowledging a Sufi or mystical experience evoking inner, cosmic, and spiritual illumination, said, "When awake, I live in the world, but when asleep the world, seen and unseen, lives in me."

Such cases of dream visions causing changes in personality or self-representations are found among Muslims in various countries. In Pakistan, for instance, a Sufi dream known as "spiritual initiation" has a powerful impact on the dreamer who is looking for a Sufi spiritual guide (*pīr*). The story of initiation is viewed along predictable lines: "A person dreams of seeing an old man or a beautiful place" when deciding to pursue a new way of life, namely the Sufi way (Werbner 2003, 135, 153). As Ewing notes, "It is not unusual for a Pakistani, particularly a man, to begin his search for a *pīr* because of a dream, thereby initiating a new social relationship, or, rather, following through on a relationship which he believes the *pīr* has initiated. The dream thus becomes a pivot in terms of which the dreamer reorients his life" (Ewing 1990, 59–60).

Shihab, a Bahraini social researcher involved in demographic and population studies, informed me, "I used to not deny or affirm the significance of dreams, but I still feel overwhelmed when I see something happen, here and now, either to me or to other people, that I already saw as part of a dream one or two days before it occurred. I do not like to talk about my dreams, but many times I found myself, on recognizing specific events happening, telling people that I saw such and such of these events in a dream." He said that he experienced a dream that changed him to become serious and alert toward symbolic images and messages coming from the unseen world.

Shihab narrated, "One afternoon, I took a nap. I saw my car in a dream. The car was clean and nice. Surprisingly, I saw a duplicate of the same car, but it looked newer, sharper, smoother and more elegant than the original one. It was a stunning experience to see the two nearly identical cars in a dream. I woke up reflecting on the significance of such a dream. I thought that the dream might be related to my work contract and to whether or not it would be renewed. Within two days, I was informed that my contract was terminated. Despite the frustration, I had a strong feeling that something good would happen. The next day, I had a phone call from a friend working in a reputable institute in a nearby Gulf country offering me a job with a much higher salary and better benefits. The strange thing is that I had to ship my car to the new location. During the process of shipping I recognized the significance of seeing the shiny duplicate of my car in the dream. Now, every time I ride my car I keep thinking of that specific dream, keeping my eyes open to other significant dreams." Shihab confirmed that he is very selective in choosing certain dreams as true, and the only criterion for that selection is his intuition or inner insight. In the process of the assessment of dreams, Shihab evades the limitations of the senses by turning his attention inward.

The following case is based on an Arabic document I translated that was sent to me by a Bahraini Shiʿi friend discussing a dream vision that occurred to a Shiʿi woman from Karbala (Iraq), who went through a serious personality transformation about forty years ago. The dream vision came to the woman when she was a girl of fifteen. At that time, she was ill and emotionally disturbed because of the brutality the Iraqi regime was directing toward her family. An elderly aunt, in an attempt to assist the girl, advised her to pray the dawn prayer for forty days along with the recitation of the "invocation of the pledge" (*duʿā' al-ʿahd*), a Shiʿi prayer dedicated to the Hidden Imam, al-Mahdi. Upon completion of the forty days of prayer, the girl was assured a full recovery. Reluctantly, the young girl complied with the serious demand from her parents and relatives. For forty days, the girl recited the specific invocation, but without good intention. On the fortieth night and before going to sleep, the girl, showing no faith in the effectiveness of the Imam's invocation, questioned the whole matter, challenging whether anything would happen the next day as promised. That night, while she slept, she had a dream vision that came with great clarity about the Hidden Imam:

> I saw a holy shrine (*rawḍa*) similar to other sacred shrines of the Prophet's family (Imams); however, this particular shrine looked more elegant and splendid than the other shrines. It had luminous pillars made of pure light. When I wanted to enter through the gate, stepping on the doorstep, I heard a voice from behind say, "Get out of my presence; you are not allowed to get in." Surprised and angered I asked, "Who are you to prevent me from entering?" He replied, "I am the person whose invocation

you ridiculed." Then, recognizing the identity of the speaker as the Imam, I started crying and shouting that the Imam had rejected me. I felt that one of the luminous pillars on which I was hanging began to generate sharp thorns that penetrated my hand and legs. I woke up paralyzed, then lost consciousness for ten days. My family took me to various Shi'i shrines such as those of Imam Husain and al-'Abbas, but nothing improved. I lost weight to nearly fifty pounds. Finally, a Sayyid, a descendant of the Prophet's who was also a religious scholar, advised my family to take me to Samarra' to the Cave of Occultation (*Sirdāb al-Ghaiba*).[31] My father aided by my uncle and some other people used a firm rope to lower me into the dark cave. I was really frightened because the cave looked very dark, yet surprisingly it was full of light from the inside. While inside the cave, the Sayyid asked me to repeat the invocation of the Imam. At the bottom of the cave, I felt as if somebody were pushing me in the back, then I could not feel anything. I became unconscious for half an hour. At that time, I later learned, my parents and friends were praying and asking the Imam to forgive me. Recognizing that I was unconscious, the Sayyid and my uncle (not my father, who was unable to act comfortably) descended into the cave and carried me out. When I came out, I heard people condoling my father, confirming that I was dead. After a few seconds, I opened my eyes, moved my hands and legs, and stood up. Surprised by my actions, people started shouting and praising God, the Prophet, and his family saying that Imam Mahdi had just displayed a great miraculous wonder [*karāma*].

After this incident, the girl became a faithful Shi'i adherent who completed her religious education and became a religious leader (*mullāya*). Although symbolic communication can make the invisible visible and the private public, it is the visible, public, and social activities that bind people together. Such incidents of dream visions may convey personal or psychological implications, but their impact on the society or the religious community cannot be overlooked.

Another case relates to an Egyptian university professor with a PhD from a reputable Western institution. He recounted that in the summer of 2001, he had a dream vision in which the Prophet Muhammad appeared to him as a very tall, masculine, and dark-skinned man wearing Arab dress. The Prophet was standing away, looking at the professor in an alarming and serious way, but not angry or disappointed. The professor was afraid and declared, "Prophet!" He then woke up. The next day he discovered that a project he had given to a colleague to review was posted on the university website as that person's own "work-in progress." The dream caused the professor to change his attitude toward the intruding and unfaithful person as well as to publish a major part of his project in a highly regarded journal so as to protect his right and change an unjust discourse. He has since gone on to become very prolific in his field. In other words, if the unseen is to become seen in the world, individuals should take their dream visions seriously. I heard of another case from 'Abd al-Hady, a highly renowned professor working in another well-thought-of Arab Gulf university. He recounted that when he was in high school, he had a dream, which he described as follows:

> I dreamed that I was walking in front of my school that was close to my house. It was nighttime. The sky was clear and the crescent was bright and attractive. I saw the crescent rising rapidly in the middle of the sky. Immediately, I reached up my hand, captured the crescent and ate it. I then woke up. The next day, I asked my father, who was a pious man, knew the entire Qur'an by heart (*ḥāfiẓ al-Qur'an*), and was gifted in the interpretation of dreams, to decipher my dream. My father, showing a happy and pleasant mood, informed me that I would be a great scholar because of the crescent, symbolizing knowledge, that I ate.[32]

'Abd al-Hady stated that he had many good dreams, but this specific dream transformed him to be a man of letters, dedicating his life to knowledge and education. He also recounted that he had the experience of hearing and composing poems in dreams. He showed me some of the precious poems in his collection. However, he insisted that he would like to keep this "divine gift" (*hiba rabāniyya*) personal. When I asked his opinion about some Sufi poets who think that they experience revelation (*waḥy*) through dreams or dream vision through which they compose religiously significant poems, he replied:

> The Sufis have their insightful interpretations of the Qur'an. They also contribute significantly to Islam through their creative and religious poetry. But certain people and more specifically highly gifted poets confuse dream vision [*rū'yā*] with revelation [*waḥy*]. They assume that because the vision equals one forty-sixth of revelation, they reduce the entire divine revelation to dream vision. Revelation, as we understand from the Qur'an and Ḥadīth (the tradition of the Prophet) does not relate to human creativity, rather relates to God, a matter that belongs to the unknowable [*al-ghaib*] which goes beyond human ability and understanding.[33] The Qur'an is not poetry; it is the Word of God [*kalām* Allah]. The Prophet Muhammad is the last Messenger to have received revelation through Jibrīl [Gabriel] and nobody else since has been able to claim such a divine event. This is one of the core religious beliefs and principles of Islam, therefore whoever says otherwise is committing heresy and blasphemy or, at least, glorifying and aggrandizing himself [*yizakī nafsuh*].

To substantiate his argument, Abd al-Hady recited the following verse of the Qur'an (36:69): "We have not instructed the (Prophet) in poetry, nor is it meet for him: this is no less than a Message and a Qur'an making things clear."

DREAMS AND SOCIAL TRANSFORMATION

The line dividing the self from the "other" and the transnatural from the natural is emphasized through dream experience. The core meaning of self-awareness is the ability to distinguish self from nonself. The differentiation between the self and the other, or nonself, a basic component of "world view" (Redfield 1962, 95), is created not only through daily social interactions, but also through dreams. Simply put, "dreaming is the process required to form the most basic distinction that exists in the universe: I and it, subject and object" (Wolf 1994, 22). Dreams help people to become aware of themselves and of "others" as well as of events that occur in their lives. The social significance of dreams is that they are interpreted as messages coming from people, dead or alive, seeking or demanding certain things. Within this context, both dream tellers and interpreters view dreams as factors of social transformation. The following ethnographic cases confirm such a statement.

This case relates to a dream vision experienced by Fikry, an old man who spent his early childhood in the Egyptian countryside. Fikry enjoyed a good reputation not only for his political power, holding the position of general in the interior ministry, but also for his status as a *sharīf* or a descendant of the Prophet. During the terrorist activities that plagued Egypt in the 1990s, Fikry experienced a dream vision that he could not dismiss. He recounted that he saw the Prophet Muhammad in a dream vision looking toward the other side in a gesture that he was unsatisfied with something. Worried about what the Prophet saw, Fikry said that he was anticipating something serious to happen. The next day, he unexpectedly received a call from a higher-ranking officer ordering him to march, supported with police forces, to a place where a group of people were designated as belonging to a group of alleged Islamist terrorists. Fikry led the forces to the location and proceeded to arrest the suspect, a man, it turned out, he knew very well. Based on personal experience, Fikry was convinced that the man would be the last person to be a fanatical Muslim or terrorist; however, he had to arrest the innocent man. The man looked at Fikry without a word and turned his face to the other side in a manner similar, if not identical, to the way the Prophet did to Fikry in the dream.

Fikry discharged the man, interpreting his dream vision as not just a sign of fantasy or false imagination, but as an actual event or message displaying the Prophet's disapproval of injustice and aggression against innocent people. Fikry would never have changed his view of the whole police operation had he not experienced his dream vision disclosing a segment of the unseen reality. Fikry's interpretations of his dream vision not only indicated the struggle against injustice, but also motivated him to change or challenge any ideological or materialistic power that precludes individuals from their rights. In brief, by narrating and interpreting his dream vision, Fikry, like many other persons, responded to the social reality and transformed or reordered it.

Dreams modify dreamers' understanding of and attitudes toward certain people and events. Certain dreams serve as cultural means for maintaining social relationships. Dreams are an important source of information that guide people in their daily interactions with each other and help them to cope with difficult and challenging realities. Egyptians use certain dream symbols and interpretations to elaborate their culturally constructed social and interpersonal relations (Herdt 1992). For example, Amal, a secretary working in an export company, recounted a dream about Said, a colleague who had a problem with the company's administration. The secretary said that she saw her colleague, Said, crying intensely in her dream. The next day she met him and told him that she was sure that he would pass the problem with no harm, whispering to him that she saw him crying in a dream, a favorable sign. The colleague's mood subsequently changed for the better. The sense of reality is reinforced by not only participating in the imaginative or inner experiences, but by acting out the internal events (Price-Williams 1987, 255).

COSMOLOGICAL DIMENSIONS OF DREAMS AND MYSTICAL PARTICIPATION

The cosmological ideas that lie behind dreaming are significant and deserve special attention. Cosmological concepts and ideas are embedded in everyday discourses as well as in the dreams and the interpretation of dreams. Dream interpretation involves an assessment of whether the dream image and its apparent meaning emanated from benevolent or malevolent beings and forces. From the Muslim point of view, the "other" not only refers to a person but also to the concept of the existence of an external or cosmological agent (invisible entity or spiritual force) beyond the human, generating or triggering dreams. Among Moroccans, for instance, "Saints and *jinniyya* manifest themselves in dreams, visions, and other states of consciousness" (Crapanzano 1980, 75). What is significant here is that the individual is part of not only the society but also the total cosmological system. The following sections focus on two themes: mystical participation with cosmic entities or forces and dream prediction (*istikhāra*).

Mystical Participation

Dreams relate to the belief in the divine creation of the seen and unseen cosmos or world, implying repetition and regeneration in the sense that the creation of the world, including life and death,[34] can be repeated and reproduced (el-Aswad 2005b, 28). "Allah is He who effects the creation, hence He repeats it" (Qur'an 10:3).[35] The cosmos refers to the dynamic process of being and becoming as exclusively exercised by God, who "when He intends a thing, His command is, 'Be,' and it is!" (Qur'an 30:82). The eternal repetition of the cosmic act "permits the return of the dead to life, and maintains the hope of the faithful in the resurrection of the body" (Eliade 1959, 62). According to Muslim worldviews, sleep is considered a partial or minor death belonging to the invisible realm. Though the invisible world is imaginary and imperceptible, it is thought to be real and have its own existence that can be traced to certain clues given in dreams. The concealed or invisible allows for possibility, rendering the cosmos or reality a dynamic structure in which parts or entities and forces are mystically fused or interconnected.

Stanley Tambiah differentiates between two coexisting modes of thinking based on notions of "participation," or mystical participation as used by

Lévy-Bruhl (1985), and "causality." Participation, a holistic, configurational, and presentational way of thinking, signifies the association between persons and things in traditional thought to the point of identity and consubstantiality.[36] Participation is a mode of relating and constructing reality. In contrast, causality is associated with a rational or logical way of thinking represented in positive science. What Western thought would consider to be logically distinct aspects of reality, the traditional may fuse into one mystic unity (Tambiah 1990, 95, 105). Men of piety or religious people experience and live in such a mystical world, at least in certain or specific periods of time designated as the dreamtime. This explains a statement made by an Egyptian Sufi, belonging to the Shinnawiyya order, that he is fully aware that what he sees in wakefulness and dreaming is not just through his eyes or heart, but through God's eyes that never sleep (*'ain Allah sāhra*).

Being of higher-order meaning or knowing, dream visions can be a source of spiritual and religious experience, connecting people with cosmological forces, beings, and realities that go beyond the ordinary boundaries of space and linear time (Casto, Krippner, and Tartz 1999; Bulkeley 1996). High-order meaning, based on participation or unification with the other, the cosmos, or the divine, may be experienced "as effects of or as *parts* of, that which they signify" (Rappaport 1999, 72). Supernatural presence is created or transmitted through dream visions, allowing for the possibility of receiving divine inspiration resulting in spiritual awakening. Dream visions are viewed not only as a source of religious inspiration and mystical participation but also as a relevant source available to a wide spectrum of people.

Cosmologically, while benevolent unseen agents or entities and forces including angels or good spirits are believed by Muslims to be present in dream visions, certain regular dreams may be induced by malevolent forces and evil spirits. Pakistanis make a basic distinction between true and false dreams. False dreams are thought to be caused either by Satan and other evil spirits or by disturbances in the body or mind of the dreamer, while true dreams are thought to be caused by God or angels and to be, often, a warning to the dreamer that harm may befall the dreamer or a family member if proper action is not taken (Ewing 1990, 58–59). To ward off malevolent spirits causing nightmares and bad dreams, Egyptians among other Muslims recite some verses of the Qur'an, especially *al-mu'awizatayn* (113, 114) and al-Kursy (2:255) before going to sleep. They also put a copy of the Qur'an underneath their pillows. In addition to the Qur'an, the Shi'a recite certain invocations composed by the Imams to deflect evil spirits during sleep.

Dream visions, justified or sanctified by the sacred text or the Qur'an,[37] separate sublime reality from superficial fantasy or illusion that might occur in regular dreams or ill-received reality. When the imaginary is sanctified through association with an unquestionable and transcendental reality, it becomes not just an idea or ideology but as real as a perceptible object. Dream visions are interpreted by

Egyptians, like other Muslims, as related to the activity of a person's soul (*rūḥ*) that transcends all psychosocial boundaries.[38] The soul is depicted as a divine secret (*sirr ilāhī*) made of the light of God (*qabas min nūr Allah*), enabling human beings to participate in the unseen, transcendental, divine, and sacred reality. The soul is a significant element in dreams related to near-death experiences (Sanders 2007). The soul is accessible through such means as dream vision, prayer, and meditation, generating a sense of encompassing cosmic oneness.

In dreams, people are networking not only with relatives and friends or humans, but also with spirits, angels, and others nonhuman beings, asking or being asked by them to do certain things. For the Muslims, Sunni and Shi'a, the self encompasses two aspects indicating that good exists side by side with evil.[39] This is to say that man has been given the ability to distinguish between right and wrong as represented in having, respectively, a righteous self (*nafs muṭma'inna*) and an evil or domineering self (*nafs ammāra*). Both contrary aspects have opposite effects on dreaming. They are also associated with two different categories of people. Mystics or those who have a "righteous self" and are known for their piety or hidden constructive knowledge are believed to be friends of Allah (*awliyā' Allah*). They are able to receive and interpret not only good dreams but also dream visions, while those who are associated with a "domineering self" and hidden destructive knowledge are viewed as friends of the devil (*awliyā' ash-shaiṭān*) whose dreams are not genuine or true.

Though the *barzakh* in Muslim cosmology indicates the intermediate realm between this world and the other world where the souls of the dead wait for the Day of Resurrection, it goes beyond this restricted notion to encompass a broader meaning as participating in differing realities, including those of the waking, the sleeping or dreaming, and the dead. Participation in the *barzakh* is the key concept in understanding the relationship between these three types of realities. With reference to dreaming, the *barzakh* here encompasses spirits of living persons interacting in dreams with invisible entities as well as with spirits of other living persons and not just with those of the dead.[40]

Dream visions, especially those with spiritual and religious contents, imply visitations from unseen worlds and, therefore, give the person spiritual strength and mystical power. Dream visions are interpreted by reference to the status of religious imagery appearing in them. For instance, the appearance and message from the dream vision of an angel would have a higher potential truth value than a message received from the dream image of a local saint. Hierarchically, highly revered and holy persons such as prophets and *awliyā'* have powerful souls (el-Aswad 2006a). Seeing sanctified beings (such as prophets, specifically the Prophet Muhammad) in dreams is interpreted both iconically and indexically.

Spiritual or mystical participation is also represented in the concept of Sufi sainthood. In the hidden dimension of reality it is the saints' loyalty or closeness to Allah that gives them the power to do extraordinary deeds. The Sufis mediate between the visible and spirit worlds, a role that shapes and contours their sensibilities and religious imagination. They, through dream visions, respond to the ceaseless transformations of the cosmos or world itself. It is common to hear that certain saints appear in people's dreams asking them to build shrines or mosques carrying the saints' names. These demands are often fulfilled because people believe that highly revered saints are alive in their tombs.[41]

In terms of mystical participation, the deceased, through dreams, show their need for many things, including praying or reading the Qur'an for their souls. Although some interviewees pointed out that they just saw images of dead persons in dreams without talking to them, they were able to infer from these images the emotional conditions of the dead as being calm, happy, healthy, sad, or disappointed.

The aforementioned statement confirms that mystical participation is not restricted to saints or mystical Sufis but extends to include regular people. Tahani, a middle-aged widow who did not pray regularly, recounted that she saw her dead father in a dream. She observed that the father looked healthy, which she interpreted positively. She tried to talk to him but found herself reciting the opening chapter of the Qur'an (the Fatiha). The surprising thing was that when she woke up, she found herself reciting the same chapter of the Qur'an loudly. Tahani said that she never had such a dream before. Recognizing the significance of the dream, she paid a visit to the grave of her father, where she recited the Fatiha for the sake of his soul. She also said that she never stopped praying after that dream. Two weeks after the dream Tahani was engaged, then married to the son of her father's best friend.

This dream narrative implies a sort of mystical participation through which the hidden aspects of the cosmos or universe are disclosed. Unlike the Moroccan Tuhami, who is "usually not so careful to differentiate the waking world from the world of dreams" (Crapanzano 1980, 116), Tahani, the Egyptian, is careful in maintaining the distinction between the two worlds, notwithstanding her participation in both of them.

The Shi'a also recognize this logic of mystical participation. Within the Shi'i worldviews, certain scholars distinguish between a law-giving prophet or messenger (*rasūl*), a non-lawgiving prophet (*nabī*), and the Imam concerning their relationships with cosmic and celestial entities such as angels as well as with dream visions. According to Amir-Moezzi, "The imam hears but does not see the angel, the *nabī* sees and hears the angel only when asleep, and the *rasūl* sees and hears the angel both awake and asleep, thus there is a clear distinction made between the imam and the prophet, and the exoteric doctrine of the religious superiority of the prophet is safeguarded" (Amir-Moezzi 1994, 71). In addition, Imams receive inspiration "from a celestial being called al-Rūḥ, a being superior to the angels, including the angel Gabriel, the angel of prophetic revelations" (Amir-Moezzi 1994, 71). "If this 'body' of the Imam can be seen 'by' or 'in' the initiate's heart . . . (*al-ru'ya bi'l-qalb*), according to cosmoanthropogonic traditions this is because they are consubstantial, both made from the same celestial matter" (Amir-Moezzi 2011, 340). Regarding the dream vision, implying mystical participation, there "can be no vision unless the subject viewing and the object viewed are of the same nature. However, the vision of the Imam may take other forms: dreams, in the awakened state or in the world of the soul, completely independent of the believer's will and practice, a meeting or encounter in the physical world with the hidden imam" (Amir-Moezzi 2011, 340–41).[42]

Dream Prediction

Individuals tend to explain unknown matters and unseen entities from such known phenomena as dreams in which they see and experience unique occurrences. At the level of popular practice, Muslims feel confident in looking to their dreams for divine guidance, especially when faced with unpredictable challenges. As a part of the seen world, society as a whole is viewed as being imperfect. The limitation of society is shown in its inability to meet its own members' needs. This shortcoming drives individuals to seek other trustworthy means of support provided by Islamic tradition, such as a predictive or intentional dream known as *istikhāra* (see figure 5.1). *Istikhāra* means seeking guidance from God in making critical decisions affecting people's lives. It is a sort of dream prediction requesting God's help. The idea here is that through the notion of unknowable and mysterious spheres of the cosmos, it is very possible for a thing to be produced, reproduced, or known through dreaming.[43]

Because of its intentional character, the *istikhāra* is restricted to functional purposes, depending on how critical and serious the matters are that people wish to accomplish. Unlike dreams that occur beyond human control or will, the *istikhāra* is thought to be controllable through certain rituals, practices, and utterances. The person recites a specific *du'ā'* or supplication through which he seeks Allah's guidance in the matter or task he intends to carry out. Then he goes to sleep in a state of cleanliness after performing ablution. If he sees anything white or green in the dream, this is considered a symbolic indication that the task is good and he should accept it. However, if he sees black or red signs or symbols, it indicates that the task is not good for the dreamer and, therefore, must be avoided. If the person does not see a dream, he should rely on his insight and intention regarding the matter under consideration. The daily difficulty of hardship (*'usr*) of this world will be eased (*usr*) in both this world or the dream world and the other world. What is thought to be unobtainable in the immediate experience might be achievable in distant and different contexts. In both mundane and transcendental terms, nothing is inaccessible or impossible for Allah.

In certain circumstances, however, people think twice before summoning the *istikhāra*. Fatima, a young woman who received a marriage proposal, showed a great fear of invoking the *istikhāra*. She pointed out that she did not like the idea of committing herself to such a practice, especially as she was not sure about her feelings toward the man. She was afraid of the supernatural punishment if she rejected the man whom *istikhāra* might approve. Such a statement implies a firm belief in the effectiveness of *istikhāra*.

CONCLUSION

The numerous case studies of dreams and their interpretations offered by both Sunni and Shi'i Muslims, elite and grassroots, professors and taxi drivers, Sufis and police officers, accentuate a broad Muslim conviction of dreaming as an integral part of their worldviews. Dreams and dream interpretations reveal folk insight of inner or psychological, social, and cosmological aspects expressed in concrete and sensuous narratives. Dreams allow Muslims to converse about hidden and unconscious motives through shared symbolism of imagination.

The chapter brings an experiential and imagined dimension to the ways in which Muslims understand and enact religious beliefs. Imagination facilitates symbolic innovation refracted in dream exegeses. Concomitant with their discontent with the overall conditions of their everyday lives, people pay great attention to dreams and visions that imply sacred meanings and divine anticipations for better outcomes in their daily lives and better conditions beyond this life.

Though the unseen and more specifically spiritual and future matters are unknown to men, dreams provide significant clues for comprehending spiritual reality and are thought to be means of anticipating future events. Imagination and dreams, inseparable from Muslim worldviews, can bring together what might otherwise be kept fragmented and separate. Dream experiences are open to possible interpretations, generating possible realities or worlds. Each of the three components of worldviews, namely the person, the society, and the cosmos, confirms, though differently, the participation of Muslims in imagination, dreams, and visions as vehicles of not only understanding certain aspects of hidden realities but also transforming these realities if needed.

The cosmological significance of dreams is embedded in the Muslim worldview that the universe is not just an object on which people practice their will but is a reality imbued with spirits and forces that can impact human beings. Dreams serve as lenses through which individuals see or glimpse the hidden or unseen aspects of the world. The known and the unknown, the tangible and the imagined, and the seen and the unseen can be balanced together through multiple experiences, including those of dreaming.

This chapter has shown that the world is constructed by Muslim worldview and imagination as a place of seen and unseen dimensions. One is related to the knowledge of everyday observation, the other to the knowledge of hidden reality, religious or otherwise. Taken in their totality, as far as they indicate psychological, social, and spiritual realities, dreams necessitate the two kinds of knowledge. Dream visions or dreams belong to the unknown or unseen sphere and assert the effectiveness of that sphere in the reconstruction of people's everyday reality.

Ordinary reality as has been explicated by case studies here can be altered or changed by serious interpretations of dreams. There is a mutual validation between the dream world and Muslim worldviews in the sense that dreams are justified or sanctified, as is the case of some dream visions, by religious worldviews, while some significant components of worldviews, especially those related to unseen dimensions, are validated by dreams.

All in all, Muslims do not consider the visible and tangible world as the only accessible world of experience; rather, there are multiple unseen and imaginary worlds from which possible realities emerge. Without the invisible and imagined domain the visible and tangible world would be devoid of meaning.

6

Multiple Worldviews and Multiple Identities of the Muslim Diaspora

Although cross-cultural studies of Muslim worldviews are scant, transnational migration and population movements are presently the focus of extensive scholarly debates dealing with such issues as hybrid identity, transnational cultural relations, the renovation of migrants' social cosmologies, and the dynamics of identity reconstruction (el-Aswad 2004b, 2006b; Axel 2004; Clifford 1988, 1997; Cohn 1987; Coutin 2003; Euben 2006; Hall 1990, 1992; Kapchan and Strong 1999; Kaplan 1996; Papastergiadis 2000; Pieterse 2009).[1]

This chapter explicates the nature of Muslim worldviews and identities of both the Sunni and Shi'a in American society through an exploration of discourses and practices related to migration and movement at global and local levels. It demonstrates the coming together of universal and local worldviews, showing how Muslims adapt their worldviews to circumstances but still by and large remain Muslim in their orientation to the social and religious world. It also examines the interrelationship between local, national, and international contexts shaping Sunni and Shi'a worldviews and the ways in which Muslims reconstruct their identities. This chapter does not provide an inclusive study of Muslim groups and their histories in the United States,[2] but rather addresses various experiences of Muslims living in the communities of Bloomfield Hills[3] and Dearborn, Michigan,[4] in the metropolitan Detroit area, with a particular emphasis on personal narratives of both men and women of different ages and socioeconomic backgrounds (figure 6.1). Notably, Dearborn has the largest Islamic center and one of the largest Muslim populations in the United States.[5]

This chapter is based on ethnographic material gathered from thirty-five case studies in which I applied participant observation and conducted in-depth interviews, with research into autobiographies, biographies, and various documents

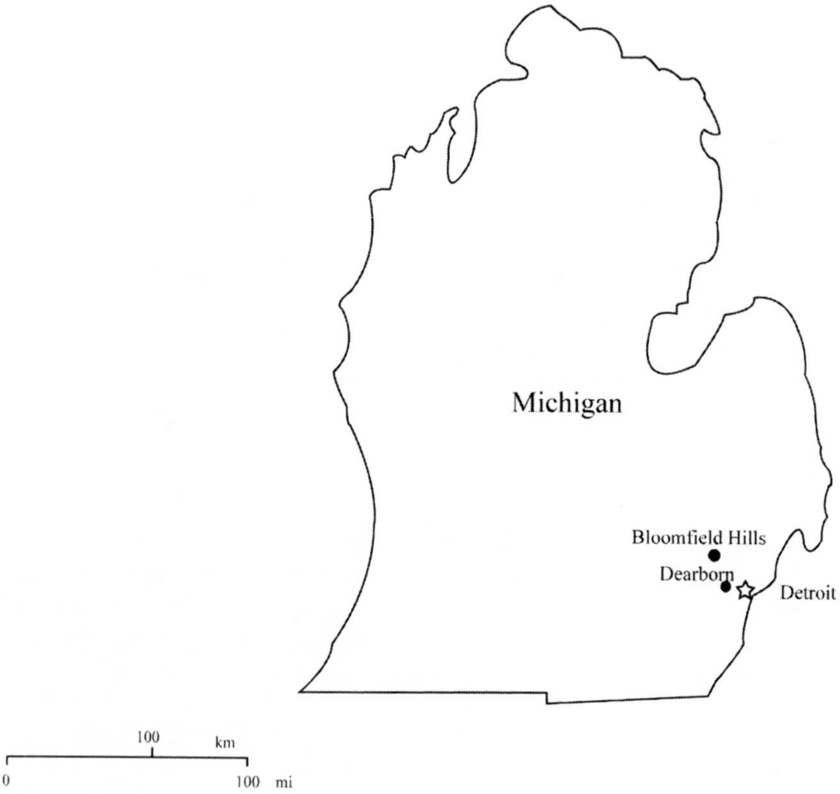

Figure 6.1. Michigan.

such as letters, books, newspapers, e-mail correspondences, and comments or essays posted on Internet websites. These case studies divulge significant cross-cultural and theoretical insights that facilitate the understanding of key features, such as the unity, diversity, plasticity, and multiplicity of the worldviews and identities of Muslim Americans. This chapter also tackles the geography of Muslim cyberspace, demonstrating the role of cybercirculations, including Internet and cyberforums, in both maintaining and changing certain elements of Muslims' worldviews and daily lives from traditional to modern forms.[6]

MUSLIM WORLDVIEWS AND AMERICAN CULTURE

Muslims are dispersed throughout various parts of the globe and adapt to different national and regional sociopolitical contexts. As a great land of opportunities, America and American society attract Muslims from all around the world.

However, since the events of 9/11, Muslim Americans, Sunni and Shi'a, have been depicted by many non-Muslim Americans as being terrorists or in sympathy with terrorism.[7] They have experienced a variety of forms of discrimination and stigmatization based on factors such as race and ethnicity, language, dress, customs, and religion.[8] The deep-seated negative interpretations of Islam in the United States affect discourses and actions of Muslim Americans who have become subject to the web of racism that includes hate crimes, media stereotypes, and dehumanizing ideology.[9]

Negative stereotyping, however, has further united Muslim Americans to counter resentment and to portray themselves not only as Muslim or Arab, but also as American.[10] Further, hate crimes have spawned an interfaith relationship that the Muslim community wants to invigorate. Muslim Americans have made open attempts to offer clarification about their heritage and to teach others about their religion (Islam) in an attempt to dissuade intolerances and injustices against them.[11] In response to the tragic events of 9/11, Muslim Americans, both Sunni and Shi'a in Dearborn and Detroit, have expressed their patriotism and full Americanness in tangible ways, including the display of American flags on clothes, cars, homes, storefront windows, and places of worship.

Muslim migrants and their immediate descendants experience profound changes in certain domains of their outlook and orientation as they move from the state of being a majority in their homeland to that of being a minority in the American pluralistic society, generating a unique sense of hybrid or multiple identities. The American pluralistic society reflects and accommodates for Muslim diversity. However, the concepts of unity of God (*tawḥīd*) and Muslim worldwide community (*ummah*) play a significant role in unifying Muslim Americans. As Gregorian notes, "It is of the greatest interest and significance that the Muslim *ummah*, or community, of North America is as nearly a microcosm of the global *ummah* as has ever occurred since Islam" (Gregorian 2003, 2).

The worldviews of Muslim Americans are generally different from those of non-Muslim Americans. Taylor (2007, 3) states, "Many milieux in the United States are secularized, and I would argue that the United States as a whole is. Clear contrast cases today would be the majority of Muslim societies." An American or Western worldview is contingent on secularism or the separation of church or religion and state (Jacoby 2004; Turner 2011) and is supported by and clearly stated within the First Amendment of the Constitution of the United States. Such a worldview, not fully recognized in Islam, either overlooks sanctified religious belief systems or renders them to private rather than public spheres.[12] The notion of secularity "stands not only in contrast with a divine foundation for society, but with any idea of society as constituted in something which transcends common actions" (Taylor 2007, 192).

According to secularist worldviews, religious beliefs stand in contrast to logic and the laws of nature. "The essence of a secularist or rationalist worldview *is* the desacralization of mysteries and taboos that defy logic and the laws of nature" (Jacoby 2004, 340).[13] Western worldviews have experienced a kind of transformation defined in terms of detachment and disenchantment with religion, the sacred, and the world of spirits (Taylor 2007, 29, 61, 77). For Muslims, the existence of God, an ultimate sacred postulate, and the prevalence of Islamic law (*shari'a*) are inseparable from their worldviews and everyday lives.[14] Certain Western scholars express their concern toward the unresolved paradox that religion, for some Americans, occupies an important place in a nation founded on the separation of church and state (Jacoby 2004, 3–4).

Muslim worldview is based on submission to Allah as the supreme guide and authority, while the secular system views religion as a form of worship separate from other aspects of life. As such, Muslim worldviews and Western ideology seem to generate conflict. But this conflict is resolved in that Western worldviews permit individuals to maintain their private beliefs, religious or otherwise, as well as to establish a connection between spiritual and secular domains as long as the law is not violated. This is attuned with the American pluralistic and free society. Moreover, secular modernity predominant in the United States has not weakened Muslim worldviews. As Berger notes, "The proposition that modernity leads to a decline of religion is, in principle, 'value free'" (Berger 1999, 3). In Islam, individuals are judged and assessed not only by their reasoning, rational behavior, and ability to choose and make the right decisions, but also by piety (*taqwā*) or the degree to which they fear, or are guided by, God.[15]

Privacy, self-interest, and individualistic orientation are prevalent components of Western or American worldviews, while connectivity, hospitality, collectivity, and strong family relations are among core elements of Muslim worldviews. "One of the specific rules that is identified as problematic about American culture is that of not being able to express oneself openly," Magnuson notes (Magnuson 2005, 383). The individualistic and family/collective orientations of Western and Muslim worldviews are expressed by 'Adel, a Sunni Muslim American scholar married to a Christian (Catholic) woman who willingly converted to Islam after twenty years of marriage. 'Adel and his wife and two children moved to the United States from Egypt seeking job opportunities and a good education for the children. The family was initially invited to stay at the house of the wife's parents. 'Adel narrated:

> One day, my father-in-law confronted me saying that he was not comfortable with the whole situation of having another family in his house. It was not easy for me to accept such a complaint. I politely responded telling him that it is "*your* family, not just *any* family." I was surprised to hear him loudly respond, "It is not my business." I immediately began to lecture him stating, "Yes, it is your business as a grandfather to take care of your family at this critical time. As a matter of fact, it is our business, not just yours or mine. It is the family business that we all should take care of and support. And, sharing and patience are good." I informed him about a family's compassion and mercy (*mawada wa raḥma*). My parents-in-law responded favorably, showing great support, understanding, and belief in the family circle. Both my

wife and I managed to find jobs and bought a nice house neighboring that of my family-in-law in Bloomfield Hills. Throughout the years, we have been able to offer reciprocal support, sharing both happy and sad times. My parents-in-law and the rest of the in-laws were and still are happy to have us visit them. We often laugh and reminisce about our time spent so closely together.

Despite the fact that not all Muslim Americans observe religious practices (including the five daily prayers), Islam is viewed as a total way of life, in both the public and private contexts. For certain Arab Americans, Islam has replaced Arabism as their primary reference point. People from different Muslim and non-Arab countries such as Egypt, India, Jordan, Iran, Iraq, Lebanon, Pakistan, Palestine, Syria, Yemen, and so forth come together at the local mosque to pray collectively and carry out other religious and social activities. Both Sunni and Shi'i Muslim Americans have become interested in establishing interfaith dialogues engaging with Christians and Jews through Islamic centers, mosques, and websites. Personal and social interactions are effective tools in eliminating or changing the misconceptions non-Muslims and Muslims have about each other's communities. In Dearborn, for example, both Muslim and non-Muslim Americans publicly and candidly share Muslim international conferences and festivals among other cultural, social, and religious activities.

Although Muslim Americans constitute a minority at the national or Michigan state level, they feel as if they were a majority, or at least a minority among a country of minorities, at the local level of the community. For Muslim Americans, the concept of "minority" in the United States differs from that in most Muslim and Arab countries, in which inequality and desecration of human rights prevail. Salman 'Ali, a Shi'i Muslim who works in a restaurant in Dearborn, describes his view as a person who belongs to a minority community by saying, "we are a minority in a country of minorities." Barbara Smith (1990, 71) states that there is "no single, comprehensive macroculture in which all or even most of the citizens of this nation actually participate, no numerically predominant majority culture in relation to which any or all of the others are 'minority' cultures, and no culture that . . . 'transcends' any or all other cultures" (Smith 1990, 71).

Muslim Americans show great interest in explaining their religious beliefs and practices to non-Muslim Americans. It happened that I invited a Christian American to attend a lecture on Islam at the Muslim Community Center in Bloomfield Hills. He recounted to me that he felt as though he were a foreigner or, at least, the people there dealt with him as a foreigner. This perception of being foreign, however, resulted from the way Muslim attendees offered him extensive information on Islam and the use of the Arabic language. Muslims from different countries, especially those from the Middle East, have become familiar faces in Dearborn among other areas and are recognized quickly by one another. Many grocery stores, bakeries, and restaurants, for instance, carry Muslim and Arabic names such as Kawthar Meat,[16] Baraka Meat and Poultry, Karbala Supermarket,

New Yasmeen Bakery, Halal Restaurant, Halal Pizza, and Iraqi Kabab (figure 6.2). Store owners and community business owners interface with the general public who come to the communities and willingly share their goods, explain the names of their stores, and offer other explanations for their services and goods as needed.

Many Muslim Americans have achieved prosperity in business, academia, engineering, and other fields and as such have been successful and mainstreamed into US society and politics. Success, however, is not entirely measured by economic progress but by maintaining Muslim values as well as good relationships with people. The pluralistic feature of American society that advocates egalitarianism has attracted Muslim Americans who seek to fill the gap between Western worldviews, secular and egalitarian in nature, and Islamic worldviews, holistic and religious in nature. In short, despite these differences in worldviews, American Muslims are interwoven into the fabric of American society. The Muslim communities in Michigan as well as other such communities (Schmidt 2004) adopted institutional structures and professional styles familiar to the American society, giving Muslim institutions a positive image of intellectual accountability attractive to the non-Muslim majority.[17]

All in all, the influence of American society is represented in such channels as seminars, lectures, conferences, speeches, media, online networking, and computer programs that the organizations have used to attain their mission. Religious

Figure 6.2. New Yasmeen Bakery, Dearborn, Michigan.

centers and organizations seek to provide Muslims, especially those of the young generation, with sufficient education to help them maintain their religious heritage. Muslim centers are also socially oriented, offering Muslim Americans a space in which to socialize with each other. During religious occasions, such as the month of Ramadan when Muslims fast, and celebratory feasts (*'Eid*), food and beverages are served free or at very low prices. However, Muslims continue to observe certain food and drink prohibitions or taboos (*ḥarām*) and are aware of permitted (*ḥalāl*) food. In addition, some of these centers have recreational facilities to attract youths and prevent them from acquiring and developing negative patterns of behavior.

Young Muslims in the United States are positively and aggressively involved in the American mainstream with strong attitudes of cooperation rather than confrontation. Muslim Americans keep an eye on what is happening inside the new homeland and another eye on what is happening in their old homeland. They are interested in knowing new ideas or interpretations of Islam offered by Muslim intellectuals both inside and outside the United States. They are not happy with the violence motivated by politically oriented religious groups, whether they are Muslim or non-Muslim.

The following is a quotation from Amir Aswad, a college student I interviewed in Bloomfield Hills in December 2011, expressing his views of American culture and homeland:

> I personally believe that I am a huge participant to the mainstream life style of America. To begin with, I have a very American social network. I interact with many "plain" and multi-ethnic Americans. It seems that no matter the ethnicity, the culture remains generally similar, as we have interests in the same American music, TV shows, video games, and sports. I dress in very American styles, including hoodies, jeans, and shoes. Also, I work hard to remain physically fit, which seems to be an obsession in American media, as a man is not a man without six-pack abs. Beyond social interaction, I interact with mainstream America by working toward an American law degree. By studying at college and working part time, I observe the American value of achievement. I definitely have "two eyes," one in the American politics and one in Egyptian/Arab politics. Every morning, before going to school, I sit on the couch with breakfast while watching American news. I like to keep up to date with both local and national events, as it may directly impact my life. I scrupulously watch American foreign agendas, especially when dealing with the Middle East. I closely pay attention to Middle Eastern affairs as they are very important to me. Although the relation is not as direct as American news, I still feel I have a duty as an Arab American to understand what is going on in the fatherland. I have always found the differences in American views of Islam compared to traditional Arabic views. From my observations, although they may be incorrect, American Muslims have a more liberal approach to Islam, as the laws and rules are more metaphorical. Traditional Arabs, on the other hand, perceive Islam more as a way of life, in which the rules are much more important. Normal Americans are terrified of Islamic groups such as Muslim Brotherhood and Hezbollah. Ironically, Americans see them as terrorist

> militant groups, while actual Arabs see them more as groups that serve the people, yet contain military power. Islam is perceived as two completely different things. One is a religion of peace and love, while the other more ignorant view is a religion of hate and destruction.

The Arab-Muslim revolutions in the Middle East (or the Arab Spring) have provoked Muslim Americans, especially those from the Arab world, to rethink concepts of violence, freedom, liberty, free information, human rights, equality, and social justice embedded in their worldviews. These recent events occurring in the old homeland have deepened and empowered Muslim Americans' awareness of the dramatic changes in the history, culture, and social structure of these Muslim countries. Further, the peaceful revolution of Egyptians in particular against their long-standing regime was much admired by mainstream Americans and provided a good opportunity to question the Western media construction of Arab-Muslim culture as violent and terrorist.[18]

Muslim Americans express their pride in the democratic changes in their homeland countries. The young generation of American Muslims takes the information revolution with its various online and electronic resources and means of communication very seriously. They are involved in a continuous process of dual assessments through which they evaluate both American culture and their homeland or Islamic heritage in order to establish novel bridges for connecting them.

SUNNI AND SHI'I MUSLIM AMERICANS

Though Muslim Americans are the most racially diverse religious group in the United States (Younis 2009), Sunni Muslims constitute the majority of Muslims in the United States, as they do worldwide. Shi'a communities, mainly Lebanese and Iraqi, however, constitute the largest ethnic groups in Dearborn, Michigan.[19] Religious communities are demarcated by specific doctrines, related rituals, worldviews, and practices. Both Sunni and Shi'i Muslims in southeast Michigan are affiliated with religious organizations and social centers serving their religious practices, spiritual inspirations, and social activities.[20] Muslims tend to organize themselves through visible, public places such as mosques and religious and social centers, in which they perform rituals and congregate for communal occasions and purposes (figure 6.3). In such places in the community and through their everyday lives and practices, they substantiate their worldviews. Overall, Islam is a medium creating and facilitating communication among people who identify themselves through Islam (Waardenburg 2003, 342).

Diversity does not hinder communication between individuals adhering to different religious sects. In southeast Michigan, the Sunni and Shi'a have engaged in cultural religious dialogue. Dialogue is viewed as a networking or exchange

Figure 6.3. Muslim Unity Center, Bloomfield Hills, Michigan.

of ideas and opinions between two or more individuals or groups with an aim to achieve better mutual understanding concerning certain issues. It implies eliminating contradictory elements that might exist between them. In May 2007 representatives of more than twenty-four Islamic centers and institutes, both Sunni and Shi'a, met at the Council of Islamic Organizations of Michigan and signed the "Muslim Code of Honor" (see the appendix) denouncing sectarianism and advocating mutual respect and peaceful coexistence of all sects within the universal Muslim community (*ummah*).[21] Muslims in metro Detroit also meet at the Islamic Council of America, in Dearborn (figure 6.4).

Despite the fact that both Sunni and Shi'i Muslims engage in respectable dialogue and peaceful relationships, some people still think negatively in terms of sectarian orientation. Ironically, scholars, in discussing the conversion of certain Americans into Shi'ism, argue that many converts "indicate that some of them accepted Shi'ism due to the proliferation of Sunni literature that vilified and denigrated the Shi'is" (Takim 2009, 209).[22]

The following narratives are examples of Muslims who expressed their religious, social, and cultural experiences in the American context. 'Asim Ahmad, a Pakistani Sunni Muslim who works at a wireless phone company, recounted, "I have to say that Americans did a superior job building a sturdy foundation for their country despite the recent financial breakdown. Also, the standard of living

Figure 6.4. The Islamic Council of America, Dearborn, Michigan.

is much higher here in America than in most Muslim countries. I have a strong feeling that Muslims in the US are more united than the Muslims in other majority Muslim countries." Mohammed el-Hadidi, a Syrian man in his midfifties working at the Ford Motor Company in Dearborn, was very proud to tell me that he had a hand in initiating and establishing a mosque in Bloomfield Hills, where he resides. His intention, however, was not only to address the needs of the Syrians, but those of all Muslims in the community.

Latifa, a middle-aged Shiʿi woman who teaches at an elementary school in Dearborn, recounted, "I read Arabic fluently and I search for information myself rather than being a passive receptive of what the imam says. In addition, I lived in Saudi Arabia for a long time, learned about Wahhabi school of thought, and married an Egyptian Hanafi Sunni, all of which exposed me to several views and hence made me selective and inquisitive of what I hear."

Latifa's younger colleague, Mariam, also an elementary-school teacher, further indicated that she was familiar with the Islamic Center on Ford Road in Dearborn. She recounted, "This mosque is liberal to a certain degree and it has a women's organization where they participate alongside with men in many activities. My two aunts, for example, volunteer every Sunday morning to make breakfast and sell it for worshipers to generate money to run the mosque. Friday's (*Jum'a*) speech or sermon and Ramadan's lectures are held in the same room for both genders; yet women usually are seated in the back rows."

The five mandatory daily prayers are observed by the Shi'a everywhere, in the homeland and new land. However, they regularly combine the noon (*ẓuhr*) and afternoon (*'aṣr*) prayers by conducting them consecutively during an acceptably designated period of time between the noon and afternoon. Similarly, they combine the sunset (*maghrib*) and evening (*'ishā'*) prayers. They consider such practice to be compatible with the principles of the Qur'an and tradition of the Prophet. The Sunni Muslims do not regularly combine mandatory prayers (*al-jam` bain al-ṣalatain*), except for certain urgent circumstances such as travel, rain, and danger. The Shi'a have argued that such practices have proven to be practical in such a busy and demanding environment as the United States.

Friday prayer (*Ṣalāt al-Jum'ah*) in mosques in Michigan is held twice on the same day: once at noon, and again around 3 p.m.[23] The reason behind such practice is to give Muslims a chance to attend the collective prayer on Fridays, which is a weekend in Muslim-majority countries but a working day in the United States. Another reason is that, on Fridays, mosques are overcrowded and cannot accommodate all those who come to pray. The Friday sermon (*Khuṭba*), for both Sunni and Shi'a, is conducted in both Arabic and English. The *shaikh* starts the sermon in Arabic and then repeats the same message in English. He switches between Arabic and English until the sermon is finished.

With the exception of a few, most Friday sermons do not address political topics but focus instead on social, ethical, interfaith, and youth-related issues. One of the Sunni sermons I attended in the mosque at the Muslim Unity Center in Bloomfield Hills (figure 6.5) addressed the social corruption (*ẓahar al-fasād fī al-bar wa al-baḥr*) that is occurring globally and locally, causing God's rage and unprecedented natural disasters of great magnitude, such as tsunamis, earthquakes, and diseases. The *shaikh* attributed further social ills to man-made disasters such as oil spills, pollution, and war.

Figure 6.5. Muslim Unity Mosque, Bloomfield Hills, Michigan.

Also, on Friday evenings at around 10 p.m., imams of both Sunni and Shi'i mosques hold religious lectures that attract a great number of Muslims and are geared toward attracting members from different generations. In a lecture also held at the Muslim Unity Center, Shaikh Muhammed Musa, the religious leader of the Muslim Unity Center in Bloomfield Hills, encouraged the people (figure 6.6), especially the young, to maintain their religious practices and added, "Sacred places are not confined to those in Muslim homelands, nor are they associated with saintly shrines, rather they are found everywhere on the earth, including America. Sacred places are not mere geographic locations, but spiritual points of reference. Any clean place is rendered sacred as far as people pray in it."

The universal Muslim worldviews have a great impact on American Muslims' understandings and explanations of the unseen realms, including dreams and dream visions. The following dream vision was announced publicly by Ayatollah Abdul-Latif Berry, the religious leader of the Shi'a community in Dearborn, Michigan, on the first annual memorial of Ayatollah Muhammad Hussein Fadlallah[24] at the Islamic Institute of Knowledge on July 8, 2011.[25] Shaikh Berry recounted that he saw Ayatollah Fadlallah in a dream vision two weeks previously:

> In the dream vision, I was in the mosque of al-Hussain when Shaikh Fadlallah approached me warmly. He was wearing his blue cloak and shook my hand. I was so surprised and wondered how Shaikh Fadlallah came back from the otherworld.

Figure 6.6. Shaikh Musa, Imam of the Mosque of the Muslim Unity Center (retired in March 2011).

He informed me of three things. First was that he was so happy in the otherworld. Second, he encouraged me to support his two sons, Shaikh Ali and Shaikh Ja'afar Fadlallah. Third was to take care of all religious institutions in Beirut, including charity societies, and those who serve in those institutes.

The message conveyed by Shaikh Berry indicates both spiritual and social participation. Spiritually, there is connection between the two souls of the highly dignified religious leaders in showing concern about maintaining the Shi'a tradition with specific reference to the sons who are themselves religious scholars. Socially, there is participation in developing various religious institutes and societies for Islamic charities with emphasis on the enhancement of their social and economic functions (figure 6.7).

The Shi'a in the United States, and more specifically Dearborn, practice 'Ashura (*ta'ziyya*) during Muharram (the first Islamic month and the month in which Imam Husain was martyred) as well as in Ramadan. I attended 'Ashura rituals at the mosque of the Islamic Center of America (figure 6.8) and the Islamic Institute of Knowledge in Dearborn. At the mosque, I saw people gathering but individually reciting the Qur'an and reading supplications. In addition, some

Figure 6.7. Shaikh Abdul-Latif Berry delivering a speech at the first annual memorial of Ayatollah Fadlallah (July 8, 2011) at the Islamic Institute of Knowledge in Dearborn, Michigan.

were praying using the stone of Karbala, on which they placed their foreheads during prayer as is done in the homeland. Then, in a sad, rhythmic tone, the *shaikh* began to address *ḥusainiyya*, chanting poems that told the story of what happened at the massacre in Karbala. When he mentioned the Prophet's family and Imams, the attendees uttered, "May Allah praise Muhammad and his family" (*allahuma ṣalli 'ala Mohammad wa āl Muhammad*). They resonated the phrase once, not three times as the Shi'a do in the homeland.[26] During the ceremony, a few children passed a basket around to collect money for the mosque. At the end of the ceremony, which lasted until 11 p.m., the mosque offered a free light meal for those who wished to eat.

At the Islamic Institute of Knowledge, the 'Ashura ritual was similar in structure to the one I observed in the mosque. The difference, however, was represented in the intellectual and religious elaboration of the tragic events of Karbala. The *shaikh*, after addressing the *ḥusainiyya*, including the historical incident and the martyrdom of Imam Husain, elaborated on the notions of sacrifice, injustice (*maẓlūmiyya*), victimization, endurance, patience, restoring justice, and love of the Prophet's family (*ahl al-bait*). Quietly and sincerely, Shi'i people cried, showing emotion and empathy toward Imam Husain. Sharing one's feelings with others is also highly valued.

Differences in certain orientations and practices are found within the Shi'i community of Dearborn. A Shi'i clerk said, "The Shi'a in Dearborn are not

Figure 6.8. Islamic Center of America, Dearborn, Michigan.

fully united. There are factions and affiliations toward certain villages in the homeland or country. For example, some major Lebanese donors to the Islamic Institute of Knowledge are not happy with the amount of Iraqi worshipers that the Shaikh of Islamic Center of America is attracting. Further, the Mahdi Marjaiya [Imam Mahdi Association Marjaeya, IMAM][27] does not believe that some Shi'a should continue following the late Fadlallah; rather, they should follow al-Sistani."[28]

Some Shi'a prefer to maintain their religious guide or source of emulation (*marja'*) in their homeland such as Iraq, Lebanon, and Iran, while others prefer to have the *marja'* in the United States. Zhara, a middle-aged Shi'i woman of Lebanese descent, informed me that she follows "the late Mohamed Hussein Fadlallah's teachings that stem from Ja'far al-Sādiq's school of thought. When I have a religious question, I call Fadlallah's office in Beirut or log on to his website, Bayynat, and try to find an answer to my question."[29]

To further exemplify the differences in Shi'i orientations, I attended the weekly meeting of the Grand Ayatollah Shaikh Abdul-Latif Berry, held at the Islamic Institute of Knowledge, on July 1, 2011, where he stated that Shi'i Muslims should distribute the charity portion of their money or excess wealth (known as one-fifth, or *khums*) among the needy Muslims in the United States instead of sending the money to the *marja'iyya* overseas. Other Shi'a, however, insist on sending the one-fifth to their *marja'iyya* in their homeland, such as Iraq.[30]

The conflict also appears on deciding which day begins the first day of the Eid (the feast following the month of Ramadan). When Grand Ayatollah 'Ali al-Sistani in Iraq, for instance, announced that a particular day was the first day of the holiday of the feast, and when the office of Grand Ayatollah Fadlallah in Lebanon announced that it would begin on the subsequent day, the Islamic Center of America announced that it would celebrate both days, respectively and independently, as the first day of the feast, to satisfy the two factions.

Muslim Americans are concerned not only with the daily activities of the living but also with the Islamic burial of the dead. A Sunni Muslim living in Bloomfield Hills lost his young child, who died in an accident in the early 1980s. He looked for a suitable place to bury his son, but nothing was available. People advised him to bury the son in a Christian cemetery, which he accepted. But when he went there, he found all graves were facing directions other than toward the *Qiblah* or the Ka'ba (or Mecca). He changed his mind and took the body of his son back to the hospital and kept him there until he found a Muslim cemetery to suit his preference.

In a reply to my question about whether Sunni and Shi'a have separate cemeteries, 'Ali, a Shi'i person belonging to the Moukalled family in Dearborn, stated, "the cemetery I know is called the Islamic Garden. Usually families collect money and buy several grave lots and reserve them for their people. For example, when my brother died suddenly, the Moukalled family donated his grave because he participated in the association when he was alive. I know there is more than one cemetery; however I am not sure if they separate Sunnah from Shi'a." However, Shaikh Musa informed me that Sunni and Shi'i Muslims have separate cemeteries and showed me advertisements indicating separate burial sites for both Sunni and Shi'a.

In Dearborn, I attended a burial ritual that was conducted in the same way as the Shi'a in the homeland (such as Bahrain and Lebanon) conduct burials. After burying the dead at the cemetery, the bereaved assembled at the Islamic Institute of Knowledge to receive relatives and friends, including Sunnis and Christians or non-Muslims, coming for the purpose of condolence. A large space or hall inside the institute was divided into two parallel sections, one for women and the other for men.

THE HYBRID IDENTITY OF MUSLIM AMERICANS

The migration of Muslims to the United States is viewed here as integral not only to the global economy but also to the global processes of the transformation of multiple identities. Hybrid identity is produced by the blending of two diverse cultures or traditions (Kapchan and Strong 1999, 240; el-Aswad 2011b). Muslim Americans' identities are the outcome of Muslim worldviews that, while maintaining their core elements, are capable of combining universal and local as well as traditional and contemporary components of cultures.

In a pluralistic society such as the United States in which hybrid identities are constructed, it is practical to understand that religious loyalty does not conflict with American identity or ethnic group.[31] Ethnic boundaries are "patterns of social interaction that give rise to, and subsequently reinforce, in-group members' self-identification and outsiders' confirmation of group distinctions" (Sanders 2002, 327). Although immigrants affirm an ethnic affinity and heritage by joining social groups that may or may not coincide with the territorial ethnicity defended by the nation (Hsu 2010; Brubaker 2010), their religious identities go beyond ethnic and national identities.[32] For the Muslim Americans I interviewed in Michigan in both previous (el-Aswad 2010b) and recent inquiries, religious identity has been more emphasized than ethnic identity (figure 6.9). Likewise, recent research reports that among young British and Scottish Pakistanis, being Muslim takes precedence over any other identity (Sanders 2002, 344).

The religious identity of Muslim Americans is viewed as part of a wide arc of global Muslim identity or community (*ummah*) encompassing differing ethnic groups from various parts of the world. This encompassing Muslim American identity is recognized by non-Muslim Americans. There are series of concentric circles that must be considered. "The smallest are families and clans; then come ethnic groups and nations; the largest, and implicitly most important, are religions" (Juergensmeyer 2005, 142).

Figure 6.9. Young Muslim Americans socializing in a backyard in Bloomfield Hills, Michigan.

To be more specific, Muslim Americans have experienced a gradually emerging sense of a unified, hybrid identity, impacted by American culture as well as by the awareness of, and identification with, the worldviews of the old homeland, encompassing, for example, religious beliefs and related values or practices, traditions, social customs, and artistic expressions.

Despite the fact that the global Muslim community (*ummah*) goes beyond the concept of citizenship or national affiliation, Muslim Americans affiliate themselves with the American society that they willingly prefer to live in. Yet they are aware that they live in a society oriented toward a secular worldview to which they adapt without overlooking their Islamic principles and values. Commenting on the drastic events occurring in Iraq, an Iraqi American, who is also a Shiʿi Muslim, expressed to me his view, articulating, "As an Iraqi American who condemns the invasion of countries by other countries, I, particularly as a Muslim, not a politician, have a real problem accepting the weird idea that my country [America] is occupying my country [Iraq]."

Some scholars argue, "Islam in the West is Western not to the extent it changes its theological framework, but because it expresses that framework more in terms of values than of legal norms, whatever the content of those values" (Roy 2004, 31–32). While it is agreeable to state that Muslim Americans have not experienced changes in theological doctrines, as is the case of Muslims in other

Western countries (Roy 2004), it is debatable to agree that they have experienced changes in the framework of values. Muslim Americans, I argue, have experienced changes in certain aspects of their worldviews and values, not the entire framework of worldviews or values.[33]

In discussing the notion of the adaptability of Muslim worldviews with both Sunni and Shi'i leaders and ordinary people, they accentuated the need to focus on a dynamic and future-oriented worldview, not just a traditional or static worldview. They discussed two kinds of change. On the one hand, changing the individual's self through self-criticism leads to change from within, not just from without. Shaikh Musa, quoting a verse from the Qur'an,[34] affirmed that God will not change people or their condition until they positively and correctly change themselves from within. The change here refers not only to a peaceful and compatible relation with oneself but also to notions of moderation, tolerance, and compatibility with modern ways of life. On the other hand, there are changes brought to the other(s) by informing or educating them about Islam as well as through providing an example of the rightful daily conduct of Muslims themselves. Change here also implies new and insightful interpretations of Islam provided by moderate scholars, which suits the progressive nature of American society.

There has been significant change among Muslim Americans as evidenced by the transition from relatively static to dynamic views of space and time as well as from a limited number of alternatives to unlimited options and open possibilities. For instance, while marriage between Sunni and Shi'i Muslims as well as between Muslims and Christians is rare in the Muslim homeland, marriages between Sunni and Shi'i Muslims and between Muslim men and Christian women have occurred. People have maintained, however, that a Muslim woman cannot marry a Christian man unless he adopts Islam as his religion. This is what happened to Suad, a media specialist who graduated from Wayne State University. She persuaded her American colleague, friend, and fiancé, Walter, to convert to Islam so that they could marry.

One of the most significant values that attracts Muslims in the pluralistic American society is freedom. In Islam, theoretically, freedom is fully guaranteed, but in practice it is not materialized in most Muslim countries. In American society, Muslims are free to practice their religion and pursue their socioeconomic aspirations, which may not be fully accessible in their home countries. Comparatively, as is the case in Western Europe (Waardenburg 2003, 337), Muslim Americans, individuals and groups alike, are in principle free to constitute their own identity and to follow what they accept or consider to be the normative Islam or Muslim worldview.

As far as freedom is a component of Muslim Americans' worldview, it provides them an unlimited number of alternatives, enabling them to integrate easily with the secular worldviews of American society. Despite the financial crisis, American society is fair in dealing with people who work hard, regardless of their religious beliefs. Peace, integrity, honesty, justice, equity, intimate family relations, hard work, accountability, and observing what is legally or religiously permitted (*ḥalāl*) and refraining from what is forbidden (*ḥarām*) are common values Muslim Americans aspire to maintain. They may also strive to maintain certain practices to support their religious worldviews. For example, in order to eat *ḥalāl* meat, Muslim Americans have established slaughterhouses that follow both local regulations and Islamic guidelines for slaughtering animals.

In her study of a Sunni Muslim community in Chicago, Garbi Schmidt (2004)[35] maintains that though Arabs, South Asians, and African Americans are the largest ethnic groups representing Islam in the United States, there is a sort of unity among them. Muslim identity, however, is not entirely to be understood as "either-or" but as "both-and" in the sense that an individual can be Pakistani or Arab, and Muslim and American at once. Walid, a Sunni Muslim and college student of Egyptian descent who works part-time in a hardware store in Bloomfield Hills, recounted, "I work with an Iraqi colleague, Kazim, a Shi'i person who, like me, identifies himself as a Muslim. He considers himself half-Iraqi and half-American, despite the fact that he was born and lives in Dearborn. His parents are from Iraq, though. If I did not know Kazim as a friend, I would not be able to recognize and appreciate the tradition of the Shi'a. He also keeps asking me about Sunni practices."

Though there are many differences between Muslim Americans, one of the most shared attributes is that they are able to choose which aspects of both the homeland and American culture they incorporate and which not to keep. For example, Samah is a second-generation veiled female Yemeni student who dresses traditionally, had a traditional marriage ceremony, prays regularly, and is not reluctant to state to others proudly that "this is our way" or "this is what we believe" when discussing her religion. Yet she wears blue jeans under her outer covering and is an avid Detroit Red Wings fan. She enjoys sports, has participated in sports, and eagerly talks about sports. This is a choice that she has been able to enjoy. Other people choose to relinquish more of their original identity. And this original identity gets weaker the longer Muslim Americans are away from their country of origin.

The awareness of the traditional and modern dimensions of the Muslim American's hybrid identity is reflected in the story of Ali Raslan, who stated that he has experienced an inimitable assimilation of both the traditional and modern sides of his identity. He further elaborated that his new or hybrid identity is an amalgamation of sameness and difference, like speaking several languages by the same person. As Lee states, "Hybrid spaces created by diasporic migrations are inhabited by bilingual and bicultural resident nomads who move between one public sphere and another" (Lee 1993, 174).

Sabry, a Sunni American married to a Shi'i woman, said that when he came to the United States twenty years ago to work in the automotive industry in Dearborn, he had a unique experience that enlightened him not only to the cultural differences, but also on how to integrate these differences into his worldviews. He related, "One day, while walking toward my relatives' house, I saw a sign in front of a large house saying 'Garage Sale,' a phrase I did not understand. I saw, displayed in front of the house, various items such as art portraits, pieces of furniture, clothes, coffee makers, TV sets, bicycles, books, lamps, and kitchen utensils. I saw people carry certain items, load them into their cars, then drive away. When I asked about such activities, I was informed that the owners of the house were having a 'garage sale' and selling the items they no longer needed. I went there and bought some books and a vase. The lesson that I learned was how to find something valuable in what might seem to be valueless." Sabry indicated that the metaphorical lesson helped him to envision ways to transform what seemed to be old fashioned into new and futuristic forms. He is now voluntarily involved in maintaining a Muslim website offering information on Islam.

CYBERSPACE OF MUSLIM AMERICANS

This section shows the impact of cybercirculation or computer-mediated communication on Muslim Americans' daily lives and vice versa. Electronic communication and websites provide information zones, enhancing people's knowledge, and interaction zones, strengthening people's relationships (Alvstad 2010, 74; Bunt 2009, 27). Muslim Americans are actively engaging in both information domains and interaction domains through making use of virtual-vernacular websites. The Internet provides a new and easily accessible arena for communication through which individuals can interact with each other, engage in dialogue and debate, and establish mutual understanding (el-Aswad 2007b). Further, the Internet has been depicted as a medium that enhances interfaith or interreligious dialogue, promoting understanding and tolerance (Brasher 2001).

Cyberdialogue, primarily in digital form, is a strong medium for social and cultural change. The Internet is an effective tool in reconstructing traditional religious identities, worldviews, and practices in unprecedented ways. Muslim worldviews have undergone a sort of "cybercirculation" or "Internetization," which means a process through which core elements of Muslim culture are mediated and transformed by the Internet. The new media of the global era have contributed to the strengthening of the ties to diasporas and also to other communities, including non-Muslim ones (Eickelman and Anderson 2003, xii).

The virtual world of the Internet, encompassing virtual information on Islam and virtual dialogue, is not separate from the real world. Sunni and Shi'i Muslim Americans have established several Islamic websites where religious services and educational programs are carried out. Topics such as Islamic education, family, neighborhood, friends, sports, social relationships, health issues, travel, and other topics are discussed online. Online social networks such as Facebook,

Twitter, MySpace, and YouTube are readily employed. Muslim cyberforums promote dialogue and interfaith communication with Muslims and non-Muslims. Much of the substance of Muslim worldviews is discussed, reproduced in new forms, and represented in various online Muslim virtual communities through both formal (or institutional) and informal (collective or individual) websites. Both formal and informal Muslim networks vigorously appropriate interactive forms of media and online worldviews, generating new religious spaces.

Institutionally, the online dialogue is a top-down communication, from specific institutional providers of Islamic heritage content to broad receivers.[36] In addition to providing information, these institutional websites encourage receivers to be active in feedback, interaction, and communication. Institutional websites concerned with Muslim culture and Islamic values provide both information and more interactive spaces where various topics of Islamic heritage can be lived and negotiated. Practical information about Shi'a and Sunni calendars is posted with daily, monthly, and annual activities, including descriptions of protocols for praying and fasting. Sacred scriptures and interpretations of religious doctrines are also accessible on the Internet, allowing people to read, interpret, and discuss religious texts. This, in turn, leads to a gradual decline in the hierarchical authorities of traditional clerks (Brasher 2001). Some sites are discussion groups, while others offer advice on religious matters, including doctrinal, legal, ethical, and social issues. Muslim websites allow people, especially the young, who constitute a sizable number of online consumers in the United States, to partake freely in discussing certain religious issues. What is striking about the proliferation of this cyberreligious culture is not only the creative adoption of new technologies, but also the challenges and possibilities these technologies offer for religious meaning making in modern society.

Responding to my inquiry about the difference between a Sunni website of the Muslim Unity Center (MUC),[37] located in Bloomfield Hills, and a Shi'i website of the Islamic Institute of Knowledge (IIK),[38] located in Dearborn, Faris, an eighteen-year-old man whose father is a Shi'i and mother is a Sunni, said:

> The website for the MUC is apparently more aimed towards the youth, recruiting members, and introducing the idea of Islam to newcomers. The site is more colorful and appears to pop out more, which gives it a casual look rather than the serious Muslim green of the IIK. The MUC caught my attention as it contains a large cafeteria serving Arabic-style foods, which seems like a great place for people to socialize with each other. Also, MUC holds special services for the youth such as a basketball league, summer camp, and father and son camping trips. The website IIK seems to be aimed for more mature audiences as it is lacking links and certain aspects that would attract younger viewers. The main feature I found interesting was a list of Questions and Answers between several people and important Shi'a imams, such as Shaikh Berry. I found this section to be quite insightful as the questions were targeted at Islamic customs, what or what not to eat or wear, lust, temporary marriage among other questions. The site also has links to Arab-American newspapers, a photo

> gallery, as well as a video gallery of key Islamic lectures. So from analyzing both sites I can come to the conclusion that the MUC is more of a youth or family-type center while the IIK deals with serious and scholarly issues.

Informally, individuals use both their face-to-face relationships and Internet interactions, meaning that dialogue relies on traditional ways as well as on modern technologies represented in the capacity of people to use the Internet to circulate their Muslim culture.[39] Muslim parents as well as some Muslim youths show concern related to problems generated by uncensored websites that contain pornography or content relating to alcohol and drug use, violence-related issues, or online dating and gambling. Parents' deep concern is justified based on the fact that censorship exists in most Muslim and Middle East countries but not in the West (Roy 2004, 30). Muslim Americans use the Internet as an effective means for opposing the negative claims of anti-Islamist extremists, who view Muslim culture as a backward and irrelevant set of beliefs and practices. Young adult Muslim Americans have become interested in developing entertainment that is mainstream and that dispels misconceptions about Islam.

Muslim American youths with their dynamic consciousness are contributing toward shaping a future worldview of Islam in the United States that is radically different from the Islam found in their parents' countries. Moreover, there is a change from static systems of interpretation to dynamic dialogues covering various issues of Muslims' daily lives.

Young people rely not only on the Internet for communication, but also on cell phone use and, more specifically, text messaging. Hafez, a Sunni Muslim pre-med student residing in Bloomfield Hills, recounted:

> Qasim, a Shiite friend who is from Lebanon living in Dearborn, contacted me via text over a cell phone, asking if I would like to come over to his house to celebrate the birthday (*wilādat*) of Imam 'Ali Zain al-'Abidīn. I didn't know what it was, so after speaking with my father, I learned that he was a prominent figure not only in Shiite Islam, but in Sunni Islam as well. I decided to attend this party and see what all this was about. I arrived at his house, and we had some well-known Lebanese desserts, including baklava, date biscuits and other things. We also had Turkish coffee. We talked about how much we liked or disliked the university we attended, the state of the Arab world, especially Bahrain and Libya, and started to poke fun at each other. Shortly after that, his father came down and greeted us, and then invited us to pray with him, so we did. I was teased for not having a stone of Karbala to use during prayer, but I dismissed their teasing. We did the standard prayer, but after that, his father invited us to do an optional prayer. Qasim excused himself and I went with him, but some of the more hardcore Shiite friends stayed to pray. When everyone was finished praying, the youth deliberated about what to do next and one of them recalled that a restaurant called "Beirut by Night" was open, and that they could go there to smoke *nargīla* or *shīsha* and walk around Dearborn. I declined the offer since it was getting late, and I didn't feel like driving half an hour to Dearborn at midnight. I departed from my friends and headed home.

CONCLUSION

The unifying doctrine of all Muslims, Sunni and Shi'a among others, is embedded in the two testimonies (*ash-shahādatain*) that there is no God but Allah and that Muhammad is His Messenger (*lā ilaha illā Allah, Muhammad rasūl Allah*). Through worldviews people make sense of themselves and the world in which they live. Differences between Muslim sects as well as within a particular sect in both the United States and Muslim homelands relate to certain details of worldviews and related practices of Muslims impacted by cultural traditions and various religious schools (*madhāhib*).

Through a focus on certain Muslim institutions in the United States as well as on personal narratives, this chapter has highlighted the significance of an overarching Muslim worldview as an effective mediation through which Muslim Americans express their identity in both public and private zones. The movement between local and global spheres has played a major role in creating a particular sense of Muslim Americans' hybrid identity attached to both local and global communities. Muslim American identity, one argues, has been shaped by many factors but particularly by continuing interactions between conditions of the Islamic tradition and the culture of the new homeland and by the interplay between their perceptions of themselves and how others see them. In brief, Muslim American identity is a hybrid of the spirituality of Islam (and the East) and the technological and material advancement of American culture.

The previous statement, however, cautions against misconceptions that the Muslim homeland, including the Middle East, is a place where people are strictly tied to tradition, believing in unseen domains, dreams, and *jinn*, whereas the United States is a place that entices Muslims to become modern, using advanced technology, cyberspace, working in academia, and engaging in interfaith discussion. As mentioned in previous chapters, Muslims in the homeland are highly motivated toward and engaged in modern and global activities.

Muslim cyberspace is considered a discursive social space, providing a novel source of the sense of rootedness associated with both old and new homelands. As minorities in the United States, Muslims are highly motivated to represent themselves positively. The implicit or explicit competition between Sunni and Shi'i Muslims adds further dimensions to such motivation. Muslim Americans now are more visible through their success in representing their identity (in virtual contexts) as well as in real, economic, political, and public life. Those who have shown a distance from their old homeland are not against their countries as such, but rather against political corruption and socioeconomic adversity.

This chapter has shown that the hybrid identity of Muslim Americans forms an enduring force unifying all Muslims living in the United States, notwithstanding the ethnic and sectarian differences. However, within this identity are multiple identities being identified with their particular Muslim homelands such as Egypt, Iraq, India, Jordan, Lebanon, Pakistan, Palestine, Syria, and Yemen. All in all, hybrid identity is not confined to geographical borders; rather it develops dual consciousness, bridging multiple real and imagined spaces. Though Muslim immigrants tend to identify themselves with the broader identity of the Muslim global community (*ummah*) as well as that of Americanism, they show a very strong sense of their fatherland tradition.

Muslim Americans are aware of the basic assumptions of their worldviews and of those implicit in Western worldviews. They experience a sense of consistency between their worldviews and their practices or everyday lives within the new American environment. Muslim Americans consider their worldview, with its spirituality, not as an alternative to but as a balancing factor to contemporary secularism and materialism.

The polarities of West and East, West and Islam, North and South, Sunni and Shi'i, home and away, among others, are reconstituted, blended, and transformed into flexible and plastic components of the new hybrid identity of Muslim Americans. People, communication, information, and material goods traverse cultural and national borders, creating all kinds of transnational and hybrid identities that change and reconstruct themselves in unpredictable ways.

In a previous study of Arab Americans (el-Aswad 2010b), I concluded that I never heard the interviewees saying such a phrase as "half Arab and half American," but rather phrases such as "half Egyptian and half American," "half Iraqi and half American," "half Lebanese and half American," and "half Syrian and half American." While such phrases signify diversity and multiplicity, the phrase "Arab American" connotes unity among Arab communities. In the present work I conclude that while such phrases as "Sunni Muslim American" and "Shi'i Muslim American" indicate diversity, the phrase "Muslim American" signifies unity among Muslim communities in the United States, notwithstanding the implicit ethnic, cultural, and racial, multiplicity.

Conclusion

This book has dealt with Muslim worldviews, which up to now have not been examined cross-culturally in sufficient depth. Further, the significance of worldviews and social cosmologies for ordinary Muslims has not been fully addressed in anthropological and religious literature. This book has examined the everyday experiences of Muslims by focusing on their worldview or cosmology, an integrative construct that includes attention not only to religious beliefs, but also to the larger systems of meanings and imagination that condition how Muslims conceive of and inhabit the world around them. The contribution of this book is not restricted to specific ideologies of Muslim groups in Muslim countries or in North America. Rather, it is essentially an inquiry of inner perspectives and transmission of Muslim worldviews in pluralistic contexts.

This book contributes to understanding the relationship between worldviews and praxes as enacted by Muslims in various social contexts. It has explicated the role of worldviews in Muslim everyday lives in both the homelands and the new land of North America. Significant differences and similarities have been shown in the worldviews and related practices of Sunnis and Shi'as in local and global contexts. An additional contribution of this study is the cross-cultural attention to religious experience as one aspect of life, with a focus on a comparative study of Muslim worldviews in predominantly Muslim places such as Bahrain, Egypt, and the UAE and in places where Muslims are minorities, such as the Muslim diaspora in the United States.

The book has reflected on the following key questions: How can Muslim worldviews be studied and understood? Is there an overarching Muslim worldview? Are there multiple and diverse Muslim worldviews? Are Muslim worldviews compatible with Muslim everyday lives? To what extent are Muslim worldviews considered as diversifying and unifying factors of their identities? To what extent does the diversity of Muslim worldviews impact positively or negatively on the overall Muslim worldview? Is there a conflict of having multiple identities and maintaining one encompassing identity? To what extent do Muslim worldviews maintain a worldwide Muslim community (*ummah*)? To what extent can Muslim Americans be viewed as cultural mediators or agents bridging the West and the East as well as the north and the south? Are Muslim worldviews static or dynamic? Are Muslim worldviews compatible with modernity and Western or secular worldviews? Do Muslim worldviews encounter any sort of challenge dealing with the notions of spirituality, sanctity, secularity, and modernity? And what is the future of Muslim worldviews?

THE STUDY OF MUSLIM WORLDVIEWS

The point of departure for this inquiry is basically cosmological insofar as cosmology or worldview encompasses a totality of the universe, society, and person. Theoretically, the connection between the levels of belief/theory or unseen/doctrine, on the one hand, and the seen/social, on the other, has been addressed through highlighting certain significant paradigms: the doctrinal, the communal, the ontological, the ritual, the spatial, and the temporal. Although Muslims share common worldviews that are contingent on shared paradigms, they interpret and employ the entailments of these paradigms in diverse manners, causing ongoing debates within Muslim discourse.

One of the important contributions of this book is to shift attention away from the prevailing focus on issues such as Islamic political ideologies and the Islamophobia industry that have received much scholarly attention in the past decade. By contrast, this book has focused on how Muslims, oriented by their worldviews, think and act in their daily lives and in various local and global contexts. As far as Muslim worldviews take into consideration inner and outer, inside and outside, unseen and seen, and spiritual and material aspects of life and seek to develop them, the research has paid attention to the emic or internalized cultural perspective concerning their images of the world in which they live and with which they interact.

Utilizing macro-cross-cultural studies and microethnographic inquiries, through conducting participant observations, in-depth interviews, and case studies, this book has provided a phenomenological account of Muslim worldviews in societies with Muslim majorities as well as in Western or American society with a Muslim minority. Dealing with worldviews as the outcome of Muslims' lived experience, this study has applied the qualitative approaches of ethnography and hermeneutic anthropology to such core concepts as sanctity, spirituality, mysticism, imperceptibility, invisibility, and the unseen world (*'ālam al-ghaib*).

Implicit worldviews become explicit through people's discursive and nondiscursive actions. Therefore, the study of worldviews necessitates the focus on both discursive and nondiscursive actions as forms of living experience. For instance, what is unimaginable, esoteric, or invisible, absent, and incomprehensible becomes, through words, recitations, narratives, rituals, bodily symbolism, and art exhibits, imaginable, visible, present, and comprehensible.

Phenomenology is concerned with wholeness through examining the parts that constitute that whole or phenomenon. Concepts and assumptions concerning the world are seen as parts of an integrated, holistic worldview. Thus, to understand the Muslim holistic worldview special attention has been given to the relationships between the parts and the whole. This means that the research has focused not on cosmological concepts as such, but on the relations within and between cosmological and conceptual orders in their integrated wholeness, relating their relevance to social and historical conditions.

Cross-culturally, examples of certain aspects of Sunni, Shi'i, Sufi, and diasporic Muslim worldviews have been provided to illustrate the similarities and differences between them. This book has also provided insightful material useful for researchers and students who seek a comprehensive, grounded, and experiential understanding of the many ways in which issues such as sanctity, secularity, modernity, authenticity, connectivity, and the seen and unseen domains of social life work together in Islam so as to create an overarching cosmology for Muslims.

OVERARCHING MUSLIM WORLDVIEW AND ITS UNIVERSAL SIGNIFICANCE

The essential thesis of this book is that Muslims in such geographically, demographically, economically, and politically diverse societies as Bahrain, Egypt, the United Arab Emirates, and the United States of America, among others, are deeply influenced by an overarching Muslim worldview, a holistic view maintained by both men of religious learning as well as by common laypeople. As has been shown, the concept of the divine oneness of God (*tawḥīd*) is considered the universal and unifying principle of all Muslims, forming a worldwide Muslim community (*ummah*). The overarching Muslim worldview, contingent on the Qur'an and the Prophet's tradition, is rooted in the two professions (*ash-shahādatain*) that there is no God but Allah (*lā ilaha illā Allah*) and that Muhammad is His Messenger (*Muhammad rasūl Allah*). The worldwide Muslim community is based on principles and values that are carried out anywhere there are Muslim people. Although there are certain inevitable sacred places revered by all Muslims (such as Mecca, Medina, and al-Quds), the Muslim *ummah* is one of the basic elements of Muslim worldviews not confined to a specific locality or place.

Islam is presented in this study as possessing an all-encompassing worldview, the core orientation of a worldwide community of believers dispersed in various places around the world. Muslim worldview encompasses entwined spiritual, mystical, ethical, material, and practical dimensions. For all Muslims, Islam is a religion that includes reciting the Qur'an, performing prayers, venerating the Prophet, maintaining his tradition, respecting all Abrahamic prophets, speculating on unseen forces, imagining possible realities, debating various aspects of life, and interacting with Muslim and non-Muslim people.

Islam has well-defined decrees, doctrines, Islamic laws or *shari'a*, spiritual principles, and well-specified rituals determining its unique features. It also encompasses a broad universal worldview as well as multiple cosmologies and worldviews with local applications bestowing meaning to Muslims' everyday lives. Such worldviews are not entirely ordered by instrumental logic or material/practical reasoning, as is case for those holding more secular worldviews. Muslim worldviews as understood and enacted by common people are tied neither to government regimes nor to Islamist militants or Muslim groups motivated by political schemes.

According to Muslim worldviews, life on earth is sacred and highly valued. Taking a life or committing suicide is forbidden and viewed negatively as an action violating the principles of Islam.[1] Muslims take care to have a happy life, but that does not divert their attention from the otherworldly life. This can be achieved through pious worshipping of God. Piety (*taqwā*), executing the commands of Allah and refraining from what is prohibited, is a common principle that Muslims endeavor to maintain in their thought and behavior. Muslims emphasize the value of purity and cleanliness not only of the heart, as represented in piety, but also of the body, as represented by ablution. Along with the five daily prayers, Muslims perform ablution, the washing or rinsing of their hands, forearms, mouths, noses, faces, foreheads, ears, and feet three times at each prayer time.

This book has shown that Islamic sacred postulates have remarkable power in maintaining Muslim worldviews in such a way that it seems difficult to understand the secular and visible aspects of life without reference to the sacred and invisible domains. In their mystic experience, both Sunni Sufis and Shi'a profoundly focus on knowing and loving God. At the same time, they show great devotion to the Prophet and his family. Also, both Sunni Sufis and Shi'as seek to reach the balance between the exterior (*shari'a*) and interior (*ḥaqīqa*) dimensions of religion in their efforts to know God. Though there are varying scales of differences mirrored in the worldviews of Sunni, Shi'i, and Sufi adherents, these differences operate within the unifying religion of Islam. This, in turn, confirms the fact that there is one Islam with multiple cosmologies or worldviews. Terminologies such as "Islams" and "local Islams" are not part of Muslims' everyday vocabulary. Rather, they reflect an outsider's view.

MULTIPLICITY AND DIVERSITY OF MUSLIM WORLDVIEWS

This study has demonstrated the complex interplay between various forms of worldviews as represented in Sufi mysticism, Shi'i esotericism, Sunni beliefs and practices, and overarching Muslim worldviews. Among conceivably comparable cultures that have differing religious outlooks, local differences in patterns of behavior may exist because of the impact of worldviews that create different social imaginaries and philosophies. Such differences are found between the Sunni worldview, emphasizing the individually and religiously oriented concept of the brotherhood of Muslims, and the Shi'i worldview that focuses on the communally oriented doctrine of the Imamate and the infallibility of the Imams.

Historical events have played a significant role in shaping certain dimensions of these Muslims' worldviews. After the death of the Prophet Muhammad, there emerged for the first time different forms of Muslim worldviews, represented mostly in those of the Sunnis and the Shi'a that continue to exist today in contemporary Muslim societies. The Sunni and Shi'a, each in their distinctive way, have developed a worldview that maintains their beliefs and practices. Each of them has a unique configuration of the same core elements. Both the Sunni and Shi'a follow the Qur'an and Prophet's tradition but differ in their worldviews regarding the religious implications of Muslim leadership as represented in the concept of *imām*. Both Sunnis and Shi'is use the word "imam" (*imām*) to refer to a person who leads Muslims in prayer. However, for the Shi'a, the term "imam" is used exclusively to refer to one of the descendants and successors of the Prophet Muhammad. Both Sunnis and Shi'is feel great devotion to and reverence for the Prophet Muhammad's family (*ahl al-bait*), but Sunnis, unlike the Shi'a, do not restrict the most prestigious religious leadership to the descendants of the Prophet. Rather, they consider religiously capable and pious persons, people of God (*ahl Allah*), as competent and religiously inspired leaders.

Among various causes generating differences between Sunni and Shi'i worldviews, the doctrine of the Shi'i Imamate is a decisive element and explains why the Shi'a add the phrase, "I bear witness that 'Ali is *walī* Allah," to the Islamic call for prayer (*adhān*). While both Sunni and Shi'a emphasize that the relationship between man and God is direct, the Shi'i doctrine of "spiritual leadership," or Imamate with specific reference to the Hidden Imam, constitutes a major difference.

The Shi'a practice what is known as emulation (*taqlīd*), but the Sunnis do not. Within the practice of emulation, a Shi'i *shaikh* or *marja'*, a person of religious learning, is believed to mediate hierarchically between the Hidden Imam and the ordinary Shi'a, providing them with religious and social advice. The Sunnis do not differentiate between religious leaders (*shaikhs*) except for those who have formal or certified religious knowledge and those who do not. The Shi'a, however, distinguish between *shaikh* and *sayyid*. Contrary to the *shaikh*, a *sayyid*, who may or may not possess religious knowledge, is a descendant of the Prophet's family (Hashimi or Quraysh tribe) and is recognized by the wearing of a black turban, especially when certified in religious knowledge. Apart from any socioeconomic hierarchy, the Shi'a are more religiously hierarchical than the Sunnis. According to Sunni Muslims, after the death of the Prophet Muhammad, no one can have the exclusive right to claim infallibility, in general, or to interpret the sacred text, in particular. In contrast, the infallibility of Imams constitutes a fundamental doctrine for the Shi'a and at the same time forms an unquestionable base for religious hierarchy.

While both the Sunni and Shi'a believe in the Mahdi, they differ in certain basic views. For the Shi'a, Imam Mahdi, the twelfth, Hidden Imam, is the "savior" who is expected to reappear before the end of the world to restore justice; then Jesus, the Messiah, will appear and call the people to follow the Mahdi.[2] For the Sunni, the Mahdi, who may be related to the Prophet Muhammad's family, will appear before Jesus, who is believed to be the redeemer who will restore justice.

In their religious worldviews, the Shi'a emphasize biology or blood, vertical in nature, represented exclusively in the hereditary line of the Prophet through his daughter Fatima (married to 'Ali, the Prophet's cousin). The Sunni emphasize brotherly ties (not in blood terms), horizontal in nature, which attract a broad spectrum of adherents. Through rituals and online discourses, the Shi'a emphasize the thesis of martyrdom predominant in their history, especially with reference to their imams and specifically with reference to Imam Husain. For the Shi'a, however, the social world outside their in-group is portrayed as having problems understanding their worldviews.

WORLDVIEW AND MUSLIM IDENTITY

Through both ethnography and a cross-cultural study, the book has considered the issues of diversity and identity within Muslim communities and thus problematizes any overarching assumptions regarding what it means to be Muslim today. This is significant specifically for Western or American and European readership, in particular, because of the ways in which Muslims continue to be represented in mainstream media and sometimes in scholarship as a homogeneous, undifferentiated, and unchanging group.

The book explains the ways in which Muslims of different communities and sects develop cosmologies and worldviews, localized belief systems, and symbolic actions within a larger framework of shared identity as well as within an overarching Muslim worldview. It has examined the relationships between shared identity as Muslim, showing the ways in which the cosmologies of specific Muslim communities belong to larger Muslim worldviews, and the variances in cosmologies across varying local contexts.

There has been a significant gradual transition from pro-Arabism or unified Arab identity predominant in the fifties and sixties into a unified Muslim identity that allows people to express their local, national, and regional identities. For example, the Bahraini Shi'a, a majority from Arab descent, differentiate themselves as *baḥārna* from the rest of the society of Bahrain, including the Persian or Iranian Shi'a (*'ajam*) and Arab Sunnis, among other religious and ethnic groups. The people of the Emirates identify themselves with Islam. They also tend to define each other on the basis of tribal identity and nationality, as presented in the dichotomous criteria of national (*muwāṭin*) versus non-national. Despite the growing feeling of national identity, the Emiratis have constructed an image of themselves as being a "minority" in their homeland, caused by the increase in the population of expatriates. According to their regional worldview, both the peoples of Bahrain and the Emirates are identified as sharing an Arab Gulf identity (*Khalījī*).

Outside the Arab or Muslim world and in the highly pluralistic society of the United States, Muslim Americans, with diverse ethnic backgrounds, emphasize their Muslim American (hybrid) identity more than regional and ethnic identities. The hybrid identity of Muslim Americans forms an enduring force unifying all Muslims living in the United States, notwithstanding the ethnic and sectarian differences. However, within this identity there are multiple identities being identified with their particular Muslim homelands such as Egypt, India, Iran, Iraq, Jordan, Lebanon, Pakistan, Palestine, Syria, and Yemen, among others. Muslim cyberspace is considered a discursive social space providing a novel source for the sense of rootedness associated with both old and new homelands.

MUSLIM WORLDVIEWS, ETHICS, AND MODERNITY

Muslims are aware of the basic assumptions of their worldviews. They experience a sense of consistency between their worldviews and their practices or everyday lives. According to Muslim worldviews, the universe is well ordered and organized. However, the order of the universe is not to be explained merely in material or physical terms, but also, and more importantly, in transcendental or religious and moral concepts.

Muslims, Sunni, and Shi'a in both local and transnational contexts share certain common values guiding their actions to be compatible with modern, global, and secular ways of life. They appreciate knowledge, industriousness, conscientiousness (*ḍamīr ḥaiy*), piety (*taqwā*), contentedness, and moral covering (*satr*).[3] In their daily lives and involvements in traditional, modern, and secular activities, Muslims wish to be morally, socially, and economically secure or covered (*mastūr*). They apply secular practices both traditional and modern in their daily activities. They also work hard to maximize their interests. Even Muslims belonging to Sufi orders are not asocial ascetic or idle persons overlooking the socioeconomic and cultural activities, but rather strive to maintain the spiritual power for achieving both worldly and otherworldly goals. Despite the growing interest in material possessions, Muslims still assert that it is not the material accumulation but the blessing (*baraka*) of what they have that matters. Muslims' daily activities are validated by the divine principle of livelihood (*ar-rizq*), a cosmological notion, which belongs to the invisible, imaginary, and unknowable world (*'ālam al ghaib*).

The accessibility of information through global cybernetworks has inspired Muslims to use various forms of traditional and modern or digital dialogue to convince others, Muslims or non-Muslims, of their views, showing tolerance toward the differing perspectives of other people.

In a discussion of Muslims in the West, certain authors argue that Muslims divide the world into believers and infidels based on the assumption that every aspect of behavior is judged according to the degree of conformity with the laws of Islam. "The world is divided into 'believers' and 'infidels,' the latter term referring not just to non-Muslims but also to Muslims who do not sufficiently observe the Law" (Cesari 2004, 54). Such a sweeping generalization is not applicable to educated and intellectual Muslims, and it does not apply to noneducated Muslims. Also, such a sweeping statement is not supported by the fact that ordinary Muslims are aware that the denial of any of the Abrahamic religions is against Islamic principles and laws. The recent interfaith dialogues in countries with a Muslim majority and those with a Muslim minority put such a statement to the test. Muslim worldviews are not against the right of non-Muslims to have their own worldviews, religious or otherwise. Further, in my research dealing with the differences and similarities between the worldviews of Sunni and Shi'i sects, I never heard anyone referring to a person from another sect as an "infidel." The factors behind those who do not accept the "other" and cannot fully cope with modern and pluralistic life are not related to religion or Islam, but rather to social environment or inadequate socioeconomic and cultural conditions.

MUSLIM WORLDVIEW AND CULTURAL MEDIATION

Within anthropological literature, there are two frameworks of orientation that represent causality and participation. Causality is viewed as the rational, linear way of thinking found in science, while participation is depicted as the associative and holistic way of thinking found in religious worldviews and traditional cultures (Tambiah 1990). Such a polar or binary distinction between causality and participation needs to be discussed in the light of Muslim worldviews within the global context. I suggest here the concept of "mediation," through which Muslim worldviews serve as "mediator," bridging or combining the two orientations of causality and participation into a new paradigm. Mediation means the ability of a concept, object, or action to occupy a middle point between two distant or opposite poles. "To mediate is basically to provide a point of contact, an intersection, a place of communication or dialogue between two different positions" (Debrix 2003, xxi). Mediation is a way that makes social meanings possible.

Within Muslim worldviews there has been a coherent mediation between the seen and unseen, between matter and spirit, between the perceptible and the imperceptible, between individuality and collectivity, and between this world and the other world. While the visible refers to material and empirical domains of life, regulated by causality, the invisible indicates cultural or philosophical spheres, articulated by the association of ideas. The seen, natural, or phenomenal world encompasses environment, nature, and tangible bodies, animate and inanimate, which form the material conditions of existence, subject to causal explanation. Also, within this material world Muslims make their history. This implies that meanings and materiality are associated. As a part of the seen or visible world, society as a whole is viewed as being imperfect. The limitation of society is evident in its injury to and inability to satisfy all the needs of its members. This limitation impels individuals to seek other higher means of social and spiritual support.

Muslim worldviews can be described not in terms of cyclical or linear causality, but in terms of mediation and transformation. This notion of mediation is associated with "moderation" (*waṣaṭiyyah*), a fundamental principle of Islam indicating a balance or midway between two extreme ways or positions. The Qur'an proclaims that the Muslim community is a middle [balanced] community.[4] Moderation proves to be practical in social interaction.

The mediation of Muslim worldviews takes distinct and different forms, with angels such as Jibril revealing the Qur'an to the Prophet Muhammad, the Ka'ba connecting the heavens with the earth, the eschatological world *barzakh* linking this life with the other life, the light uniting the celestial world with the mundane world, and the dreams linking the visible with the invisible. With regard to the afterlife, the concept of mediation implies transition through which Muslims perceive the world only as a transit for corporeal man to the perpetual or transcendental world in the hereafter. In their mystic experiences Sufis mediate between the visible and spirit worlds, a role that shapes and contours their sensibilities and religious imagination. Also, the concept of intercession (*shafā'a*) of the prophet Muhammad (or Shi'i Imams) at the Day of Judgment is frequently called upon in Muslim worldviews. Meanwhile, Shi'i religious scholars (*marja'* or *'ulama*) mediate between the Hidden Imam and the common Shi'a.

In this study, dream phenomena and related notions of spirituality and unseen realities are not dealt with within the oppositions of participation versus causality, tradition versus modernity, dream reality versus commonsense reality, or belief versus science because such oppositions do not exist in Muslim multidimensional worldviews, in which there is always an intermediate realm (*barzakh*) connecting them. Rather, this study has shown the significance of dreams as cultural and symbolic mediation between the visible and the invisible. As the eschatology (*barzakh*) in Muslim cosmology bridges this life with the other life, dreams also constitute the *barzakh* linking the seen with the unseen and the living and the dead.

Mediation is also represented in the mutual validation between dream worlds and Muslim worldviews in the sense that dreams, especially dream visions, are justified by religious worldviews, while some significant components of worldviews, especially those related to unseen dimensions, are validated by dreams. This book has shown the significance of dreams by bringing an experiential and imagined dimension to the ways in which Muslims understand and experience religious belief, an approach that complements in an important way the prevailing focus on textuality or on politics that seems to dominate much contemporary scholarship on Islam.

Within the pluralistic context of American society, the hybrid identity of Muslim Americans mediates between different ethnic groups, nations, and geographies. Through worldviews Muslims make sense of themselves and the world in which they live. The key features of cultural mediators are understanding, communicative skillfulness, and reasonable knowledge of the cultures of both the hosting and homeland countries. The cross-cultural misunderstanding occurs when persons, holding specific worldviews, interpret and judge the behaviors of people belonging to another culture as if they were holding the same worldviews.

In effect, the notion of invisibility and related concepts of subjectivity and spirituality provide the *possibility* of a more complete social or cultural and religious experience. The invisible allows for possibility, a core concept in Muslim worldview, and renders the whole cosmos a dynamic structure. Anything is possible because there is always room for the invisible, benevolent or malevolent, to work. This explains Muslims' dynamic, open, and flexible worldview and attitude of alertness for any possible event, peculiar or normal, to occur (el-Aswad 2002, 62).

THE FUTURE OF MUSLIM WORLDVIEWS

Worldview serves as an interpretative framework through which people construct and comprehend how their world is ordered. As indicated, the Muslim worldview is a holistic construct based on the integrated relationship between conceptual or cosmological elements and the religion of Islam as a whole. The visible and invisible aspects of reality are interwoven into a whole. For the Muslims in this study, the sacred is not detached from the mundane world, where most social relationships as well as economic and material gains are perceived in religious terms.

Muslims keep their future in perspective by positioning the past in the present in preparation or anticipation of the future. Muslim worldviews are not rigid or static paradigms. And Islam is a lived religion, not a utilitarian force imposing its worldviews on its adherents. Muslim worldviews are characterized by being culturally, ethnically, and regionally different. This diversity, however, strengthens the underlying unity and sustains the future of the overall Muslim worldview.

Muslim worldviews affect Muslims' everyday lives. They provide pictures of what is morally good or bad in their lives and play a significant part in determining their actions, practices, and moral choices. It is quite possible that local worldviews and practices continue to prevail as popular worldviews, satisfying people's certain pragmatic and social needs, along with the core tenets of formal religion serving more spiritual and transcendental aspirations.

The belief in the divine unseen realm (*al-ghaib*), a principal constituent of faith, brings about an imaginary world of possibilities generating hope in a good life as well as fostering high expectations of a promising and prosperous future. According to Muslim worldviews, people, individually and collectively, are free to choose and make decisions in their daily lives, but they are also responsible for their choices or decisions, whether good or bad. Worldviews are strong predictors of changes or transformations of Muslims' lifestyles.

By transformation of worldviews, I mean the way in which certain or all assumptions individuals and groups have about the world, including society and persons, can be altered or changed from being closed, static, or fixed in nature to being open, dynamic, and flexible as a consequence of interaction with other people's worldviews. Muslims seek to change their lives through becoming more emotionally open, more loving, and more supportive, while at the same time being self-critical, spontaneous, and progressive. They seek a world that is more communal and more spiritual and one that reaches a higher level of justice, liberty, and equality. The events of the Arab Spring are viewed as serious attempts to transform Arab-Muslim societies, implementing values of justice, freedom, dignity, democracy, and peace.

Muslim worldview, with its features of unity and diversity, provides Muslims with a unified spiritual-social-meaning system, which, though not in essence politically oriented, can be mobilized for building a unified Muslim power structure. The future of Muslim worldviews is not a matter of purely local, national, regional, or global concern but is linked to the future of universal Islam as a whole.

Appendix

Muslim Code of Honor

بسم الله الرحمن الرحيم

In The Name of God, The All Merciful, Bestower of Mercy

Council of Islamic Organizations of Michigan

Preamble

Reports of sectarian tension overseas, particularly in aftermath of the American invasion of Iraq, have prompted the Muslim American leadership to speak out against communal divisions and all sectarian violence. Such expressions of sectarianism, if unchecked, may add fuel to the fire, engulfing the Community in historical grievances that magnify theological differences and minimize the common 'Pillars of Faith' on which all Muslims agree, irrespective of their school of thought *(madhhab)*.

As Muslim Americans who live and struggle for a dignified existence for Islam and Muslims in a spirit of peaceful coexistence and respect for all, we believe that the practical challenges of the future supersede the ideological differences of the past. Moreover, in recognition of our communal duty to promote goodness and peace, we remain eager to offer any help we can and to join hands with all those who wish well for the Family of Believers *(Ummah)* in stopping the senseless, inhumane violence in Iraq and elsewhere in the world.

In our view, we must begin by preventing such tragic sectarianism from spilling over into our Muslim communities in the United States. As a first step toward this goal, we agree to live in peace and respect each other in accordance with a 'Muslim Code of Honor.' We remain committed to this Muslim Code of Honor not only during times of agreement and ease but, more importantly, when faced with contentious issues and in times of mutual disagreement.

Muslim Code of Honor

- No group or individual should use, spread or tolerate the rhetoric of *takfir* (branding others nonbelievers) against anyone who believes in the oneness and supremacy of God, the prophethood of Muhammad Ibn 'Abd Allah, peace be upon him, as the last of God's messengers, and in the reality of the Last Day, agreeing on the authenticity of the Holy Qur'an and facing Mecca *(qibla)* in daily prayers.
- Muslims should respect one another and the people, places and events that any Muslim group or individual holds in esteem, even when they disagree about the relative importance of such people and events. Such disagreements, moreover, should only be expressed in a respectful manner, avoiding inflammatory language and insulting verbiage.
- As to differences in the performance of worship *('ibâdât)*, we agree to respect the rules in effect and the authority of the leadership that endorses them in the particular mosque or religious institution where they are the norm.
- We agree that steps should be taken to protect the general Muslim population in America from the distribution of divisive, inflammatory or irrelevant literature, primarily from overseas, in order to maintain the integrity and protect the future of Islam in America and curb the spread of harmful and misleading propaganda.
- We support the establishment of objective, scholarly study groups *(halaqas)* to examine Muslim history, creed and law, in an effort to increase our knowledge and understanding of one another and to aid in mutual reconciliation. In the event, however, that problems should arise in this regard, a joint body of Muslim scholars from both Shia and Sunni traditions should be consulted in order to prevent schism.
- Finally, we encourage all Muslims in the United States to work to emphasize their commonality, in accordance with God's statement:

  "And hold fast, all together, to the rope of God, and be not divided among yourselves. And remember with gratitude God's favor upon you, when you were enemies and He joined your hearts in love. Thus by His grace you became brethren. And you were on the brink of the Fire, and He saved you from it. Thus doth God make His Signs clear to you, that you may be guided. So let there arise out of you a band of people inviting to all that is good, enjoining what is right and forbidding what is wrong. They are the ones to attain felicity. And be not like those who are divided amongst themselves and fall into disputations after receiving clear signs. For them is a dreadful penalty." (3:103-05)

We, the undersigned, on 10 May, 2007 *(22 Rabi'll, 1428)*, endorse the contents of this Code of Honor and commit ourselves to upholding it. We encourage, moreover, all Muslims to honor the terms set forth herein to the best of their ability. We ask God the Exalted to aid us in this and all our efforts to conduct ourselves in a manner that is most pleasing to Him *(in alphabetical order)*.

Imam Jowad Al-Ansari
As-Sojood Muslim Hospice

Sheikh Ali Suleiman Ali
Muslim Community of Western Suburbs, Canton

Imam Husham Al-Husainy
Karbala Islamic Educational Center, Dearborn

Imam Hassan Al-Qazwini
Islamic Center of America, Dearborn

Dr. Main Al-Qudah
Islamic American University, Southfield

Imam Abdullatif Azom
Masjid Alfalah, Detroit

Hajj Ghalib V. Begg
Chair, Council of Islamic Organizations of Michigan

Imam Abdul Latif Berry
Islamic Institute of Knowledge, Dearborn

Imam Kassem Baydoun
Islamic House of wisdom

J-TAYEB
CAIR

Imam Baker Berry
Islamic Institute of Knowledge, Dearborn

Imam Abdullah Bey El-Amin
Muslim Center of Detroit

Imam Mohammad Ali Elahi
Islamic House of Wisdom, Dearborn Heights

Imam Mustapha Elturk
Islamic Organization of North America, Warren

Imam Shuajb Gerguri
Albanian Islamic Center, Harper Woods

Arif Huskic
Bosnian Islamic Center Gazihusrevbeg, Hamtramck

Dr. S. Abd al-Hakim Jackson
University of Michigan, Ann Arbor

Imam Aly Mohammad Lela
Islamic Association of Greater Detroit, Rochester Hills

MPAC
Muslim Public Affairs Council

Imam Mohamad Mardini
American Muslim Center, Dearborn

Malek Menad
Muslim American Society, Detroit

Imam Muhammad Musa
Muslim Unity Center, Bloomfield Hills

Imam Achmat Salie
American Muslim Diversity Association

Imam Omar Soubani
Islamic Society of Greater Lansing

Sheikh Mostafa Tolba
MAS Quran Institute, Southfield

Imam Mohammad Muyeen Uddin
Al-Islah Islamic Center, Hamtramck

Hajj Dawud Walid
Executive Director, Council of American Islamic Relations
Michigan Chapter

Turkish Center of F. Hills

Source: http://ciomonline.com/about-us/preamble

Notes

INTRODUCTION: WORLDVIEW, IDEOLOGY, AND GEOGRAPHY

1. According to James Olthuis (1989, 27), "A worldview (or vision of life) is a framework or set of fundamental beliefs through which we view the world and our calling and future in it. The vision may be so internalized that it goes largely unquestioned; it may be greatly refined through cultural-historical development; it may not be explicitly developed into a systematic conception of life; it may not be theoretically deepened into a philosophy; it may not even be codified into creedal form. Nevertheless, this vision is a channel for the ultimate beliefs which give direction and meaning to life." For a review of the concept of worldview as used in the social sciences, see Smart (1995), el-Aswad (1990b, 2002), El-Shamy (1977, 2008), Foltz (2003), Hail (2003), Hiebert (2008), Kearney (1984), Kiernan (1981), Kluckhohn (1949), Jones (1972), MacLean (2009), Naugle (2002), Rambachan (2006), Redfield (1968), Sire (1997, 2004), Valk (2009), Wilkens and Sanford (2009), and Wolters (1989).

2. Contrary to the advocates of secularism who claim that religion is vanishing, religion is not disappearing from the modern world. Young generations in the postindustrial societies of the West today show a renewed interest in religious and spiritual matters (Berger 1997, 1999).

3. According to a recent report entitled "Religion in the News: Islam Was No. 1 Topic in 2010," published by the Pew Forum on Religion and Public Life, "Events and controversies related to Islam dominated U.S. press coverage of religion in 2010." See http://pewforum.org/Politics-and-Elections/Religion-in-the-News--Islam-Was-No-1-Topic-in-2010.aspx.

4. Globalization refers to all those processes by which the peoples of the world are incorporated into a single global society (Albrow 1996). In other words, globalization can be defined as the intensification of worldwide social relations that link distant localities in such a way that local happenings are shaped by events occurring many miles away and vice versa (Appadurai 1990, 2001; Featherstone 1990, 1995; Giddens 1990; Kennedy 2001).

To understand globalization is to "grasp the 'proximity' that comes from the networking of social relations across large tracts of time-space, causing distant events and powers to penetrate our local experience" (Tomlinson 1999, 9). For a discussion of the relationship between globalization and hybridization or the mixture of culture, see Pieterse (2009).

5. The English word "worldview" is derived from the German term *Weltanschauung*, coined by Immanuel Kant (Naugle 2002, 4). *Weltanschauung* denotes a broad view or standpoint through which people understand the world in which they live as well as their life as forming an ordered whole (Naugle 2002, 7). "Basic to the idea of *Weltanschauung* is that it represents a point of view on the world, a perspective on things, a way of looking at the cosmos from a particular vantage point which cannot transcend its own historicity. A 'worldview' tends to carry the connotation therefore of being personal, dated, and private" (Wolters 1989, 18).

6. Geertz (1973, 218–19) states, "The function of ideology is to make an autonomous politics possible by providing the authoritative concepts that render it meaningful, the suasive image by means of which it can be sensibly grasped. It is, in fact, precisely at the point at which a political system begins to free itself from the immediate governance of received tradition, from the direct and detailed guidance of religious or philosophical canons on the one hand and from the unreflective precepts of conventional moralism on the other, that formal ideologies tend to emerge and take hold."

7. For further information on Imam Mahdi, see chapters 1, 3, 4, 5, and 6.

8. In Egypt, for instance, the informal and spontaneous way through which preachers interact with members of the communities has resulted in the formation of small, moderate groups interested in discussing religious issues with political implications. Further, local religious scholars, *shaikhs* or preachers, through sermons and religious sessions, have been involved in public debates criticizing and opposing the intrusion of the center, at both national and global levels, in people's lives.

9. For a review of Muslim orthodox worldview or cosmology, see Burkhalter (1985), Daud (1989), el-Fandy (1961), Heinen (1982), Izutsu (1964), Nasr (1964), Netton (1989), Rahman (1966;), al-Taftāzānī (1975), and Wensinck (1916, 1932). It is interesting to note that "Nasr has argued that there is a strong tendency of Islamic cosmologies to employ the concept of the unity of God (A. *Tawhid*) as a starting point for cosmological speculation about the natural world, the mystical path leading to union with God, planetary astronomy and the human mind. The result is a rich and highly varied corpus of cosmological texts and doctrines" (Woodward 2010, 140).

10. The Sunni, derived from the Arabic word "Sunnah," meaning the tradition of the Prophet Muhammad, is the largest branch of Islam, constituting 90 percent of the religion's followers and stretching from Indonesia to Morocco (el-Aswad 2012a). Following the Sunni, the Shi'a is the second largest denomination of Islam. Shi'a Muslims are followers of 'Ali ibn Abi Talib, the Prophet Muhammad's cousin and son-in-law. They believe that Imam 'Ali ibn Abi Talib should have been the first imam (caliph) or successor of the Prophet (el-Aswad 2012b, 2010c).

11. Diaspora may be understood here as a globally mobile category of identification as well as something objectively present in the world today with regard to something else in the past, the place of origin (Axel 2004, 28).

12. Religious leaders do not have "a monopoly on sacred authority where Sufi shaykhs, engineers, professors of education, medical doctors, army and militia leaders, and others compete to speak for Islam" (Eickelman and Piscatori 1996, 211).

13. There are various schools of interpretation with different orientation not only between Sunni and Shi'a but also within Sunni and Shi'a themselves.

14. For further information on Salafism and Wahhabism, see chapter 2.

15. Terrorism is a political act, ordinarily committed by an organized group, involving the death or the threat of death to noncombatants (Screiber 1978, 20).

16. Since 9/11, there has been a transition from Orientalism, criticized by Edward Said (1978), to Islamism, leading to a new Orientalism (el-Aswad 2008a). The "Orient" or "East" has become the "Arab East." For instance, Thomas Friedman, in his attempt to distinguish between the West and the "Arab East," focuses on certain symbols. Friedman (quoted in Lockman 2004, 219) argues, "The symbol of the West is the cross—full of sharp right angles that begin and end. But the symbol of the Arab East is the crescent moon—a wide ambiguous arc, where there are curves, but no corners." Lockman comments, stating, "Friedman's dichotomization of the West and the Arab world, each neatly equipped with a symbol that purportedly expressed its essence, its core cultural attributes and fixed mentality, was no doubt crude and simplistic, even laughable; but at a critical moment it offered Americans an easy way both to make sense of a complicated and often confusing world and to reassure themselves about their innocence, righteousness and rationality" (Lockman 2004, 219).

17. See, for example, Corbin (1969), Eickelman and Piscatori (1996), Haddad (2011), Netton (1989), and Said (1981). Similarly, many Muslim scholars, including anthropologists, "carefully separate their faith from their fieldwork accounts" (Varisco 2005, 117).

18. Literature on Islamophobia has recently increased. See, for example, Allen (2010), Esposito and Kali (2011), Gottschalk and Greenberg (2008), Hamdon (2010), and Sheehi (2010).

19. Most Middle East countries suffered economically and politically after the events of 9/11 and the declaration of global war on terror in which two Muslim countries, Afghanistan and Iraq, were invaded.

20. See, for example, Barber (1995), Diner (2009), Karsh (2006), Kepel (2004), Lewis (2003), Lincoln (2003), Perry and Negrin (2008), and Wiktorowicz (2005).

21. The relationship between space or locality and Muslim identities in various American and European communities is meticulously discussed in Barbara Metcalf's work (1996). See also the study of Aitchison, Hopkins, and Kwan (2007) dealing with different Muslim groups on five continents within various urban, rural, regional, and national contexts.

22. Tanta, the capital city of the al-Gharbiyya province located nearly sixty miles north of Cairo, is the largest and most active commercial center in the Middle Delta and comprises a mixed urban-rural population (el-Aswad 2004a; Mayeur-Jaonen 2004a, 2004b). Tanta is also known as a center for religious festivals related to the revered Sufi Sidi Ahmad al-Badawi. The villages of Shibshir al-Hissa and al-Rajdiyya are in the environs of Tanta; Shibshir al-Hissa is located five miles north of Tanta, and al-Rajdiyya is located less than four miles northeast of Tanta. For more information, see chapters 2 and 4. I conducted fieldwork in Tanta and the adjacent villages during the following periods: September 2000 to January 2001, March to June 2001, July to October 2002, and February to May 2003. A short fieldwork session was conducted in August 2008.

23. For more information regarding Manama and other villages, see chapters 2 and 3. I conducted fieldwork in Bahrain during the following periods of time: December 2004 to June 2005, August to December 2005, February to July 2006, and November 2006 to February 2007.

24. The fieldwork in the UAE (al-Ain and Umm Ghafa) was conducted during the following periods of time: from October 2008 to March 2009, and from September 2008 to April 2009.

25. In the United States (Bloomfield Hills and Dearborn, Michigan), I conducted fieldwork as follows: June to September 2007, January to March 2008, and June to August 2010. A short fieldwork session was conducted in December 2011.

26. Although some have challenged the correctness of the use of the word "saint" with reference to Islam on the grounds that it derives too closely from the language of Christianity, this book uses the terms "saint" and *Sayyid* or *Sidi* (*Sīdī*) interchangeably. The word *Sidi*, derived from the most widely used term *Sayyid*, is an honorific addressing a revered *shaikh* or religious (Sufi) leader and can be used as an equivalent to "saint."

27. Phenomenology was founded by Edmund Husserl (1859–1938), developed by Martin Heidegger (1889–1976), and applied by Maurice Merleau-Ponty and Paul Ricoeur, among others (Sokolowski 2000, 3). Charles Sanders Peirce (1839–1914) contributed significantly to phenomenology through his work on experiential phenomena. Phenomenology is currently used by anthropologists among other scholars in their symbolic and hermeneutic studies.

28. Phenomenology is "the analysis of what kind of constituents there are in our thoughts and lives (whether these be valid or invalid being aside from the question)" (Rosensohn 1974, 103). This is also known as the phenomenological analysis of the lived experience (Lakoff and Johnson 1999, 108).

29. See, for example, Geertz (1960) and Gilsenan (1982).

30. Drawing on Peirce's tripartite classification of signs, Rappaport (1999, 70–73) makes a distinction between three hierarchical levels of meaning. They are low-order meaning, which is based on distinction (as in taxonomy), middle-order meaning, which is founded upon similarity (as in metaphor), and high-order meaning, which is grounded in identity or unity.

31. For more information on the doctrine of *al-ghaib*, see Ibn Kathir (1937, vol. 41) and el-Aswad (2002).

32. "He Who created the seven heavens one above another: No want of proportion wilt thou see in the Creation of (Allah) Most Gracious." "And we have, (from of old), adorned the lowest heaven with Lamps, and We have made such (Lamps) (as) missiles to drive away the Evil Ones, and have prepared for them the Penalty of the Blazing Fire" (Qur'an 67:3–5). See also el-Aswad (2002), el-Fandy (1961), and Izutsu (1964).

33. Muslims constitute a majority in Java (Geertz 1960; Kim 2007; Woodward 2010). In Java more than 90 percent of the people are Muslim (Geertz 1960, 7).

34. On the Muslim concepts of *jinn* and Satan in Java, see Geertz (1960, 125) and Kim (2007, 150–54, 160).

35. For the meaning of 'Ashura, see chapter 3.

CHAPTER 1: MUSLIM WORLDVIEWS

1. Islam is the world's fastest-growing religion and will soon be the world's largest. Muslims make up approximately one quarter of the world's population. The world's Muslim population is expected to increase by about 35 percent in the next twenty years, rising from 1.6 billion in 2010 to 2.2 billion by 2030, according to new population projections

by the Pew Research Center's Forum on Religion and Public Life. See http://pewforum.org/The-Future-of-the-Global-Muslim-Population.aspx.

2. The complicated issue of the unity and diversity of Islam and Muslim cultures has been debated by scholars from various disciplines. See, for example, the classic collection of essays by von Grunebaum (1955), Arjomand (1995), Hess (1976), and Said and Sharify-Funk (2003). However, the literature addressing this problem concentrates on political rather than cultural diversity.

3. For the Sunnis, there are four schools of law (*madhāhab*) reflecting different opinions on the laws and obligations of the *shari'a*. These schools include the Shafī'ī, Malikī, Hanafī, and Hanbalī. They are not sects and have no major doctrinal differences; rather, they represent scholarly opinions on details of Islamic applications and behavior. For further information on Sunni schools of law, see Bearman, Peter, and Vogel (2006) and Melchert (1997).

4. Both Sunni and Shi'i Muslims constitute minorities in the United States and other Western countries.

5. See chapters 2 and 3, in which the worldviews of the Sunni and the Shi'a are discussed, respectively.

6. The phrase "Twelver Shi'a" is used interchangeably with "Ja'fari Shi'a" and "Imami Shi'a" in various literature. The Ja'farī school of thought is a religiously correct school to follow in worship, as are other Sunni schools of thought, according to the "al-Azhar Verdict [*fatwa*] on the Shi'a," announced on July 6, 1959. For more information, see http://www.al-islam.org/encyclopedia/chapter1b/14.html.

7. The twelve imams are 'Ali ibn Abi Talib, Hasan, Husain, 'Ali ibn al-Husain ('Ali Zain al-'Abidīn), Muhammad al-Bāqir, Ja'far al-Sādiq, Musa al-Kāẓim, 'Ali al-Riḍā, Muhammad al-Taqī, 'Ali al-Hādī, Hasan al-'Askarī, and Muhammad al-Mahdī.

8. These doctrines will be subsequently discussed. *Taqlīd* is the commitment of the Shi'a to follow the advice or utterances of a certain religious scholar (*'ālim*, *marja'*, or *mujtahid*). According to Ayatollah Sayyid Muhammad Kazim, without "this commitment the action and prayers of all Muslims were void even though in reality they were correct and in conformity with *sharī'a*" (Lawson 2005, 527). But these doctrines are completely different from the Catholic priesthood, in which a priest exercises authority over a person or group of people through a connection with the Divinity.

9. It is interesting to note that the Shi'a refrain from eating certain seafood, such as squid and lobster, or certain animals, such as rabbit, that Sunni regularly consume.

10. Although the Sunni and Shi'a consider the Prophet's tradition (Hadith) as an authentic source for understanding the Qur'an, jurisprudence, and other aspects of life, they rely on different Hadith collections. The Sunnis, for example, prefer *Ṣaḥīḥ al-bukhhārī* (al-Bukhārī 1966), *Ṣaḥīḥ Muslim* (al-Qushayrī 1911), and *Jāmi' al-Tirmidhī* (al-Tirmidhī 1900), while the Shi'a prefer *Uṣūl al-Kāfī* (Kulaynī 1969), al-Istibṣār (al-Ṭūsī 1970), *Tahdhīb al-aḥkām* (al-Ṭūsī 1981), and *Man lā yaḥḍuruhu al-faqīh* (Ibn Bābawayh 1992).

11. For further information on the differences between the Shi'a and the Sunni, see chapters 3, 4, 5, and 6.

12. The Shi'i call for prayer at dawn (*fajr*) includes the phrase "*ḥayi 'ala khayr al-'amal*" (good deeds), while the Sunni version includes "*aṣ-ṣalāt Khair min an-naum*" (prayer is better than sleep). While Sunni Muslims pray five times daily, the Shi'a always combine the prayer (*al-jam' bain aṣ-ṣalāt*) of the noon (*dhuhr*) with that of the afternoon (*'aṣr*) and the prayer of the sunset (*maghrib*) with that of the evening (*'ishā'*). The Sunnis

tend to combine prayers only under certain circumstances such as traveling a long distance, for instance. For further information, see "Joining Prayers and Other related Issues," at http://www.al-islam.org/encyclopedia/chapter7/5.html.

13. For more information concerning the doctrine of Imamate and the Hidden Imam (al-Mahdi), see chapter 3.

14. While the Arabic term *madrasa* is used by both Sunni and Shi'a to mean a school, the Shi'a use the term *ḥawza* to refer to a center of learning or seminary school of higher education where clerics are trained in religious, philosophical, and social studies.

15. Members of a family might have different *marāji'*. Locally and hierarchically, a Shi'a might follow a low-rank clerk representing an influential or high-rank *marja'* who might reside outside Bahrain—in Iraq, Lebanon, or Iran, for example. A Shi'i person is required to pay one-fifth (*khums*) of excess wealth and a charitable contribution (*zakat*) to his or her *marja'* to be distributed to the needy (Fuller and Francke 1999, 15).

16. For more information on mystic worldviews, see chapter 4.

17. In Indonesia, Sufism engages in ritual practices with the ultimate end being the "annihilation" of the self in the oneness of Allah. "The mystical journey into self-annihilation is undertaken to acquire 'divine power,' an ancient Southeast Asian preoccupation" (Farrer 2009, 141).

18. Sufis travel from place to place to gain knowledge and establish, after sufficient spiritual training, their own orders.

19. Qur'an 3:110.

20. Saqr recited this verse from the Qur'an, namely 49:13.

21. For a detailed discussion of some of these Sufi orders, particularly Ahmadiyya and Shinnawiyya, see chapter 4.

22. According to Anderson (1983, 6), imagined community contains members of people who never know or meet each other, but "in the mind of each lives the image of their communion."

23. See the website http://ccm-inc.org/iqra/. Other examples of online Umma forums include Ummah.com-Muslim Forum, http://www.ummah.com/forum/; MuslimDot, http://muslimdot.com/; Ummah.community, http://www.ummah.co/; Shi'a community forums, http://www.shiaforums.com/vb/content.php. There is also "Ummah Radio," http://ummahradio.com/, whose goal is to provide the online community with 100 percent religiously and ethically accepted *halal* entertainment with a secure source of education. It offers modern songs praising Allah, the Prophet, and the *ummah*. For further information regarding cyber-Islamic environment, see, for example, Bunt (2003, 2009), el-Nawawy and Khamis (2009), and Roy (2004).

24. See, for example, the Qur'an (2:22, 117), (3:188–190), (6:2–3, 14, 73, 97, 103), (7:54, 121), (10:5), (13:2), (14:33), (15:26), (16:12, 16), (21:33), (22:18, 65), (23:17), (24:35), (25:45), (29:44, 61), (31:10), (35:43), (36:38, 40, 82), (37:5–6, 40), (39:5), (41:37), (51:47), (53:1, 49), (55:5–8), (67:3–5), (71:15–16), (75:9), (78:12–13), (81:2), (82:2), (85:1), (86:3), (91:1–10). For more information on cosmic verses mentioned in the Qur'an, see el-Fandy (1961), Rahman (1980), and Wadud (1971). See also http://www.ymsite.com/books/ocvr/default.htm.

25. Relying on textual analysis, some scholars concentrate on "the way in which sets of more general cosmological concepts are used in the construction of particular cosmologies" (Woodward 2011, 140). It is clear, however, that the constructions of cosmologies

made by scholars using certain classical texts do not reflect the cosmologies of ordinary Muslims.

26. The world of *jinn* refers to invisible beings, good and bad, Muslim and non-Muslim, created of fire by God (el-Aswad 2002).

27. Mecca is at 21° 25' N and 39° 49' E.

28. Islam recognizes the existence of magic (*siḥr*), but the practice is forbidden because it is regarded as the work of evil creatures such as the devil (*shaitan* or *Iblis*) and the 'infidel' jinn (bin Osman 1972, 225). For instance, Egyptians view magical thought and action as either an affiliation with devils and evil forces or an abuse of hidden knowledge and sacred power. For Egyptians, the magician (*sāiḥr*) is considered an enigma or extraordinary person who possesses remarkable religious knowledge, yet he abuses it (el-Aswad 2002).

29. For more detail on the Shi'i esoteric worldview, see chapter 3.

30. One story, showing the place of *jinn* in Malay worldviews, "goes that a man underwent this training and became invisible, but because the invisible man abused his power, he stayed that way. Becoming invisible means that 'you are not just invisible but you're in a *jinn* world'" (Farrer 2009, 152).

31. The Arabic word *dīn* means religion, but it also means the afterlife, especially when preceded by the Arabic word *yaum* or "day" (*yaum ad-dīn*). It is noteworthy that the following invocation (*taḥiyyāt*), emphasizing merits in both this world and the other world, is uttered twice in each prayer, as part of five prayers performed by Muslims every day. "Our Lord! grant us good [*ḥasanah*] in this worldly life [*dunyā*] and good in the otherworldly life [*ākhira*], and save us from the chastisement of the fire."

32. Various verses of the Qur'an deal with the divine features of Allah as being simultaneously visible (*zāhir*) and invisible (*bāṭin*). "He is the First and the Last, He is the Visible and the Invisible; and He has full knowledge of all things" (Qur'an 57:3). See also, for example, Qur'an 13:9; 32:6; 34:48; 39:46; 59:22; 64:18.

33. Also, Muslims have the option to perform the minor pilgrimage (*'umrah*) at various times throughout the year. But most Muslims prefer to do the *'umrah* during the month of Ramadan.

34. "O our Lord! I have made some of my offspring to dwell in a valley without cultivation, by Thy Sacred House; in order, O our Lord, that they may establish regular Prayer: so fill the hearts of some among men with love towards them, and feed them with fruits: so that they may give thanks" (Qur'an 14:37).

35. Al-Isrā' is a title of one of the chapters (*sura*), namely 17, of the Qur'an.

36. The Arabic word *burāq* (b-r-q) means "lightning." However, the *al-burāq*, mentioned in the mystic night journey of the Prophet, is described as a mythical horselike creature or steed that transported the Prophet horizontally (from Mecca to Jerusalem) and vertically (from Jerusalem to the heaven and back to Mecca) that sacred night that occurred twelve years after the Qur'an was revealed to the Prophet in the seventh century. According to *Saḥīḥ al-bukhhārī*. (5:58:228), the sights that Allah's Apostle was shown on the night journey were actual sights, not dreams. See al-Bukhhārī (1966, *kitab fadā'il al-anṣār*, ch. 58, no. 228).

37. See the section on the cosmic dimension of the mystic worldview, chapter 4.

38. "Sufi mystics claim the ability to exist in multiple places simultaneously. For example, Shaykh Habib Nor is buried atop a pyramidical tomb (*keramat*) in a stone sarcophagus in Singapore. Habib Nor is credited with supernatural power: transcending time and place (mundane reality) he can transform himself anywhere at will, and is said to appear every

Friday in Mecca" (Farrer 2009, 141). The "double of an exceptional person or charismatic saint can exist in two or more places simultaneously" (el-Aswad 2002).

39. Among other important holy places in Iraq are Kazimiyya and Samarra. Kazimiyya contains the shrines of Musa al-Kāzim, the seventh Imam, and his grandson Muhammad al-Jawad, the ninth Imam. Samarra encompasses shrines of the tenth Imam, 'Ali al-Hādī, and his son Hasan al-'Askarī, the eleventh Imam. It is also the place of the twelfth (Hidden) Imam Muhammad al-Mahdi.

40. Al-Azhar Mosque-University (in Cairo) is the foremost school of Sunni Islam.

41. The city of Qum is the largest center for Shi'a scholarship in the world.

42. Regarding certain periods of time in which spirits are believed to be active in Java, "twelve noon and twelve midnight are unusually dangerous times" (Geertz 1960, 20).

43. In his study of Java, Geertz (1960, 14–29) discusses the ceremony of *slametan*, which is a communal ritual symbolizing the social unity of those participating in it. The ceremony's name relates to the Javanese word *slamet*, derived from the Arabic term *salam*, which means "peace." The *slametan* rituals concern temporal cycles centering on the crises of life: birth, circumcision, marriage, and death. The ceremony of *slametan* represents a reassertion and reinforcement of the Javanese general cultural order and its power to hold back the forces of disorder.

44. According to the Javanese local system of a five-day week, each day signifies a color and a specific direction. For example, Legi indicates white and east. Wage refers to black and north. Paing indicates red and south. Pon denotes yellow and west, while Kliwon signifies center (Geertz 1960; Kim 2007).

CHAPTER 2: THE WORLDVIEW OF THE SUNNI

1. For more information on the duration of fieldwork, see Introduction, note 22.

2. The percentage of rural population in the Emirate of Abu Dhabi in 2006 was 60.82, while it reached 2.30 in Dubai (UAE in Figures, 2007). Despite the fact that most al-Ain residents are expatriates, it has a higher proportion of Emirati nationals than elsewhere in the country.

3. Islam is the official and predominant religion of both Egypt and the UAE. Of the population of national citizens in the UAE, Sunni Muslims make up 80 percent, while Shi'a Muslims make up 16 percent (el-Aswad 2005d). Religion is not included in the 2006 general population census of Egypt. Also, the distribution of population based on religious affiliation is not recorded in Egypt's official website of the Central Agency for Public Mobilization and Statistics: http://www.capmas.gov.eg/?lang=2. However, approximately 90 percent of the population of Egypt is Muslim (dominantly Sunni) and 10 percent is Christian (9 percent Coptic, 1 percent other Christian). See Central Intelligence Agency (2012).

4. The proximity of the Emirates or Arab Gulf countries to the birthplace of Islam as well as their common Arab (Bedouin) ancestry bestows meaning to these societies. The UAE state has to cope with the growing demands of modernization and globalization as well as with the demands of the locals to maintain their heritage and national Muslim identity. These demands are especially critical if we consider the short period of time in

which their tribal identity has been in the process of transformation into a national identity following the establishment of the federation in 1971 (el-Aswad 2005d; Al Abed and Hellyer 1997).

5. The UAE shares fundamental features with other small and wealthy Arab Gulf countries, such as being a culturally and ethnically diversified and heterogeneous society. For further information on the history of Islam in the UAE, see King (1997).

6. The Central Agency for Public Mobilization and Statistics (United Arab Republic of Egypt, posted January 2, 2012), http://www.capmas.gov.eg/?lang=2.

7. The actual population census of the United Arab Emirates was conducted in 2005. See United Arab Emirates (2009). Since 2006, all population figures depend on the estimate because of "the lack of actual population figures due to the fact that the 2010 census, which was scheduled to take place in April 2010, was not conducted because of lack of financial resources" ("Population Estimates 2006–2010," posted March 31, 2011, http://www.uae statistics.gov.ae/ReportPDF/Population%20Estimates%202006%20-%202010.pdf.

Emirati nationals are a "minority" (11.7%) with regard to the fast-growing population of Arab and non-Arab expatriates (88.3%) needed for undertaking developmental projects and other economic enterprises. In contrast, Egypt is the most populous Arab country whose population is not affected by such a discrepancy.

8. Income group: Economies are divided according to the 2008 GNI per capita, calculated using World Bank figures. The groups are low income, $975 or less; lower-middle income, $976–$3,855; upper-middle income, $3,856–$11,905; and high income, $11,906 or more. http://web.worldbank.org/WBSITE/EXTERNAL/DATASTATISTICS /0,,contentMDK:20420458~menuPK:64133156~pagePK:64133150~piPK:64133175~the SitePK:239419,00.html.

9. For more information, see "Doing Business in United Arab Emirates," http://www .doingbusiness.org/exploreeconomies/?economyid=195Doing.

10. The expression "the open-door economic policy" appeared on April 21, 1973, in a government statement referring to the role of Arab and foreign capital in the housing and construction sectors. However, it acquired a high political sanction in 1974 when the president issued it in the October Paper and it was approved in a referendum (Richards 1984, 323–38).

11. The seven emirates are Abu Dhabi, Dubai, Sharja, Ras al-Khaimah, al-Fujairah, Ajman, and Umm al-Quwain.

12. For further discussion of the notion of patriarchy as a dominant ideological force shaping both family structure and state politics, see Barakat 1993 and Sharabi 1988.

13. In the Emirates, the term *shaikh* is used positively to designate the good features of an object. For instance, when describing a specific and fine food item, such as a high-quality fish, a person says, "This is the 'chief' [*shaikh*] of fish" (el-Aswad 1999a). In the Emirates the religious leader is referred to as the *miṭawa'*, and not *shaikh* as is the case in Egypt. Basically the *miṭawa'* is the person who runs the *kuttāb*, a local traditional institute for teaching and memorizing the Qur'an.

14. See al-Bukhārī (1966), *Saḥīḥ al-bukhhārī* (*Kitāb al-Imāra*, 20, no. 4496). The Hadith says, "Everyone is a shepherd, and every shepherd is responsible for [the well being of] his subject" (*Kullukum rā'in wa Kullu rā'in mas'ulun 'an ra'iyyatih*).

15. The official religious institutions, both Muslim (al-Azhar and Dar al-Fatwa, or religious verdict) and Christian (the Coptic Church), were supporting Mubarak's regime, especially during the first week of the revolt.

16. See, in the Hadith, Ṣaḥīḥ Muslim (*kitab al-Iman*), chapter 21, no. 0079. On Thursday, March 3, 2011, the Dubai-based television channel Al-Arabiya hosted Ahmad al-Tayyeb, Shaikh of al-Azhar or the Grand Imam of al-Azhar since 2010, in a program titled, "Egypt after Mubarak," discussing the ambivalent position of al-Azhar toward the January 25 revolution as well as the continuous support of the former regime of Mubarak. Ahmad al-Tayyeb was criticized for asking demonstrators to go home after Mubarak's departure. Shaikh al-Azhar recounted that he preferred silence as a way of resisting power or authority. He referred to the aforementioned Hadith of the Prophet, emphasizing that he chose to resist using his heart, which is the weakest form of resistance. He also recounted that the Grand Imam should be appointed by the state but should be independent in thinking and in making decisions.

17. Discussion of political Islam and Islamist militants or Islamic societies (*al-jamā'āt al-Islāmiyya*) is beyond the scope of this study.

18. Egypt's two main Islamist parties, the Freedom and Justice Party (*al-ḥuriyya wa al-'Aadāla*), representing the Muslim Brotherhood, and the Salafi al-Nūr (Light) Party, have won almost two-thirds (65.3%) of the vote in three-round elections for the Egyptian Parliament (national assembly, or Majlis al-Sha'b). Results were revealed on Sunday, January 22, 2012. Out of 498 seats, the Freedom and Justice Party (Muslim Brotherhood) gained 235 seats (37.5%), and the al-Nūr Party of the Salafis gained 127 seats (27.8%). See *Al-Ahram* (no. 45702), Sunday, January 22, 2012. The Muslim Brotherhood, through expansive nationwide networks, has provided valuable services to the poor and needy grassroots, including selling food items (flour, sugar, cooking oil, and meat, among other items) at wholesale prices, helping with medical treatment, and offering subsidized school supplies. Labor unions and professional syndicates, including those of doctors, lawyers, engineers, and journalists, have been run by members affiliated with the Muslim Brotherhood.

19. See chapter 4 for a discussion of mysticism with specific reference to the Sufi order (*ṭarīqa*) of al-Ahmadiyya al-Shinnawiyya.

20. It is not in the scope of this book to discuss the debate between elites or intellectuals defining their religious or secular positions. This book concentrates on common people's views. For a detailed discussion of the debate between advocates of secularism and those of religion in Muslim societies, see Asad (2003).

21. The UAE Marriage Fund is more than just a financial sustenance arm; it is an initiative that educates Emirati youth on cultural and religious values and the sanctity of marriage. However, the applicant must be employed with a monthly salary less than 16,000 AED. See the official website: http://zawaj.gov.ae/.

22. Wahhabism is the foremost form of Sunni Islam in Saudi Arabia and other Gulf countries. The Wahhabi movement came to be allied with the Qawasim tribes of the Emirates in the mid-eighteenth century (el-Aswad 2005d).

23. The GCC, established in May 1985, includes six countries: Bahrain, Kuwait, Oman, Qatar, Saudi Arabia, and the United Arab Emirates.

24. Local men wear traditional cloth in a gownlike dress called *kandūrah*, whose color varies according to the seasons. In summer it is white and made of cotton or silk, and in winter it is gray or brown and sometimes worn with a matching, usually Western-style, jacket. Men wear a head-cap (*quḥfiyya*) and a square headscarf (*ghutrah*). Men of high rank complete their attire with a cloak (*'abāyah* or *bisht*). Women wear the traditional dress (*kandūrah*) made from indigo-stained cloth that has a slit around the neck. The over-

garment (*thūb* or *thaub*) is made of black lace over which a cloak (*'abāyah*) is frequently worn. Women also follow Islamic codes by wearing a hair veil or face veil (*burgu'*) (el-Aswad 2005e, 2010d).

25. The word *wide* is a colloquial form of the Arabic word *wājid* that means "plenty of" or "whatever exists in abundance." In most Arab Gulf societies, /j/ or /g/ is pronounced /y/. However, this is observed in some Arabic words.

26. For more information on the impact of wealth on changing patterns of behavior among the youth of the United Arab Emirates, see el-Aswad 1996c, 1996d.

27. Qur'an 57:3.

28. For a detailed discussion of the value of patience in Egyptian society, see el-Aswad 1990a, 1990c.

29. See Eickelman and Piscatori (1990) for further information regarding Muslim travelers to sacred places.

30. The government of the United Arab Emirates offers 600 AED ($164) a month to a male citizen (not expatriate) to whom a child is born.

31. Ibn Khaldun (1981) indicated that the history of the ruling class or dynasty moves in cycles, starting with a less civilized group of people of common descent united by their tribal solidarity (*'aṣabiyah*). When this group seizes power, it establishes the dynastic state, which gradually disintegrates due to both internal factors (represented by indulgence in luxury and the production of unnecessary goods and services) and outside challenging forces that eventually overthrow the state. It gradually loses power and collapses, replaced by another powerful group of people of a new *'aṣabiyah.*

32. Egyptian and Emirati Muslims show a great concern for the growing materialistic attitudes among people, Muslim and non-Muslim, which threaten their social relationships and cause God to take revenge. For further discussion of the same idea, see Kepel (1994).

CHAPTER 3: THE ESOTERIC WORLDVIEW OF THE SHI'A

1. Manama, located in the northeastern part of the country, is one of most active economic centers in the Arab Gulf (Fuccaro 2005, 28).

2. For more information on the duration of fieldwork, see Introduction, note 23.

3. 'Ashura means "the tenth of Muharram," the first month of the Islamic calendar, in which Imam Husain was martyred by Umayyad forces in the Battle of Karbala in 680.

4. The term *ḥusainiyya*, derived from the name of Imam Husain, means Husain-related recitation as well as a building where such recitation is performed. The term *ma'tam* will be subsequently addressed.

5. For a brief history of the Twelve Imams, see Amir-Moezzi (1994), Momen (1987), and Newman (2000).

6. Imam Husain was martyred, along with his seventy-two family members and followers, by the mighty army of Yazid ibn Mu'awiya under the command of 'Umar ibn Sa'd ibn Abi al-Waqqas. See Halm (2007) and al-Mutahhari (2003).

7. The Shi'a, like all Muslims adhering to the Qur'an and Islamic tradition, maintain that a martyr (*shahīd*), a person who sacrifices his soul defending his religion, country, honor, and property, lives on in heaven and enjoys the prominent status of being close to Allah (Qur'an 2:154, 3:169). As a martyr, Imam Husain is depicted as Master of the Youths of Paradise.

8. Louër (2008a, 19) argues, "Bahrain is one of the few places, if not the only one, where Akhbarism has maintained a strong presence to this day, becoming the distinctive attribute of Bahraini Shiism." In a discussion with Shi'i authorities in Bahrain, they state that Akhbarism is declining at the intellectual level of the *'ulama*, while it is still held among common lay Shi'a.

9. *Ḥusainiyya* discourses include lectures, speeches, and sermons delivered by *shaikhs* or religious leaders addressing and commemorating the significance of the martyrdom of Imam Husain, his family, and his companions.

10. See chapter 4, which discusses the mystic worldview of Sufism.

11. Literature dealing with the concealment and unseen dimension of the infallible Imam, al-Mahdi, is extensive. See, for example, al-'Amily (2004), Amir-Moezzi (1994), al-Majlisi (1965), Sachedina (1981), Sulayman (2004), and al-Tusi (2004).

12. This Shi'i view postulates that prophetic hermeneutics is not concluded and will continue to bring forth secret meanings until the return of the awaited Imam, of him who will still be the "seal of the Imamate" and the signal for the resurrection of resurrections (Corbin 1969, 29).

13. The "minor occultation" (*al-Ghaiba al-ṣughra*) of the Hidden Imam started in 873 and ended in 941. The "major or prolonged occultation" (*Ghaiba al-kubra*) began in 941 when the last representative of the Twelfth Imam died, and this occultation will continue until his appearance (*ẓuhūr*) (Corbin 1969, 29).

14. Shi'i intellectuals are cautious not to reduce the existence of the Imams to a political and militant role or lessen their doctrine to an ideology of subversion. "In fact, what characterizes the existence of the imam is not his political role but his initiatory and esoteric kind of knowledge (*'ilm*), and his occult and supernatural powers (*a'ājib*)" (Amir-Moezzi 1994, 69).

15. Green, the Prophet's beloved color, is the natural color of paradise. I saw women wearing green bracelets to identify themselves as Shi'i. Also, Shi'a's saintly shrines are covered with green material.

16. Compare these practices of intercessions with those of Indians studied by Pinault (1999, 285–305).

17. Such incidents are documented in literature on the events of Karbala. See, for instance, al-Muqarram (1963, 341–42).

18. Concerning the emotion of sorrow among Shi'i women of Iran, see, for example, Flaskerud (2005) and Torab (1996). For the notion of sorrow among the Shi'a of Iraq, see al-Haydary (1999) and Nakash (2006).

19. According to the Qur'an (18:60–81), al-Khiḍr, whom Moses met at a place where two seas conjunct, is alive.

20. Interviewees recounted that certain persons claimed to see al-Mahdi in their dreams. For the impact of dreams on people's everyday lives, see chapter 5 and el-Aswad (2010a).

21. For the Shi'a, the Prophet's birthday is the seventeenth of Rabi' al-Awwal, but for the Sunni it is the twelfth.

22. Among Sunni Muslims of Durrani Pashtuns, in Afghanistan, "food values and commensal practices are part of a wider system which is held to locate all Muslims cosmologically and to afford them contact with the supernatural and the possibility of an afterlife in paradise" (Tapper and Tapper 1986, 65).

23. Shi'i women practice the *laṭmah* in private when they beat their laps. In public zones, however, they use the cloak (*'abaya*) to hide their hands while beating their breasts.

24. Regarding *zangīl* or *ḍarb al- zangīl*, a performance in which Shi'i men use chains made of light metal to beat their backs until bleeding, some Shi'i *'ulama* do not approve; however, others do if the intention is good, showing sincere love of al-Husain.

25. Certain parts of the body are used symbolically in Shi'i culture. The hand and the head are dominant symbols embodying martyrdom, sacrifice, wisdom, and strength. If the head is directly associated with the martyrdom of Imam Husain, the hand is related to the hands of al-'Abbas, Husain's brother, that were cut off by the enemy while he was fetching water for his thirsty companions under siege.

26. Regarding the differences between ritual, drama, and theater, see, for example, Asad (1993), Schechner (1985, 2006) and Turner (1969).

27. Zaynab is the daughter of Imam 'Ali ibn Abi Talib and granddaughter of the Prophet Muhammad. She played a significant role in al-Husain's revolution after Karbala.

CHAPTER 4: THE MYSTIC WORLDVIEW OF SUFISM

1. The concept "mystic" can be defined as "a state of consciousness that surpasses ordinary experience through the union with a transcendent reality" (Dupré 1987, 246).

2. The literature addressing Sufism is extensive. For various definitions and approaches dealing with Sufism and mysticism, see, for example, el-Aswad (2004a, 2006a), Crapanzano (1973), Evans-Pritchard (1949), Johansen (1996), Lings (1975), Renard (1996, 2004), Schimmel (1975), al-Sha'rani (2004), Sirriyeh (1999), Trimingham (1971), and Weismann (2007).

3. Ethnographic research was conducted in Egypt, Bahrain, and the Emirates during the period of 2004–2010. In Egypt, ethnographic material was collected from the city of Tanta and two of its adjacent villages (Al-Rajdiyya and Shibshir al-Hissa) in March–June 2001 and July–October 2002. Shibshir al-Hissa (located five miles north of Tanta) is where Sidi Abdullah and Sidi Ahmad Jamal ad-Din are buried. Al-Rajdiyya (located nearly four miles northeast of Tanta) is the place of the shrines of Shaikhs Muhammad Yusuf and Muhammad Said al-Shinnawi. In Bahrain, ethnographic material was collected from Manama city and two villages, Blad al-Qadim and Duraz, in January–June 2005 and February–July 2006. Cross-culturally, the ethnographic accounts are examined against other studies related to Sufism in other societies.

4. The Sufi order of Ahmadiyya, named after the first name of the saint, has other names, such as Badawiyya (after the last name of the saint, Badawi) and Suṭūḥiyya. Suṭūḥiyya is derived from the Arabic word *as-saṭḥ*, which means the roof of the house on which the saint Sayyid al-Badawi (1199–1276) and his close disciples used to spend time together contemplating and praying. Al-Badawi was also known for his chivalry (*futuwwa*), with which he managed to release Muslim captives (*gāb al-'asrā*) from the French forces in the thirteenth century.

5. Al-Badawi, known as the Master of Travelers (Sayyid al-Sālikīn), succeeded in establishing spiritual chains of genealogies located in Egypt and different parts of the Muslim world. For the Sufis, travel and migration are prototypical rites of passage involving transition in space, territory, and group membership. They represent bodily engagement in the world resulting in the achievement of mystical experience and divine knowledge. Travelers of "all kinds, past and present and from many directions, produce knowledge

about others and themselves" (Euben 2006, 8). Born in Fez, al-Badawi visited Mecca and Iraq and then resided and was buried in Tanta, Egypt ('Ashur 1998; Maḥmud 1993). One of his spiritually certified descendants who was born and raised in Fao village in Upper Egypt and who traveled to Tanta seeking the Sufi path was Sidi 'Umar al-Shinnawi, the patron saint and founder of the Shinnawiyya Sufi order.

6. Shaikh Said, born in Rajdiyya village (Tanta district) on September 13, 1961, was appointed vice patron of the Shinnawiyya Sufi order in 1986, then head of the order on June 28, 2008, after the death of his father. He has also been the head of the Ahmadi Association in Tanta since 2008. He graduated from the Faculty of Agriculture, University of Menufiyya, Egypt, in 1985.

7. For example, Arberry (1950, 122) states that "ignorant masses" are drawn to Sufi orders. Another example of the Orientalist view of Sufism is clearly shown in Nicholson's statements that "the beginning of wisdom, for European students of Oriental religion, lies in the discovery that incongruous beliefs—I mean, of course, beliefs which *our* mind cannot harmonize—dwell peacefully together in the Orientalist brain; that their owner is quite unconscious of their incongruity; and that, as a rule, he is absolutely sincere. Contradictions which seem glaring to us do not trouble him at all" (Nicholson 2002, 93–94 [italics in original]). He also states, "To the Muslim who has *no sense of natural law*, all these 'violations of custom' seem equally credible. We, on the other hand, feel ourselves obliged to distinguish phenomena which we regard as irrational and impossible from those for which we can find some sort of 'natural' explanation. Modern theories of psychological influence . . . have thrown open to us a wide avenue of approach to this dark continent in the Eastern mind" (Nicholson 2002, 99–100 [italics added]).

8. See al-Ghazālī (1979). See also Griffel (2009).

9. For the contribution of 'Abd al-Ḥalīm Maḥmud to Islamic mysticism, see Maḥmud (1981, 1993).

10. Abū al-Wafa al-Taftazānī was also the Shaikh of Mashaikh al-Turuq as-Sufiyya in Egypt (the president of Sufi orders in Egypt). He wrote extensively on Islamic Sufism (1974, 1975).

11. Similarly, in the sixteenth and seventeenth centuries "most learned men . . . were also Sufis. . . . [M]ysticism had come to penetrate the madrasa curriculum being taught" (Robinson 1997, 164).

12. "The Sufis aspire to total concentration upon God and upon the approach to Him, in order to obtain the mystical experience of gnosis and Divine oneness" (Ibn Khaldun 1981, 85).

13. The council officially belongs to the Ministry of Social Affairs and is responsible for Sufi affairs in Egypt. In 1976 (and 1978), new legislation was promulgated, giving largely increased powers to the Supreme Council of Sufi Orders, in which legislative, judiciary, and executive powers were, and still are, vested. In accordance with the 1976 law, the council has exclusive authority to approve all Sufi activities, whether private or public. See http://weekly.ahram.org.eg/2000/512/special.htm.

14. This statement is derived from one of the Prophet's sayings or Ḥadīth; see al-Bukhari (1966, *Kitab al-Iman*, chap. 2, 47).

15. See al-Bukhari (1966, *Kitab al-riqaq*, chap. 38, 6502).

16. The reference to Muslim brothers is used here within a metaphorical context and is not related to the well-known politically oriented Muslim Brotherhood established by

Hasan al-Banna in Egypt in the first half of the twentieth century. For information on the history of al-Banna's Society of Muslim Brothers, see Lia (2006) and Mitchell (1969).

17. The Prophet is frequently mentioned as the exemplary model for those who deal with people guided by principles of mercy, compassion, and peaceful dialogue. I heard many interviewees quoting the following verse of the Qur'an: "It is part of the Mercy of Allah that thou dost deal gently with them. Wert thou severe or harsh-hearted, they would have broken away from about thee" (3:159).

18. "Men who have followed Sufi training have, as is well known, as acts of divine grace, obtained perceptions of supernatural things" (Ibn Khaldun 1981, 82).

19. Among the Sufis of Iran, the spiritual stations (*maqāmat-i-'irfānī*) are based upon the inner spiritual states of persons. "The spiritual stations of the Prophet and the Imams leading to union with God can be considered as the final goal toward which Shi'ite piety strives and upon which the whole spiritual structure of Shi'itism is based" (Nasr 2009, 112).

20. "Saints are recognized as having a hierarchical worth or value exceeding that of ordinary believers, based very simply on the understanding that they have achieved a special closeness to God" (Smith and Haddad 1981, 184).

21. See subsequent discussion.

22. This is also mandated by the Qur'an: "When the Qur'an is read, listen to it with attention, and hold your peace: that ye may receive Mercy" (7:204).

23. The Qur'an "is strewn with verses which have an obvious spiritual and esoteric dimension" (Geoffroy 2010, 36). This view is compatible with al-Sharani's (1965) definition of Sufism, as based on the Qur'an, the Sunna, and the virtuous ways of prophets and pious persons. According to Michael Winter, "al-Sha'rani belonged most fully to the Ahmadiyya, a popular and moderate Egyptian *ṭarīqa*, which held the best model of relations between a Sufi shaikh and his followers to be a strict one of adherence to *Shari'a*, obedience, benevolence, and structured testing" (quoted in Hudson 2004, 47).

24. Ibn Khaldun (1981, 73) states that the Qur'an, revealed to the Prophet, "is the greatest, noblest, and clearest miracle. . . . It is itself the wondrous miracle. It is its own proof."

25. Shaikh Yasin has a sharp memory, enabling him to recall and recite verses of the Qur'an quickly and easily.

26. Shaikh Yasin asserted that the obedience to God and the Prophet is the main source of mercy, and then he recited, "And obey Allah and the Messenger, that ye may obtain Mercy" (3:132). Further, Shaikh Yasin states that the Prophet, being a "mercy" to all creatures, is also the intercessor (*shafī'*) who intercedes for Muslims on the Day of Judgment.

27. See the Qur'an (2:105, 118; 3:74; 4:96, 113, 175; 6:12, 54, 133; 7:57, 156; 9:71, 99; 10:58; 23:118; 12:56).

28. Other verses indicating the Qur'an as "mercy" (*raḥma*) include, for example, 4:113; 6:64, 89, 155, 157; 7:52; and 17:82.

29. See chapter 1 for a full discussion of this point.

30. Shaikh Yasin was referring to two Qur'anic verses (17:1; 53:18). He also mentioned a verse indicating mystical revelation, "And He revealed unto His slave that which He revealed" (53:10).

31. Unlike the English word "patient," the Arabic word *ṣabr* does not refer to a sick person. A person might be sick but not patient, and conversely, a person might be patient but not sick. Mystic *shaikhs* I interviewed emphasized the virtue of patience as the first step toward the Sufi path. They support their statement by saying, "Allah is with the patient"

(*inna Allah ma'a aṣ-Ṣabirīn*). They also refer to various verses of the Qur'an: "And those who remain patient, seeking their Lord's Countenance; establish regular prayers; spend, out of (the gifts) We have bestowed for their sustenance, secretly and openly; and turn off Evil with good: for such there is the final attainment of the (eternal) home" (13:22); "And their recompense shall be Paradise, and silken garments, because they were patient" (76:12); and "And certainly, We shall test you with something of fear, hunger, loss of wealth, lives and fruits, but give glad tidings to the patient" (2:155). See, for example, Qur'an (3:17, 146, 200; 5:14; 12:90; 13:24; 52:48; 70:5; 103:3).

32. Egyptians plant the evergreen trees of aloe inside pots and place them on the graves of beloved persons, praying and saying, "May Allah have mercy on the dead."

33. Mystical knowledge, emanating directly from God (*'ilm ladunnī*), and divine mercy (*raaḥmah*) are mentioned together in numerous verses of the Qur'an.

34. The narrative of al-Khiḍr is mentioned in the Qur'an (18:60–82). For further details on the place of al-Khiḍr in Muslim life, see A. J. Wensinck (1978).

35. "So they found one of Our servants, on whom We had bestowed Mercy from Ourselves and whom We had taught knowledge from Our own Presence" (Qur'an 18:65).

36. The grand *shaikhs* and founders of Sufi orders such as 'Abd al-Qadir al-Jilani (d. 1167), Ahmad al-Rifa'i (d. 1182), Abu al-Hasan ash-Shadhili (d. 1258), Ahmad al-Badawi (d. 1276), and Ibrahim ad-Disuki (d. 1277) conveyed that they were descendants of the Prophet Muhammad. Some of them specified a certain descent line (el-Aswad 2006a).

37. The Arabic word *wirātha* implies multiple meanings ranging from hereditary transmission to social or spiritual heritage. Within the Sufi discourse, *wirātha* refers to the doctrine of prophetic heritage that first appeared among the earliest Sufi authors and was later articulated by Ibn 'Arab. According to this doctrine, "Muslim saints receive the spiritual heritage of past prophets, starting with the Prophet Muhammad, who recapitulated and encompassed all of the previous prophetic types" (Geoffroy 2010, 18).

38. The genealogy goes back to al-'Abbas Ibn 'Abd al-Muttalib (the Prophet's father's brother). However, there is not a specific reference cited by Shaikh Hasan to support the kin relationship between Sidi 'Umar and al-Bistami or al-Suhrawardi. Though the exact identity of Shihab al-Din al-Suhrawardi (1144–1234) is not clearly delineated, it seems that he is the person Shaikh Hasan refers to as forefather of Sidi 'Umar. Shihab al-Din al-Suhrawardi is known for his popular Sufi manual *'awarif al-Ma'arif* as well as for his moderate Sufi views associated with al-Suhrawardiyya Sufi order, which advocate the concept of *futuwa*, a multiple-meaning concept referring to bravery, generosity, and hospitality in both mundane and spiritual zones (Bigelow 1999; Hoda 2004).

39. Al-Bistami (d. 874) is known for his ecstatic utterances (*shaṭḥāt*) as well as for his theory of mystical annihilation (*fanā'*) (Awn 1987; Trimingham 1971).

40. The annual birthday celebration (*mawlid*) of al-Badawi is held in October. Almost two million people from around the Delta and other parts of Egypt and the Muslim world come to celebrate this exceptional occasion (especially on the grand Thursday night, *al-lila al-kabīra*) in which vows are carried out. Ordinary people as well as followers of different Sufi orders perform various *dhikrs* during the *mawlid*. Also, relatives, friends, and members of Sufi orders, motivated by love, respect, and loyalty, get together to celebrate the occasion until dawn. The last day of the *mawlid* is Friday, on which the procession begins in the morning at the mosque and where the successor (*khalīfa*) of al-Badawi mounts a horse and leads the procession of innumerable Sufi orders, government representatives, and ordinary people. The procession lasts until noon or the Friday prayer (el-Aswad 2006a).

41. There is a debate among scholars regarding the impact of Shi'ism on Sunni Sufism or vice versa. For example, Ibn Khaldun argues that Sufism was impacted by Shi'a theories (Nasr 2009; Ridgeon 2010). Other scholars, however, maintain neither Shi'ism "nor Sunnism, nor Sufism within the Sunni world, derive from one another. They all derive their authority from the Prophet and the source of Islamic revelation" (Nasr 2009, 106).

42. It seems that certain scholars relate the esotericism only to the Imams. "From his own light, God made a luminous ray spring forth, and from this ray he made a second ray proceed; the first was the light of Muhammad, that of Prophecy (*nubuwwa*), that of exoteric (*ẓāhir*); the second was the light of 'Ali, that of the Imamate or of *wlāya*, of the esoteric (*bāṭin*)" (Amir-Moezzi 2011, 135).

43. Such allusive sayings can easily be compared with the famous "ecstatic utterances (*shaṭaḥāt*) of the mystic" (Amir-Moezzi 2011, 114).

44. The Arabic word *al-Khawwas* connotes a person whose job is to treat palm reeds. Ali Khawwas, al-Sharani's most influential master, was illiterate (Hudson 2004, 51).

45. In a recent study conducted in Palestine, the author mentions that in their legal works, the scholars and jurists, particularly those within the Shi'i community, not only favored but strongly encouraged visitations to the shrines of their holy figures and considered such practice an essential, practical act of worship. The same study shows the impact of the Shi'a on the Sunni practice of visitations to saintly shrines in Palestine, where "these visitations were and are associated with making vows and performance of ritual duties" (al-Houdaleih 2010, 378–79).

46. Opponents of mystic worldviews of Sufism and related sainthood practices include disciples of the Hanbali theologian Ahmad ibn Taymiyya, specially the Wahhabis (Weismann 2007, 8) and the Salafis, advocating a return to the example of the pious forefathers of Islam. *Al-Ahram* (Arabic version, no. 45407—Saturday, April 2, 2011) stated that a group of religious scholars and students from al-Azhar marched in Cairo streets denouncing the attempt of the Salafi men to destroy the shrines of saints established in various places in Egypt. Shaikh 'Ali Jum'a, Grand Mufti of Egypt, was quoted as saying that he was praying that God would cut the hand that touches the shrine (mosque) of Husain (grandson of the Prophet). The following day, April 3, 2011 (*Al-Ahram* no. 45408—page 1), Shaikh Muhammad 'Abd al-Maqsud, a prominent Salafi leader, commented on the shameful events in which some Salafi Muslims actually destroyed some saintly shrines. He said that destroying these shrines is a fanatic action and does not represent an Islamic value. Islam forbids such irrational actions, he recounted. On April 9, 2011, Egyptian news, under the rubric "Sufis to form popular committees to protect tombs," stated, "The Supreme Council for Sufi Orders held an emergency session Wednesday to discuss the continued attacks on shrines and the need to rebuild the demolished and vandalized tombs. Shaikh Abdul Hady al-Qasaby, head of the council, said 'The council decided in its emergency session to form popular committees to protect the tombs in all governorates. Sufi sheikhs will form and supervise the committees to aid local agencies in putting an end to the continued attacks on Sufi tombs.'" See http://news.egypt.com/en/2011040914226/news/-egypt-news/sufis-to-form-popular-committees-to-protect-tombs.html.

47. All over Bangladesh there are popular shrines of Sufi saints (*pirs*). All of these saints are said to be from points west of Bengal, especially the Middle East. "These saints and their devoted followers constructed mosques and *mazars* throughout Bengal. These sites became local sacred sites and the locations for the offering of *ziyarat* (visitation)" (Uddin 2006, 147, italics in original).

48. For more information, see chapter 3.

49. As a place of regional sanctuaries, Tanta has forty saints (*awliya'*) (Wahbi 2000).

50. Similar examples are found in different Muslim places. For instance, John Renard observes that in Ottoman Turkey the "founder of the organization (tariqa), and often the spiritual leader's successors as well, are buried within the structure, either in a separate room or in a space continuous with that used for communal prayer rites" (Renard 1996, 66).

51. Some of these phrases include, for example, "Blessings and peace be upon the Prophet, his Family, and his Companions."

CHAPTER 5: MUSLIM WORLDVIEWS, IMAGINATION, AND THE DREAM WORLD

1. Discussing the relationship between imagination and science, in addition to religion, Lakoff and Johnson (1999, 93) write, "What has always made science possible is our embodiment, not our transcendence of it, and our imagination, not our avoidance of it." Similarly, Thomas (1997, 109) argues that the reason that imagination is thought to be particularly relevant to the arts arises from the ability of artists to see and to induce the rest of people to perceive aspects of reality differently or more fully than is ordinary.

2. "The reality of the objective significance of the dream is guaranteed by the Holy Book" (von Grunebaum 1966, 7).

3. The Prophet Muhammad had several dream visions related to various circumstances. In some of these dream visions he received divine support, immediately before the battle of Badr, rendering his enemy insignificant. "Remember in thy dream Allah showed them to thee as few: if He had shown them to thee as many, ye would surely have been discouraged, and ye would surely have disputed in (your) decision; but Allah saved (you): for He knoweth well the (secrets) of (all) hearts" (Qur'an 8:43). There is also a dream vision through which the Prophet Muhammad was confirmed entering Mecca victoriously (Qur'an 48:27).

4. There is a verse of the Qur'an that relates to a vision through which the Prophet Abraham received God's command to sacrifice his son, Isma'il. "'O my son! I see in vision that I offer thee in sacrifice: Now see what is thy view!' (The son) said: 'O my father! Do as thou art commanded: thou will find me, if Allah so wills one practicing Patience and Constancy'" (Qur'an 37:102).

5. In the Qur'an, chapter 12, titled "Yusuf" (Joseph), contains 111 verses in which Joseph is depicted as an exemplary man of truth and piety upon whom God bestowed the gift of interpreting dreams (*ta'wīl al-aḥādīth*). It is interesting to note that the Arabic word "*aḥādīth*" (sing. "*ḥadīth*") means speech, talk, conversation, or story.

6. Dreams played a significant role in the lives of medieval Muslim communities. They were considered decisive elements in changing reality. For example, the caliph al-Ma'mun's decision to translate Greek philosophical texts into Arabic was made after he had a dream conversation with the Greek philosopher Aristotle (von Grunebaum 1966, 12). "In 1169 Asad ad-Dīn Shīrkūh, the Zengid general in Egypt, has a dream which he interprets as foretelling that he would arrest and replace his rival, the Fatimid commander Shāwar. Encouraged by his dream he proceeds with his plot which leads to the capture and execution of his opponent" (von Grunebaum 1966, 13).

7. For more information on the independent ontological status of imagination addressed by medieval Muslim scholars such as Ibn al-ʻArabi, al-Farabi, and Avicenna, among others, see Bulkeley (2008), Corbin (1966), Davidson (1992), Halligan (2001), Murray and Cocking (1991), and Rahman (1966). In his discussion of Sufi experiences of Sohrawardi and Ibn al-ʻArabi, among other Sufis, Corbin refers to an ontological reality called *mundus imaginalis* or the imaginary and imaginal world that "is a perfectly real world preserving all the richness and diversity of the sensible world but in a spiritual state. The existence of this world presupposes an imaginative power that makes it possible to leave the sensible state without leaving physical extension" (Corbin 1966, 407).

8. "In putting complete faith in reason, the West forgot that imagination opens the soul to certain possibilities of perceiving and understanding not available to the rational mind" (Chittick 1989, ix).

9. Ethnographic material related to dreams in societies of both Bahrain and Egypt is based on in-depth interviews and case studies with persons of both genders from different social, economic, educational, and occupational backgrounds. In Bahrain, I conducted fieldwork in the capital city of Manama and two villages, al-Duraz and ad-Dayh. In addition to interviewing sixteen persons of both genders, I concentrated on ten case studies. In Egypt, I conducted fieldwork in Tanta and two of its adjacent villages (Shibshir al-Hissa and al-Rajdiyya).

10. From the psychological point of view, Jung had long argued that the experiences of religion or God are archetypal realities, inherited as psychic structures (which have the possibility of producing images) by all human beings. The experience of God occurs in the psyche but is usually projected outward (Smyers 2002, 485). Freud's psychoanalytic theory (1950), viewing dreams as forms of fulfillment of unconscious wishes and unfulfilled sexual desires, overlooks that the symbolic basis of dream work lay in culture, transformed into language for dream reports and not mere privates fantasies (Herdt 1992, 81). For Jung (2002, 78–79), however, there are two kinds of unconscious: a *personal* unconscious, causing "little" dreams or nightly fragments of subjective impressions and fantasies, and a *collective* unconscious, causing "big" or archetypal dreams concerned with symbolic images or general ideas (containing the accumulating experience of all humanity) whose significance lies in their intrinsic meaning and not in any personal experience and its association. Jung (2002, 9) said, "The human psyche is unique and subjective or personal only in part, and for the rest is collective and objective." Interestingly, what Jung calls collective unconscious is essentially the realm of the "active imagination" of Ibn ʻArabi (Halligan 2001, 277).

11. Dreams and dream visions have been extensively studied within religious contexts. For the religious role of dreams and visions in Islam, see, for instance, Corbin (1966), Ewing (1990, 1994), Green (2003), Hermansen (1997a, 1997b), Hoffman (1997), Katz (1997), and Sirriyeh (2000).

12. Jung recounted, "I prefer to regard the symbol as the announcement of something unknown, hard to recognize and not to be fully determined" (Jung (2001, 22).

13. Basso points out that the core cosmological and ontological principles of the worldview of the Kalapo people "can just easily govern the manner of dream interpretation. The specific content of that world view—upon which the daily fears, anticipations, and joys of participants avidly feed—in turn affects the manifest content of the dreaming experience and conditions how it is to be communicated" (Basso 1987, 102).

14. These different interpretations of seeing a camel in a dream differ from those given by Ibn Sīrīn, according to whom seeing a camel in a dream represents prosperity, trials, a tree, or women's holdings. A tamed camel in a dream represents a learned person. Collecting camel's fur in a dream means acquiring money (Ibn Sīrīn 2000, 67).

15. For further discussion of Peirce's contribution, see Mitchell (1986), Parmentier (1994), and Singer (1984).

16. Concerning the contribution of Arab and Muslim intellectuals to the symbolic interpretation of dreams, see Al-'Akili (1992) and Ayoub (1992).

17. The Prophet Muhammad said that a good dream is one of forty-six parts of prophecy (al-Bukhari 1966, *Kitab al-Ta'bir*, chap. 2, no. 6983; chap. 4, nos. 6987, 6988, 6989; chap. 10, no. 6994). He also said that nothing would be left after his death except good dream visions or glad tidings (*mubashshirat*) (al-Bukhari 1966, *Kitab al-Ta'bir*, chap. 5, no. 6990). This implies that dreams are a small but legitimate source of divine knowledge.

18. The Arabic word *istihlam* (derived from the root *h-l-m*) locally connotes the sexual sensation a person experiences in dreams after which he or she usually cleanses the whole body, especially if signs of fluids have been found.

19. It is questionable to claim that the phrase "*ḥadīth nafsī*" (talk of the self) is used by ordinary Egyptians to refer to a specific kind of dream implying subconscious desires (Mittermaier 2011, 98). This specific phrase, however, does not refer to "a category of dream," but is used more in "texts" or by religious scholars (*'ulamā'*) (or those who follow the classical exegesis), not by ordinary or folk people. In his everyday life, an Egyptian person may say, "I have/had a dream," "*anā ḥalamt*," not "I have/had a *ḥadīth nafsī*." In addressing dreams, one must take into consideration people's points of view. However, in discussing the relationship between prophecy or revelation (*waḥy*) and dream vision, Mittermaier, in certain contexts, seems to impose her view on Egyptian interviewees. This is obvious in the reaction of "Shaykh 'Abdullah," a member of a local Sufi order in Upper Egypt and known for being well versed in the spiritual worlds (as the author maintains), who, questioning the motive of the author, said, "It's obvious that you want to damage Islam. You want to say that the Prophet didn't receive revelation but only dream-visions" (Mittermaier 2011, 135).

20. There are numerous publications dealing with dreams in Muslim countries. For instance, in Egypt, books on dreams and their interpretations, written in Arabic by various authors with different perspectives, circulate in cheap and accessible editions, such as al-'Afifi (1993), 'Ali (1987), 'Ārif (1996), Ibn Sīrīn (2000), al-Nabulusi (1972), al-Qardawi (1966), and al-Sha'rawi (1998). However, in countries with a Shi'a majority, such as Bahrain and Iraq, books on dreams written by Shi'i scholars or Imams, such as the collection of *tafsīr al-aḥlām* by Imam Ja'afar al-Sādiq (2000), are widely circulated. Similarly, "Pakistani dream theory and techniques of interpretation are to be found in printed manuals which are readily available in book bazaars" (Ewing 1990, 59). Dreams play a central role in the lives of many Pakistanis.

21. The earliest known records of dreams can be found on Egyptian papyri dating from the Twelfth Dynasty, around 2000 and 1790 BC (Mahrer 1989, 3–4). More than a century ago Lane recounted that the "Egyptians place great faith in dreams, which often direct them in some of the most important actions of life" (Lane 1973, 261).

22. Ibn Sīrīn (2000) affirms that the meaning of a dream is not fixed but instead depends on the personality and social circumstances of the dreamer.

23. Among the Kalapalo Indians of central Brazil, dreaming is said to occur as well when a sleeper is visited by a powerful being (Basso 1987, 88–89).

24. In addition to *hātif*, the word *khayāl*, which means "image" or "imaginary," is used with reference to dreaming.

25. In this phrase the name "Muhammad" refers to the Prophet of Islam, while that of "'Ali" indicates 'Ali ibn Abi Talib, the Prophet Muhammad's cousin and son-in-law and the fourth of the "Rightly Guided Sunni Caliphs."

26. Concerning the issue of seeing different images of the Prophet Muhammad in a dream vision, Muslim scholars' views (according to al-'Asqalani 1959, 386–87) can be summed up as follows. In all cases the images of the Prophet as seen in dream visions are true, but the differences of images are related to the inner state or condition of the dreamer. If the image of the Prophet appears in a dream vision as being identical to his real or actual image (as described in the authentic classical tradition such as those of Ṣaḥīḥ al-Bukharī and Ṣaḥīḥ Muslim), it means that the dreamer is in peaceful and perfect state of mind. If otherwise (seeing a different image of the Prophet), it means that the dreamer's state of mind is imperfect or troubled. This latter case necessitates a deeper interpretation of the dream vision (al-'Asqalani 1959, 387).

27. Edward Lane referred to an incident in which a religious leader announced publicly that the head of the revered Imam al-Husain, grandson of the Prophet Muhammad, was not in al-Husain's mosque in Cairo. Nonetheless, a disciple had a vision in which he saw the Prophet accompanied by 'Ali ibn Abi Talib, the father of al-Husain, and intimate companions visit the head of Imam al-Husain in his shrine or mosque in Cairo. The religious leader, being informed of the dream vision, took the disciple and together they went to visit the shrine of al-Husain. When they entered the mosque, the religious leader said, "Peace be on thee, O son of the daughter of the Apostle of God. I believe that the noble head is here, by reason of the vision which this person has seen; for the vision of the Prophet is true; since he hath said, 'Who sees me in my sleep sees me truly; for Satan cannot assume the similitude of my form'" (Lane 1973, 216).

28. According to Ibn Sīrīn (Al-'Akili 1992, 6), seeing 'Ali ibn Abi Talib "in a dream means victory over one's enemy. Seeing him in a place or a mosque where people are mourning him or performing the funeral prayer on him or carrying his coffin or prostrating to him in dream means becoming a Shia'it or gathering one's strength for a rebellion or to create divisiveness, or it could mean hypocrisy. If a scholar sees 'Ali in a dream, it means that he will earn increased knowledge, asceticism, reverence and strength. Seeing him in a dream also means capture by one's enemy, migrating from one country to another and mostly to die as a martyr. Seeing him in a dream also means having blessed progeny, vanquishing one's enemy, presiding over the believers, hardships during travel, booty, manifestation of blessings and miracles, acquiring extraordinary knowledge, following the leading practices of God's Messenger."

29. For more on the Sufi order of al-Shinnawiyya, see chapter 4.

30. Qur'an 18:60–82.

31. Shi'a believe that this Twelfth Imam hid himself in a cave below a mosque in Samarra in Iraq. This cave is blocked by a gate called the "Gate of Occultation" (*Serdāb al-Ghaiba*), a sacred site at which the faithful gather to pray for the return of the Hidden Imam.

32. When I heard that in the dream the crescent was interpreted as a sign of knowledge, I consulted Ibn Sīrīn's book on dreams. I found that the crescent has many positive meanings but no specific indication of knowledge or learning. This indicates that people

have their own insights or interpretations of certain dreams. According to Ibn Sīrīn, the crescent or new moon, when it appears in its correct position in a dream, means begetting a blessed son or receiving an important appointment or profits from one's business. If a crescent falls to the earth in a dream, it means a newborn. Seeing the new moon at a time other than the time of its birth in a dream means happy news, glad tidings, the return home of a long-awaited traveler, or having a newborn. The birth of a new moon in a dream also denotes the truth of one's promise, or it could mean receiving money, for rent is usually due at the beginning of each month (Al-ʻAkili 1992, 101–2).

33. According to the Islamic worldview, revelation or the power of prophecy is believed to come from God (El-Shamy 1995).

34. "That it is He Who granteth death and life" (Qur'an 53:44).

35. The creator often integrates opposites and contraries into one unity, being simultaneously visible and invisible, first and last, creator and destroyer, and very near and very remote (el-Aswad 2005a, 3).

36. Lévy-Bruhl refuted the criticism that he depicted traditional (primitive) people as irrational or prelogical. He clarified the notion of participation by stating that for traditional society there is a continuum of forces and agencies found in animate and inanimate entities (Evans-Pritchard 1934, 19–20).

37. See the Qur'an (8:43; 12:6, 36–37, 41, 43, 46; 30:23; 37:102, 105; 48:27).

38. "Sleeping and dying persons, being about to die or to fall asleep, likewise speak about supernatural things. Men who have followed Sufi training have, as is well known, as acts of divine grace, obtained perceptions of supernatural things " (Ibn Khaldun 1981, 82).

39. Persons I interviewed frequently mentioned the verses of the Qur'an (91:7–9) accentuating this statement.

40. Some verses of the Qur'an, especially al-Zumar (39:42), affirm that Allah takes the souls of people at death and during their sleep. He keeps the souls of those on whom He has passed the decree of death and returns the souls of the sleepers until their assigned period of life is fulfilled. The interpretation of this verse, however, "led to the view that the souls or spirits during sleep share a condition with those of the dead, and that by means of that shared circumstance they are said to interact and communicate" (Smith 1980, 225).

41. See chapter 4, which discusses the views of the Salafis among other conservatives toward such beliefs.

42. "It is also reported by Jaʻfar that at the moment that the seed of an imam is conceived in the womb of his mother, she . . . will then be visited in a dream by 'a man' (*rajulan*, an angel who has taken a human form . . .) who will later tell her the good news" (Amir-Moezzi 1994, 57).

43. Ayoub argues that dreams are messengers to people from the unknown. Dreams "are often prophetic voices of the future. Hence, they have at times directed the course of the history of nations" (Ayoub 1992, xii).

CHAPTER 6: MULTIPLE WORLDVIEWS AND MULTIPLE IDENTITIES OF THE MUSLIM DIASPORA

1. Peoples, information, communication, and material goods traverse cultural and national borders, creating all forms of transnational and subnational identities that transform

and reconstruct themselves in unpredictable ways (Euben 2006, 3). The contemporary work in hybridity is cross-disciplinary, evident in studies of popular culture, media, immigrant populations, subaltern studies, and history, as well as expressive culture (Kapchan and Strong 1999).

2. The Muslim American community embraces African Americans, immigrants from every part of the world, but mostly from the Middle East and South Asia, and white converts. Muslims began arriving in the New World at the turn of the sixteenth century when European explorers and colonists crossed the Atlantic in search of new trading routes. In the period between the First and Second World Wars, Islam was a means to deflect the stigma associated with the black race. Muslims were negotiating their own understanding of the relationship between Islam and the United States through the establishment of mosques and Muslim organizations as well as through their political activities. In 1920, Muslim immigrants in Detroit initiated the Detroit Chapter of the Red Crescent and purchased plots for Muslim burials. They also founded a mosque in the Highland Park area in 1921. Another mosque was established in Cedar Rapids, Iowa, in 1934. In 1930 Fard Muhammad went to Detroit, where his teaching of Islam led to the establishment of the Nation of Islam. Fard's mission was to restore black Americans to their original divine nature, language, and culture through Islam. Under Elijah Muhammad's leadership, and with the help of Malcolm X, the Nation of Islam in the 1950s and 1960s grew to become the most successful black nationalist movement in the United States. During this period, influential organizations such as the International Muslim Society (later renamed the Federation of Islamic Associations of the United States and Canada), the Uniting Islamic Society of America, the Islamic Mission of America, and the Islamic Center of New York Foundation were established. In the past four decades, Muslim immigrants from Africa, Asia, and the Middle East came to the United States in large numbers. During the Gulf War and after 9/11, Islam was portrayed as an antidemocratic and violent religion. One of the most notable American Muslim political organizations to emerge to negotiate relations between Islamists and the United States was the Council of American-Islamic Relations (CAIR). American Muslim organizations came to present a wider spectrum of Muslims' diversity, in terms of theology, politics, and gender, in the American public square. For more information regarding major waves of Arab immigration to the United States, see Curtis (2009), Elkholy (1966), Ghanea Bassiri (2010), Naff (1993), Nyang (1999), and Orfalea (2006).

3. Bloomfield Hills, five square miles, is located in Oakland County, Michigan, about twenty miles northwest of Detroit. As of the 2010 census [retrieved August 2011], Bloomfield Hills had a population of 3,869. See http://factfinder2.census.gov/faces/tableservices/jsf/pages/productview.xhtml?src=bkmk.

4. Dearborn, 24.5 square miles, is located in the Detroit metropolitan area and Wayne County, Michigan. As of the 2010 census, it had a population of 98,153 (33.4% were of Arab ancestry). See http://quickfacts.census.gov/qfd/states/26/2621000.html.

5. The growth can be seen in the increase in the number of Islamic centers, schools, and businesses run by Muslims. There are about forty-five mosques in metro Detroit, roughly double the number ten years ago (http://www.michigan.statenews.net/story.php?rid=42441166). President Barack Obama, in his speech at Cairo, Egypt, on June 5, 2009, referred to "nearly 7 million American Muslims in our country today who, by the way, enjoy incomes and educational levels that are higher than the American

average" (http://www.whitehouse.gov/the_press_office/Remarks-by-the-President-at-Cairo-University-6-04-09/).

6. Rifa'a Rafi' al-Tahtawi (1801–1873), an Egyptian scholar (al-Azhar graduate) who spent five years (1826–1831) in Europe (Paris) as a chaplain of a group of students, emphasized that the values and principles of Islam are compatible with those of Western modernity. For Tahtawi, the most effective way to protect the homeland culture is to be receptive to the changes coming with modern cultures (Gelvin 2005, 134).

7. Ethnic stigmatizing and negative stereotyping of Arab Americans have been discussed by scholars such as Edward Said (1979, 1983, 2001), Jack Shaheen (1997, 2001), Nacos and Torres-Reyna (2007), Alia Malek (2009), and Salait (2006), among others. In his recent article, "Jihad against Islam," Robert Steinback (2011) argues how, ten years after the 9/11 attacks on the United States, a second wave of anti-Muslim hatred is sweeping the country. The outrage seems largely ginned up by politicians and others seeking to capitalize on Americans' fears. http://www.splcenter.org/get-informed/intelligence-report/browse-all-issues/2011/summer/jihad-against-islam.

8. Two factors, mainly an individual's ethnicity/religion and a "Muslim name," remained the primary causes of discrimination. On June 23, 2011, the Council on American-Islamic Relations (CAIR) and the University of California, Berkeley's Center for Race and Gender released a report based on available data and interviews with experts that documents growing Islamophobia in the United States and offers recommendations about how to challenge the troubling phenomenon.

9. Indicative of this is the recent visit of Qur'an-burning Pastor Terry Jones to Dearborn to speak at the Islamic Center of America against radical Islam. The reaction of the community, according to the *Arab American News*, was, "Terry Jones and his supporters are wrong about Islam and the Qur'an. We know it and we should show it. We welcome the opportunity to meet this man with a strong interfaith coalition and show of support for the Muslim community in Southeast Michigan. Let's meet hate with love and show Americans of other faiths what Islam is really about." For further information, see http://www.cair.com/ArticleDetails.aspx?ArticleID=26818&&name=n&&currPage=1&&Active=1. See also the 2010 legal report of the Arab American Anti-Discrimination Committee, http://www.adc.org/media/adc-publications/.

10. According to the Dearborn *Press & Guide* (January 13, 2010, vol. 93, no. 4, p. 3-A) and under the headline "Area Muslim Protestors: The Message Got Out," about 150 protesters, wearing shirts with signs that read "Not in the name of Islam," gathered outside a federal courthouse in Detroit to condemn the alleged actions of a Nigerian man charged with trying to blow up a Northwestern Airlines flight en route from Amsterdam to Detroit Metropolitan Airport. Marchers, identifying themselves as Arab Americans, were telling the world, "Islam is against terrorism."

11. Despite the negative implication of the topic, "Muslim-Western Tensions Persist," the latest Pew Global Attitudes survey (released July 21, 2011) finds somewhat of a thaw in the United States and Europe compared with five years ago. A greater percentage of Western countries' publics now see relations between themselves and Muslims as generally good compared with 2006. In four of the six largely Christian nations included in the study, most say they have a positive opinion of Muslims: United States (57% favorable), Britain (64%), France (64%), and Russia (62%). The exceptions are Germany (45%) and Spain (37%), although views toward Muslims have improved in both countries since 2006. See http://pewglobal.org/2011/07/21/muslim-western-tensions-persist/.

12. This, however, does not negate the fact that secularism (*'almāniyya*) or a secular worldview (*'almānī*) can be found, for example, among certain classes in Muslim-majority countries such as Turkey (Silverstein 2011), Iran (Osanloo 2009; Wright 2010), and Pakistan (Ziring 1997). Silverstein states that Muslims in "Turkey have religious reasons for having a secular attitude toward religion and politics" (Silverstein 2011, 15).

13. "The tension between secularism and religion was present at America's creation; a secular government, independent of all religious sects, was seen by founders of diverse private beliefs as the essential guarantor of liberty of conscience" (Jacoby 2004, 4).

14. For most Muslims, Islamic law (*shari'a*), derived from the Qur'an and Sunnah, is inseparable from daily life. Several Muslim-majority countries initiated constitutional amendments requiring that the state law conform to Shari'a principles (Hefner 2011, 3).

15. "When asked whether religion is an important part of their daily lives, 80% of Muslim Americans answer in the affirmative" (Younis 2009).

16. For the meanings of the Arabic words used in the names of these local businesses, see the glossary.

17. Muslim Americans have established institutions and organizations such as the Arab-American Anti-Discrimination Committee (ADC), American Moslem Society (AMS), Council on American-Islamic Relations (CAIR), Islamic Center of Detroit (ICD), Muslim Unity Center (MUC), Muslim Public Affairs Council (MPAC), and Islamic Cultural Institute (ICI), among others.

18. A similar spirit of protest was evident in US culture and represented by the demonstrations of public workers in Wisconsin against their state government, which they viewed as taking away their rights and privileges. In an article published in the *Nation* magazine (on February 15, 2011), John Nichols states, "Many of those who showed up for one of the first of what [was] expected to be days of ever-expanding protests borrowed . . . language and themes from the crowds that filled the streets of Cairo and other Egyptian cities to call for the end of President Hosni Mubarak's dictatorial reign." Nichols recounted that one of the phrases the protesers were using was "If Egypt Can Have Democracy, Why Can't Wisconsin?" See http://www.thenation.com/blog/158609/tens-thousands-protest-move-wisconsins-governor-destroy-public-sector-unions.

19. For further information on the history of Dearborn's Shi'a community, see Marion Mourtada (posted October 7, 2007): http://islamicinsights.com/index2.php?option=com_content&do_pdf=1&id=54.

20. The largest Sunni Muslim institutes and centers include the Islamic Association of Greater Detroit, Rochester; Islamic Center of Detroit, Detroit; Islamic Cultural Institute, Clair Shores; Muslim Community of Western Suburbs of Michigan, Canton; and Muslim Unity Center, Bloomfield Hills. The largest Shi'i Muslim institutes and centers in Michigan are in Dearborn and include the Islamic Center of America, Islamic Institute of Knowledge, Islamic House of Wisdom, and Karbala Islamic Educational Center.

21. Imam Muhammad Musa and Imam Abdul-Latif Berry, whom I interviewed, participated in the religious dialogue and signed the Code of Honor. For more information on the Muslim Code of Honor, see the appendix or http://ciomonline.com/about-us/preamble.

22. The same statement is applicable to African Americans. After calculating many negative factors, the author asserts, "These factors, plus the Wahhabi denouncement of Shi'ism have encouraged many African Americans . . . to look at Shi'ism as an alternative articulation of normative Islam" (Takim 2009, 208). It is still not clear why the converts

prefer Shi'ism. Sympathy to a sect being criticized by another sect is not enough to be fully faithul to that chosen sect.

23. For Muslims, Friday (*Jum'ah*) is the holy day of the week on which Muslims attend mosques, listen to a sermon (*Khuṭba*), and perfom congregational or collective prayer (*ṣalāt al-Jum'ah*).

24. Ayatollah Muhammad Hussein Fadlallah (1935–2010) was a renowned Lebanese Twelver Shi'a leader or *marja'*. The website of Ayatollah Fadlallah is http://www.bayynat.org.lb/.

25. The Islamic Institute of Knowledge, under the guidance of Ayatollah Shaikh Abdul-Latif Berry, has been active in the intellectual awakening of Shi'i Muslims in Dearborn. The institute has several publications, both in Arabic and English, including the *Islamic Times* (*Al-'Asr al-Islami*) as well as a website (http://iiokonline.org/) in addition to Shaikh Berry's website (www.imamberry.org).

26. For more on the *ḥusainiyya* discourse in the homeland, particularly Bahrain, see chapter 3.

27. For further information regarding Imam Mahdi Association Marjaeya, IMAM, see http://www.imam-us.org/Home/tabid/112/Default.aspx. The website has a section dedicated to the Shi'a Ayatollah and grand *marja'* al-Sistani.

28. The website of al-Sistani (http://www.sistani.org/) is accessible in six languages: Arabic, English, French, Persian, Turkish, and Urdu.

29. The Bayynat website (http://www.bayynat.org/), established in 1997, is accessible in four languages: Arabic, English, French, and Persian.

30. For more informattion on the Shi'i practice of the one-fifth (*khums*) of excess wealth, see chapter 1, note 15.

31. Most definitions of ethnic groups emphasize cultural and geographical elements. "The first of these elements is usually viewed as a social construction involving insiders and outsiders mutually acknowledging group differences in cultural beliefs and practices. Insiders and outsiders do not necessarily agree over the details of the acknowledged cultural division, nor do groups necessarily develop similar interpretations of the relative merits of the various distinguishing cultural attributes. The second basic element used to define an ethnic group pertains to geographical origins, and therefore social origins, that are foreign to the host society. While this element usually has an objective basis, it is also partly subjective. The native-born generations of an ethnic group sometimes continue to be identified by outsiders, and in-group members may self-identify, in terms of their foreign origin" (Sanders 2002, 327).

32. Although "American identity has also been more fragile than other national identities, which have been moored in commonalities beyond the state: in ethnicity, religion, language, and histories far more ancient," it has always been ahead of its time (Spiro 2008, 7).

33. Examples displaying the impact of Muslim values on changing certain negative patterns of behavior of non-Muslim Americans are numerous. "In the struggle against drug sales and drug-related crimes in Brooklyn, for example, a mosque took an active role in cooperation with the police. Reports of this noted that Muslims 'risked personal safety to defend the area against drug dealers' and resulted in local non-Muslims saying, 'Thank God for the Muslims.' A similar activist Muslim program has helped reduce drug dealing in some housing projects in Washington" (Voll 1993, 112).

34. The verse is "Verily never will Allah change the condition of a people until they change it themselves [with their own souls]" (Qur'an 13:11).

35. In her study of Muslim communities in Chicago, Schmidt (2004) focused on two main Sunni Muslim immigrant ethnic groups from the Middle East and the South Asian peninsula.

36. Some examples of the websites of Muslim institutes and centers that are actively used by Muslims in Michigan include, for example:

American Moslem Society, Dearborn: http://www.masjiddearborn.org/
Al-Islah Islamic Center, Hamtramck: http://www.umich.edu/~biid/FM_Al_Islah_Islamic_Center.html
Council of Islamic Organizations of Michigan, Detroit: http://ciomonline.com/
Islamic Association of Greater Detroit, Rochester: http://www.iagd.net/
Islamic Center and Mosque of Grand Rapids: http://icgr.homestead.com/
Islamic Center of America, Dearborn: http://www.waymarking.com/waymarks/WM2ZAC_Islamic_Center_of_America_Dearborn_Michigan
Islamic Center of America, Columbiaville: http://www.icofa.com/
Islamic Center of Detroit: http://icd-center.org/
Islamic Center of Greater Lansing: http://lansingislam.com/
Islamic Insight, Dearborn: http://islamicinsights.com/about-us.html
Karbala Islamic Educational Center, Dearborn: http://karbala.org/
Islamic Cultural Institute, Clair Shore: http://www.icionline.org/
Muslim Unity Center, Bloomfield Hills: http://www.muslimunitycenter.org/
Flint Islamic Center: http://www.flintislamiccenter.com/
Albanian Islamic Center Michigan, Harper Woods: http://www.facebook.com/pages/Albanian-Islamic-Center-Michigan/143500942353031
Kalamazoo Islamic center, Kalamazoo: http://kiconline.org/
Islamic Institute of Knowledge, Dearborn: http://iiokonline.org/
Islamic Organization of America, Warren: http://www.ionaonline.org/
Islamic Society of Greater Jackson, Jackson: http://www.lansingislam.com/contact.htm
Muslim Center, Detroit: http://www.muslimcentermcc.org/
Muslim Community of Western Suburbs of Michigan, Canton: http://www.mcws.org/home
Muslim Community Association of Ann Arbor: http://www.mca-aa.org/
Tawheed Center, Detroit: http://www.masjidtawheed.org/
Imam Mahdi Association of Marjaeya, Dearborn: www.imam-us.org

37. For more information on the Muslim Unity Center, see http://www.muslimunity-center.org/.

38. For more information on the Islamic Institute of Knowledge, see http://iiokonline.org/.

39. On one online forum (http://muslimonline.org/forum/), posted on July 11, 2011, people were encouraged to "Come. Meet somebody new. Sunni or Shia. Share ideas. Have some fun. Words not guns. In this city, you'll be helped. To be united, be yourself."

CONCLUSION

1. "If any one slew a person—unless it be for murder or for spreading mischief in the land—it would be as if he slew the whole people: and if any one saved a life, it would be as if he saved the life of the whole people" (Qur'an 5:32).

2. This statement is based on an interview with Shaikh (Sayyid) Muhammad Baqir al-Kashmiri, the chair of the Imam Mahdi Association of Marjaeya (IMAM) in Dearborn, on July 20, 2011.

3. The concept of "cover" (*satr*) is not restricted to the notion of covering things or bodies (veil or curtain). In the Muslim and Arab contexts, "cover" (*satr*) is metaphorically used to indicate social cover/shelter (in terms of modesty or chastity), economic security (financial improvement), integrity (self-reliance), divine protection, and religious tranquility. One of the glorious names of God is the "Coverer" (*as-Sattār*).

4. "Thus We have appointed you a middle community [*ummah waṣaṭ*], that ye may be witnesses against mankind, and that the messenger may be a witness against you" (Qur'an 2:143).

Glossary of Arabic Terms

adab	Literally, "literature." Good manners or propriety.
adhān (*azān*)	Islamic call to prayer that is broadcast from mosques five times a day.
'ahd (*al-'ahd*)	Literally, a pledge; in Sufism, a covenant between a Sufi leader and a disciple *(murīd)*.
ahl al-bait	Literally, "people of the house," but in the Muslim context, the Prophet Muhammad's family and descendants, who are revered by all Muslims.
ahl al-kitāb	Non-Muslim adherents to a religion that has a revealed book, including Jews and Christians.
'ālam	World or universe (see also *kaun*).
'ālam al-ākhira	The other world, the hereafter or afterlife.
'ālam al-mlā'ka	The world of angels. Angels are believed to be created of light. They neither eat nor drink.
'ālam ar-rūḥ	The world of spirits.
'ālim (pl. *'ulamā'* or *'ulama*)	A scholar or person of religious learning.
'almānī (*'almāniyya*)	Secular or secularism.
arba'īn	Literally, "fortieth," referring to the forty days that follow the death of a person. It is also used to signify the forty days that follow the birth of a baby. For the Shi'a, it indicates the forty days that follow the day of 'Ashura.

'ārif bi-Allah	A person (Sufi) who is acquainted with God or Allah.
'aṣabiyyah	Tribal or social solidarity that is based on blood or kin relationships, supported by religious beliefs and political affiliations.
ash-shahādatain	The two witnesses, "there is no God but Allah and Muhammad is His Messenger," that are considered the first of the five pillars of Islam.
'Ashura (*'āshūrā'*)	The tenth day of Muharram, the first month of the Islamic calendar. On this day in 680 CE, Husain, the grandson of the Prophet Muhammad, was martyred. Muslims commemorate that day, but the Shi'a mourn it through various rituals (see also *Muharram*).
baraka	A cosmic benevolent force, blessing, or divine grace that has the power of both healing and making wonders. It plays a significant role in mystical or esoteric modes of thought.
barzakh	Eschatology, or a period of time between death and resurrection, the life beyond the grave, between and betwixt, liminal, mediation, or intermediary between two entities.
bāṭin	What is hidden, interior, invisible, or esoteric.
dhikr (*zikr*)	Oral, bodily, or ritualistic remembrance of God.
fiṭrī	Natural or innate disposition.
futuwwa	Literally, young manliness; but within Sufi context it connotes a combination of chivalry, bravery, and nobility.
ghaib	Literally, "absence," or what exists but is invisible or not present. The belief in the unseen or invisible, *ghaib* (known only to God) is a basic doctrine of Islam. Parts of the mysteries of the unseen, not the absolute *ghaib*, may be disclosed through revelation (as in the case of the prophets) or visions and dreams.
al-ghaibah (*al-ghaiba*)	The occultation of the twelfth and last Imam (al-Mahdi). In the Shi'i worldviews, there is a minor occultation (*al-ghaiba al-ṣughrā*) as well as a major or prolonged occultation (*al-ghaiba al-kubrā*).

hadith	The tradition, exemplary sayings, and actions of the Prophet Muhammad.
Hadith Qudsi (*ḥīdth qudsī*)	The divine or sacred tradition believed to be words of God revealed to the Prophet Muhammad but not found in the Qur'an.
ḥaḍra	Within Sufi contexts, a gathering to participate in the discourse and performance of the *dhikr*.
ḥajj	A pilgrimage, one of the five pillars of Islam, which includes certain rituals performed at the Ka'ba (in Mecca), Mina, and Mount 'Arafat (in Arabia, during the month of Dhu al-Ḥijjah, the last month of the Islamic calendar).
ḥalāl	What is legally permissible and acceptable according to Islamic law and ethics.
ḥarām	What is forbidden according to Islamic law and ethics.
ḥasad	Envy or a malicious desire to possess what somebody else has.
ḥawza	A term used by the Shi'a to refer to a center of learning or school.
ḥidāya	Guidance. The Qur'an and the tradition of the Prophet are the core sources of religious guidance in Islam.
ḥijra	Literally, "migration." In Islam, it refers to the migration of the Prophet Muhammad and his companions from Mecca to Medina in 622 CE. It also indicates the beginning of the Muslim calendar (*Hijriyya*).
ḥulm (*ḥilm*, colloquial in Egypt)	A general category of dreams, both good and bad.
ḥusainiyya	Derived from the name of Imam Husain, Husain-related recitations and rituals as well as a building in which such recitations and rituals are performed. *Husainiyya* and *ma'tam* are used interchangeably by the Shi'a.
iḥrām	A necessary spiritual and physical state a Muslim must experience in order to perform the pilgrimage (*hajj*) properly.

'ilm ladunnī	Knowledge bestowed by God on specific people (such as prophets, saints, and pious persons).
imām (Imam)	A religious leader; a person who leads Muslims in prayers. Also used by the Sunni as a formal title like "the Grand Imam of al-Azhar" or as an honorific title, such as Imam Shafi'ī. For the Shi'a, Imam is one of the Twelvers, descendants of the Prophet Muhammad.
imamate (*Imāmah*)	A Shi'i doctrine of the spiritual leadership (*walāyah*) of the Twelve Imams, including the Hidden Imam (al-Mahdi) and his occultation (*ghaiba*).
infitāḥ	Open-door or free-market policy introduced in Egypt in the 1970s.
'irfān	A spiritual position based on the inner spiritual state of a person, mostly Shi'i, seeking unity with God through mystic or Sufi practices (see also *m'arifa*).
iṣlāḥ	Social, economic, and political reform.
al-isrā' wa al-mi'rāj	The Prophet Muhammad's Night Journey, including two events: *Isrā'*, the journey from the sacred mosque in Mecca to the farthest mosque of Jerusalem, and *Mi'rāj*, his ascendance to the highest point of the seventh heaven.
istikhāra	A nonobligatory prayer, followed by supplications in which a person asks God's guidance in making the right decision concerning critical matters. Through dreams or visions the answer is often realized or predicted.
ithna'ashariyya	The "Twelver Shi'a," or those who believe in the Twelve Imams. It is used interchangeably with Ja'fari Shi'a.
Ja'farī (Ja'fari)	The Ja'fari School, established by Ja'far as-Ṣādiq, the sixth Shi'a Imam, which differs from the four Sunni schools in jurisprudence and certain religious matters. The Ja'fari School is recognized by the Sunni institutes, including al-Azhar.
jihād (*Jihad*)	Literally, "struggle"; refers to people's spiritual struggle to control their inner life. The objective

	of *jihād* is to attain salvation or liberation through one's own efforts. *Jihād* is not restricted to the popular meaning of a religiously and politically externalized and mobilized war.
jinn	A category of invisible beings also known as *'afārīt* (sing. *'ifrīt*), believed to be created of fire. There are good (Muslim) and bad or evil *jinn*. They eat, drink, and procreate.
jum'ah	Friday, which is the holy day of the week on which Muslims attend mosques, listen to a sermon (*Khuṭba*), and pray together as a congregation (*ṣalāt al-Jum'ah*).
Ka'ba	The holy site or building in Mecca toward which Muslims direct themselves during prayers.
kābūs	A nightmare or a category of dreams that always contain stressful, terrible, and evil matters causing negative emotions in the dreamer.
Karbala	One of the holiest cities for the Shi'a, located about sixty-two miles southwest of Baghdad, Iraq.
kashf (*al-kashf*)	Within Sufi contexts, the disclosure or unveiling of what is hidden or veiled.
kaun	Cosmos or universe (see also *'ālam*).
kawthar	A river in Paradise.
khair	Goodness, blessing, or unlimited good.
khayāl	Mental and social imagination.
khums	One-fifth of the interest accrued, paid by a Shi'i person to the *shaikh* or *marja'*; different from almsgiving (*zakāt*), which must be given by all Muslims.
kuttāb	A local traditional institute for teaching and memorizing the Qur'an.
madhhab (*mazhab*)	A Muslim school of thought concerning Islamic jurisprudence (*fiqh*). Sunni jurisprudence schools include Shafi'i, Maliki, Hanafi, and Hanbali, while Shi'i jurisprudence schools include, for example, Ja'fari.
madrasa	A center of learning or school.
al-Mahdī (al-Mahdi)	The rightly guided one who is believed by all Muslims to appear before the end of the

	world to restore justice. For the Shi'a, however, al-Mahdi is identified as the twelfth and last Imam, and he will reappear from his occultation.
majdhūb (*jadhb*)	A state of mind in which a person is described as being attracted to divinity.
m'arifa (pl. *ma'ārif*)	Literally, "knowledge"; in Sufism, a direct and spiritual knowledge of God through heart (*qalb*). See *'irfān*.
marja' al-taqlīd (*Marja'iyya*)	For the Usuli Twelvers Shi'a, *marja'* (pl. *marāji'*) means a cleric or immanent scholar serving as a source of emulation for his followers (*muqallidūn*, [sing. *muqallid*]).
marqad (pl. *marāqid*)	Literally, a "grave." Also used to refer to a Shi'i holy shrine (in Najaf and Karbala in Iraq, for example).
ma'ṣūmiyya	The notion of infallibility of the Shi'i Imams as being descendants of the Prophet through his daughter Fatima.
mawlid	A birthday celebration of a prominent Muslim figure or Sufi leader.
mawlid an-nabī	The Prophet's birthday celebration.
Muharram	The first month of the Islamic calendar. Muslims commemorate the tenth day ('Ashura) of Muharram in which Husain, grandson of the Prophet, was martyred. The Shi'a mourn that day through annual rituals and liturgies of Muharram (see also *'Ashura*).
muntada	A Muslim online forum.
murīd	A Sufi disciple.
muwāṭin	A citizen or "national" of a specific country.
nafs	Self or psyche.
qurbān	An offering for sacrifice.
Raḥma	Mercy, compassion.
Rasūl	A messenger of God.
Risālah	Implies multiple meanings such as a message, letter, book, or thesis written to fulfill higher-education requirements.

al-rizq (*ar-rizq*)	Livelihood that, when associated with religious meanings, implies cosmic and divine sustenance.
rūḥ	Soul, spirit.
ru'yā	A dream vision or revelatory dream that enjoys higher-order meaning and differs from other categories of dreams. In accordance with Islamic tradition, dream vision is one of forty-six parts of prophecy.
ru'ya	Waking vision or sight.
ṣabr	Patience, a value referring to the ability to tolerate pain or illness as well as to undertake and tirelessly endure arduous activities without complaining. Patience is emphasized by Sufi and mystic worldviews.
salafiyya (Salafism)	A Sunni purist-reform movement of the late nineteenth and early twentieth centuries calling for a return to Islam as understood and enacted by the pious forefathers or ancestors.
ṣalāh or *ṣalāt* (pl. *ṣalawāt*)	Muslim prayer. A Muslim must perform five prayers a day, every day, starting at dawn and ending at nighttime.
satr (*as-satr*)	A social, economic, and divine cover, akin to the notion of divine providence.
Sayyid	A name of a person as well as a title equivalent to "Mr." as used in the West. For the Shi'a, "Sayyid" refers to one of the descendants of the Prophet Muhammad's family (Hāshimī or Qurayshī). Another version of Sayyid is Sīdī (see also *Sīdī*).
shafā'a	Literally, "intercession" or "mediation"; religiously refers to invocations and prayers to God on behalf of other persons. Among the folk, however, it is believed that prophets, saints (*awliyā'*), or righteous imams may intercede with God on behalf of their followers.
shahādatain (sing. *shahāda*)	The two testimonies declaring that there is no God but Allah and that Muhammad is His Messenger. They constitute the basic doctrinal condition for a person to be a Muslim.
shahīd	A martyr or a person who sacrifices his soul defending his religion, country, honor, and

	property. The *shahīd* is believed to be alive in heaven and enjoys the prominent status of being close to Allah.
shaikh (fem. *shaikha*)	A person of religious learning. Also a title indicating an elderly and/or political figure (mainly in the Arab Gulf countries, including the Emirates).
shari'a	Islamic law that is derived from the Qur'an and the tradition of the Prophet Muhammad.
Shi'a	The second-largest denomination of Islam (after the Sunni) that includes those whose forebearers supported 'Ali Ibn Abi Talib, cousin and son-in-law of the Prophet, who was to be the fourth caliph but who was killed in 661 AD. Shi'i Muslims are divided into various divisions (the Twelvers, Ismaili, Zaydi, Druz, Nizari, and Bohara, among others).
Sidi (Sīdī)	An honorific used in addressing a revered *shaikh* or religious (Sufi) leader. In Muslim context, I suggest the term "Sīdī" to be used as equivalent to the term "Saint" (see also *Sayyid*).
siḥr	Magic, or the manipulation of supernatural forces or occult-hidden knowledge to achieve certain goals, mostly destructive.
ṣilat ar-raḥim	A Muslim moral principle motivating people to maintain blood or kin and affinal relationships.
Sunni	The largest denomination of Islam that follows praxis and sayings (tradition) of the Prophet Muhammad. The Sunnis have various schools of jurisprudence (*Madhhābih*).
tafsīr	Exegeses or interpretations of the Qur'an.
ṭahārah (*ṭuhr*)	Purity or cleanliness. The purification of the body and the place as a necessary condition for performing religious rituals.
taqiyya	Dissimulation or extreme caution practiced by the Shi'a in times of critical threat where they are rendered religiously and politically undetectable by means of concealment, abstinence, withdrawal, avoidance, or reservation.
ṭarīqa (pl. *ṭuruq*)	A Sufi order headed by a Sufi leader.

taṣawwuf	Muslim mysticism or Sufism (*ṣufiyya*, *ṣufī*) including different Sufi orders (*ṭuruq*, sing. *ṭarīqa*) whose aim is to reach the truth (*ḥaqīqa*) and achieve unity with God.
tawḥīd	The Muslim doctrine of the oneness of God.
ta'ziya	Condolence offered to the bereaved for their lost or dead one. Within the Shi'i context, mournful elegies commemorating the martyrdom of Imam Husain.
'umāmah	A turban of different shapes and colors Muslim leaders or *shaikhs* wear on their heads. Sunni *shaikhs* wear a red fez wrapped with a white sheet. A Shi'i *shaikh* or Sayyid who is a descendant of the Prophet's family (*ahl al-bait*) wears a black turban.
ummah	Universal Muslim community.
wahhābiyya (Wahhabism)	A movement within the Sunnis established in Saudi Arabia by Mohammad ibn 'Abd al-Wahhāb (1703–1792) that regards the Qur'an and Hadith as fundamental texts and considers folk religion and practices of Sufism and sainthood as forms of non-orthodox Islam.
waḥy	Revelation.
walīy (pl. *awlyiā'*) (*walī*, colloquial in Egypt)	A pious person who is near to and protected by God. For the Shi'a, *walīy* refers to an imam.
waqt	Time. Also indicates a certain period or interval of time determined or measured for certain activities. See also *zaman*.
ẓāhir	What is apparent, exterior, visible, and exoteric.
zaman (*zamān*)	Time that denotes either a long period of time, such as a century, or a short period of time, such as an hour (see also *waqt*).
zamzam	Blessed water gushing from a miraculously generated well located within the Ka'ba or Masjid al-Haram in Mecca.
ziyāra (*Ziyara*)	Literally, "visitation," but in a religious (Islamic) context, paying a visit to a sacred place or shrine.

Bibliography

Al Abed, Ibrahim, and Peter Hellyer. 1997. *United Arab Emirates: A New Perspective*. London: Trident Press.

al-'Afifi, Abd al-Hakim. 1993. *Al-Ahlam wa al-Kawabis: Tafsir'ilmi wa-Dini*. Cairo: Dar al-Misriyya al-Lubnaniyya.

Aitchison, Cara, Peter Hopkins, and Mei-Po Kwan. 2007. *Geographies of Muslim Identities: Diaspora, Gender and Belonging*. Williston, VT: Ashgate.

Al-'Akili, Muhammad M. 1992. *Ibn Seerin's Dictionary of Dreams according to Islamic Inner Tradition*. Philadelphia: Pearl.

Albrow, Martin. 1996. *The Global Age: State and Society beyond Modernity*. Cambridge: Polity Press.

'Ali, 'Isam al-Din Muhammad. 1987. *Tafsir al-Ahlam: Ru'ya Islamiyya Jadida*. Alexandria, Egypt: Al-Markaz al-'Arabi li al-nashr wa al-tawzı'.

Allen, Chris. 2010. *Islamophobia*. Surrey, UK: Ashgate.

Alvstad, Erik. 2010. "Encounters between Believers and Non-Believers in a Symbolic Universe: Religious Dialogue and Controversy on the Internet." *Nordic Journal of Religion and Society* 23 (1): 71–86.

al-'Amily, 'Ali al-Kurani. 2004. *'Aṣr al-ẓuhūr*. Beirut: Dar al-Muhjjabah.

Amir-Moezzi, Mohammad Ali. 1994. *The Divine Guide in Early Shi'ism: The Sources of Esotericism in Islam*. Translated by David Streight. Albany: State University of New York Press.

———. 2011. *The Spirituality of Shi'i Islam: Belief and Practices*. London and New York: I. B. Tauris.

Anderson, Benedict. 1983. *Imagined Communities: Reflections on the Spread of Nationalism*. London: Verso.

Appadurai, Arjun. 1990. "Disjuncture and Difference in the Global Cultural Economy." *Theory, Culture and Society* 7 (2): 295–310.

———. 2001. "Grassroots Globalization and the Research Imagination." In *Globalization*, edited by Arjun Appadurai, 1–21. Durham, NC: Duke University Press.

Arberry, A. J. 1950. *Sufism*. London: Allen & Unwin.

'Ārif, Abū al-Fidā Muammad Izzat Muammad. 1996. *Tafsīr al-Ahlām bi-al-Qurān*. Beirut: Dar Uli al-Nuha.

Arjomand, Said Amin. 1995. "Unity and Diversity in Islamic Fundamentalism." In *Fundamentalisms Comprehended*, edited by Martin E. Marty and R. Scott Appleby, 179–98. Chicago: University of Chicago Press.

Asad, Talal. 1986. *The Idea of Anthropology of Islam* (Occasional Papers Series). Washington, DC: Center for Contemporary Arab Studies, Georgetown University.

———. 1993. *Genealogies of Religion: Discipline and Reasons of Power in Christianity and Islam*. Baltimore: Johns Hopkins University Press.

———. 2003. *Formations of the Secular: Christianity, Islam, Modernity*. Stanford, CA: Stanford University Press.

———. 2007. *On Suicide Bombing*. New York: Columbia University Press.

'Ashur, Said Abd al-Fattah. 1998. *Al-Sayyid Ahmad al-Badawi: Shaikh wa Tariqa*. Cairo: Al-Haiya al-Misriyya lil-ktab.

al-'Asqalani, Ahmad Ibn Hajar. 1959. *Fatḥ al-Barī fī Sharḥ Ṣaḥīḥ al-Bukharī [Kitab al-Ta'bir]*. Vol. 12. Damascus: Dār al-Fikr.

Aswad, Barbara C., and Barbara Bilge, eds. 1996. *Family and Gender among American Muslims: Issues Facing Middle Eastern Immigrants and Their Descendants*. Philadelphia: Temple University Press.

el-Aswad, el-Sayed. 1987. "Death Ritual in Rural Egyptian Society: A Symbolic Study." *Urban Anthropology and Studies of Cultural Systems and World Economic Development* 16 (2): 205–41.

———.1988. "Patterns of Thought: An Anthropological Study of World Views of Rural Egyptian Society." Unpublished PhD thesis, University of Michigan, Ann Arbor.

———. 1990a. *Aṣ-ṣabr fi at-turāth ash-sha'bī al-misī: Dirāsa anthropolojiyya* (*The Concept of Patience in Egyptian Folklore*). Alexandria, Egypt: Munsha'at al-Ma'raf.

———. 1990b. "Tasawwur ru'yat al-'ālam fī al-dirāsāt al-anthropolojiyya (The Concept of 'World View' in Anthropological Inquiries [with English abstract])." *National Review of Social Sciences* (Cairo) 27 (1): 9–54.

———. 1990c. "Ath-thaqāfa wa at-tafkīr ru'yat anthropolojiyya (Culture and Thought: An Anthropological View) [with English abstract]." *National Review of Social Sciences* (Cairo) 27 (3): 71–104.

———. 1993a. "At-tanshi'a al-igtimā'iyya wa takwīn ru'a al-'ālam lada at-tifl: Dirāsa muqāranah bain mugtama' khalijy wa mugtama' misrī(Socialization and the Construction of World Views of the Child: Comparative Study between a Gulf Society and a Rural Egyptian Society)." *Dirasat* (Studies). Sharjah, UAE: Emirates Writers and Literates Union, vol. 6: 7–30.

———. 1993b. Rumūz mihwariyya fī at-turāth ashsha'bī al-misrī: Dirāsa anthropolojiyya. *Al-Ma'thurat al-Sha'biyyah* (Qatar) (29): 77–91.

———. 1994. "The Cosmological Belief System of Egyptian Peasants." *Anthropos* 89 (4/6): 359–77.

———. 1995. "Bedouin World Views: Stability and Change in Visions of the Bedouins of the United Arab Emirates." Paper presented at the ninety-fourth annual meeting of the American Anthropological Association, Washington, DC, November 14–19.

———. 1996a. *Al-bait ash-sha'bī: Dirāsa anthropolojiyya lil 'imāra ash-sh'abiyya wa ath-thqafa at-taqlidiyya li mujtama' al-Imārāt* (*The Folk House: An Anthropological Study of Folk Architecture and Traditional Culture of the Emirates Society*). Al-Ain: UAE University Press.

———. 1996b. "Ru'ā al-'ālm fī al-adab ash-sha'bī bi mujtama' al-Imārāt." *al-Ma'thurat al-Sha'biyyah* 38 (April 10): 7–26.

———. 1996c. "Ṣurat al-ākhar bain ath-thabāt wa at-taghayyur: Dirāsa anthropolojiyya muqārna litullāb min mujtama'ain 'arabiyyain." *Journal of the Social Sciences* (Kuwait) 24 (1): 207–41.

———. 1996d. *Athar al-rafāhiya 'ala anmāṭ as-sulūk ladā ash-shābāb bi mujtama' al-Imārāt* (*The Reality of the Youth of the United Arab Emirates*). Sharjah: Sociological Association of the UAE, 15–38.

———. 1999a. "Manāhij at-taḥlīl ar-ramzī fī al-anthropolojiya wa al-folklore." *Al-Ma'thurat al-Sha'biyyah* 53–54 (January/April): 30–55.

———. 1999b. "Hierarchy and Symbolic Construction of the Person among Rural Egyptians." *Anthropos* 94:431–45.

———. 2001a. "The Ethnography of Invisible Spheres." *AAA Anthropology Newsletter* (Middle East Section) 42 (6).

———. 2001b. "Key Symbols in the Folklore of the Emirates." Translated from Arabic by Salwa Al-Misned and reviewed by the author. *Al-Ma'thurat al Sha'biyyah* 16 (62): 8–27.

———. 2002. *Religion and Folk Cosmology: Scenarios of the Visible and Invisible in Rural Egypt*. Westport, CT: Praeger.

———. 2003a. "Sanctified Cosmology: Maintaining Muslim Identity with Globalism." *Journal of Social Affairs* 24 (80): 65–94.

———. 2003b. "Islam in Two Worlds: Global Violence and Changing Images of the Muslims in the Homeland and Diaspora." Paper presented at the Society for Anthropology of Religion meeting, Providence, RI, April 24–26.

———. 2004a. "Sacred Networks: Sainthood in Regional Sanctified Cults in the Egypt Delta." In *Yearbook of the Sociology of Islam*, Vol. 5, edited by Georg Stauth, 5:124–41. Bielefeld, Germany: Universität Bielefeld.

———. 2004b. "Viewing the World through Upper Egyptian Eyes: From Regional Crisis to Global Blessing." In *Upper Egypt:Identity and Change*, edited by Nicholas Hopkins and Reem Saad, 55–78. Cairo: American University in Cairo Press.

———. 2005a. "The Nature of the Creator." In *Archetypes and Motifs in Folklore: A Handbook*, edited by Jane Garry and Hasan El-Shamy, 3–8. Armonk, NY: M. E. Sharpe.

———. 2005b. "Creation Myth: Cosmogony and Cosmology." In *Archetypes and Motifs in Folklore: A Handbook*, edited by Jane Garry and Hasan El-Shamy, 24–30. Armonk, NY: M. E. Sharpe.

———. 2005c. "Magic Bodily Members: Human Eye and Hand." In *Archetypes and Motifs in Folklore: A Handbook*, edited by Jane Garry and Hasan El-Shamy, 139–146. Armonk, NY: M. E. Sharpe.

———. 2005d. "The United Arab Emirates." In *Worldmark Encyclopedia of Religious Practices*, edited by Thomas Riggs. Farmington Hills, MI: Gale Group.

———. 2005e. "At-tamāthul wa at-tamāyuz fī al-zayy al-'Arabī al-Khalījī: Ru'iyah wa qirā'ah fī al-dilālāt al-ramziyyah fī thaqāfat as-Satr." *Journal of Human Sciences* 11 (4): 158–92.

———. 2005f. *Al-Dīn wa al-taṣawwur ash-shabī lil-kaun: Sinario al-ẓāhir wa al-bāṭin fi al-mujtama' al-qarawī al-miṣrī.* Cairo: Al-majlis al-A'la lil-thaqafa.

———. 2006a. "Spiritual Genealogy: Sufism and Saintly Places in the Nile Delta." *International Journal of Middle East Studies* 38 (4): 501–18.

———. 2006b. "The Dynamics of Identity Reconstruction among Arab Communities in the US." *Anthropos* 101 (1): 111–21.

———. 2007a. "Dreams and the Construction of Reality: Symbolic Transformations of the Seen and the Unseen in the Egyptian Imagination." Paper presented at the AAA Annual Meeting, Washington, DC, November 28–December 2.

———. 2007b. "Ethnography of Cyberspace: Globalism, Localism and Cyber-Grassroots in Bahrain." *CyberOrient*. Accessed July 4, 2007. http://www.digitalislam.eu/article.do?articleId=3793.

———. 2008a. "Al-Istishrāq al-Jadīd: Jadaliyyat al-Thunā'iyya al-Thaqāfiyya bayn al-Gharb/al-Sharq wa al-Gharb/al-Islam." *Thaqafat* (University of Bahrain Press) 21: 204–33.

———. 2008b. "Art, Religion and History: The Case of Bahrain." *Tabsir: Insight on Islam and the Middle East* (February 9, 2008). http://tabsir.net/?p=452.

———. 2009. "Heritage in a Global Era: The Integration of Modernity and Tradition in the UAE." *Tabsir: Insight on Islam and the Middle East* (March 23, 2009). http://tabsir.net/?p=834#more-834.

———. 2010a. "Dreams and the Construction of Reality: Symbolic Transformation of the Seen and Unseen in the Egyptian Imagination." *Anthropos* 105 (2): 441–53.

———. 2010b. "Narrating the Self among Arab Americans: A Bridging Discourse between Arab Tradition and American Culture." *Digest of Middle East Studies* 19 (2): 234–48.

———. 2010c. "The Perceptibility of the Invisible Cosmology: Religious Rituals and Embodied Spirituality among the Bahraini Shi'a." *Anthropology of the Middle East* 5 (2): 59–76.

———. 2010d. "Al-Dilālāt al-Ramziyya lil-Zayy al-'Arabī al-Khalījī." *Turath* (periodicals published by the Zayed Center of History and Heritage) 129 (5): 29–35.

———. 2010e. "Athar al-thaqāfah al-sha'biyya 'ala ashkāl al-itisāl al-aliktroni bayn al-shabab bi mujtama' al-Imarat (The Impact of Folk Culture on Electronic Communication among the Youth of the Emirates Society)." *Turath* (periodicals published by the Zayed Center of History and Heritage) 130:47–51.

———. 2011a. "Breadom." *Tabsir: Insight on Islam and the Middle East* (February 13). http://tabsir.net/?p=1370#more-1370.

———. 2011b. "Arab Americans' Hybrid Identity." *Tabsir: Insight on Islam and the Middle East* (February 23). http://tabsir.net/?p=1364#more-1364.

———. 2011c. "Social Networking: United Arab Emirates." In *Encyclopedia of Social Networks*, edited by George A. Barnett, vol. 1, 897–98. Thousand Oaks, CA: Sage.

———. 2011d. "Authenticity, Identity and the Spirit of the UAE Union." *Tabsir: Insight on Islam and the Middle East* (November 23). http://tabsir.net/?p=1635#more-1635.

———. 2011e. "Negotiating Heritage and Identity: Cases from Arab Gulf Societies." Paper presented at the 110th Annual Meeting of the American Anthropological Association, Montreal, Canada, November 16–20.

———. 2011f. "Religious Rituals in the Making of Sacred Space: An Ethnographic and Cross Cultural Study of Sunni and Shi'i Communities in the Middle East." Paper presented at the Annual Meeting of the American Academy of Religion, San Francisco, CA, November 18–21.

———. 2012a. "Sunni: 1920 to Present." In *Middle East*, vol. 1 of *Cultural Sociology of the Middle East, Asia, and Africa: An Encyclopedia*, edited by Andrea L. Stanton. Thousand Oaks, CA: Sage.

———. 2012b. "Shi'a: 1920 to Present." In *Africa*, vol. 2 of *Cultural Sociology of the Middle East, Asia, and Africa: An Encyclopedia*, edited by Edward Ramsamy. Thousand Oaks, CA: Sage.

Austin, Lewis. 1977. "Visual Symbols, Political Ideology, and Culture." *Ethos* 5:306–25.

Awn, Peter J. 1987. "Sufism." In *The Encyclopedia of Religion*, edited by Mercea Eliade. New York: Macmillan.

Axel, Brian Keith. 2004. "The Context of Diaspora." *Cultural Anthropology* 19 (1): 26–60.

Ayoub, Mahmoud. 1992. Foreword to Muhammad M. Al-Akili, *Ibn Seerin's Dictionary of Dreams According to Islamic Inner Tradition*. Philadelphia: Pearl.

Bahry, Louay. 2000. "The Socioeconomic Foundations of the Shiite Opposition in Bahrain." *Mediterranean Quarterly* 1 (3): 129–43.

Barakat, Halim. 1993. *The Arab World: Society, Culture, and State*. Berkeley: University of California Press.

Barber, B. R. 1995. *Jihad vs. McWorld*. New York: Times Books.

Barth, Fredrik. 1987.*Cosmologies in the Making: A Generative Approach to Cultural Variation in Inner New Guinea*. Cambridge: Cambridge University Press.

Basso, Ellen B. 1987. "The Implication of a Progressive Theory of Dreaming." In *Dreaming: Anthropological and Psychological Interpretations*, edited by Barbara Tedlock, 86–104. New York: Cambridge University Press.

Bearman, P., Rudolf Peter, and Frank E Vogel. 2006. *The Islamic School of Law: Evolution, Devolution, and Progress*. Cambridge, MA: Islamic Legal Studies Program, Harvard Law School.

Berger, Peter L. 1997, October 29. "Epistemological Modesty: An Interview with Peter Berger." *Christian Century*, 972–78.

———. 1999. "The Desecularization of the World: A Global Overview." In *The Desecularization of the World: Resurgent Religion and World Politics*, edited by Peter L. Berger, 1–18. Grand Rapids, MI: Eerdmans.

———. 2002. Introduction to *Many Globalizations: Cultural Diversity in the Contemporary World*, edited by Peter Berger and Samuel P. Huntington, 1–16. Oxford: Oxford University Press.

Beyer, P. 1994. *Religion and Globalization*. London: Sage.

Bigelow, Anna. 1999. "The Sufi Practice of Friendship, the Suhrawardi *Ṭarīqa* and the Development of a Middle Road." *Jusur* 15:14–49.

bin Osman, Mohd Taib. 1972. "Patterns of Supernatural Premises Underlying the Institution of the Bomoh in Malay Culture." *Bijdragen tot de Taal-Land-en Volkekunde* 128: 219–34.

Bloch, Maurice. 1977. "The Past and Present in Future." *Man* 12 (2): 278–92.

Bonnemaison, Joel. 2005. *Culture and Space: Conceiving a New Geography*. London: I. B. Tauris.

Boosahda, Elizabeth. 2003. *Arab-American Faces and Voices: The Origins of an Immigrant Community*. Austin: University of Texas Press.

Boulding, Kenneth E. 1956. *The Image: Knowledge in Life and Society*. Ann Arbor: University of Michigan Press.

Bourdieu, Pierre. 1963. "The Attitude of the Algerian Peasant toward Time." In *Mediterranean Countrymen: Essays in the Social Anthropology of the Mediterranean*, ed. J. Pitt-Rivers, 55–72. Paris: Mouton.

———. 1977. *Outline of a Theory of Practice*. Translated by Richard Nice. Cambridge: Cambridge University Press.

Brasher, Brenda E. 2001. *Give Me That Online Religion*. San Francisco: Jossey-Bass.

Brenneis, Donald. 1987. "Performing Passions: Aesthetics and Politics in an Occasionally Egalitarian Community." *American Ethnologist* 14 (2): 236–50.

Brubaker, Roger. 2010. "Ethnicity in Post–Cold War Europe, East and West." In *Ethnic Europe: Mobility, Identity, and Conflict in a Globalized World*, edited by Roland Hsu, 44–62. Palo Alto, CA: Stanford University Press.

Buehler, Arthur F. 1998. *Sufi Heirs of the Prophet: The Indian Naqshbandiyya and the Rise of the Mediating Sufi Shaykh*. Columbia: University of South Carolina Press.

al-Bukhārī, Muhammad ibn Isma'īl. 1966. *Ṣaḥīḥ al-bukhhārī*. Cairo: Al-Majlis al-'Ala li al-Shu'n al-Islamiyya, Lajnat Ihya Kutub al-Sunna.

Bulkeley, Kelly. 1996. "Dreaming as a Spiritual Practice." *Anthropology of Consciousness* 7 (2): 1–15.

———. 2008. *Dreaming in the World's Religions: A Comparative History*. New York: New York University Press.

Bunt, Gary R. 2003. *Islam in the Digital Age: E-Jihad, Online Fatwas and Cyber Islamic Environments*. London: Pluto Press.

———. 2009. *iMuslims: Rewiring the House of Islam*. Chapel Hill: University of North Carolina Press.

Burkhalter, Sheryl L. 1985. "Completion in Continuity: Cosmogony and Ethics in Islam." In *Cosmogony and Ethical Order: New Studies in Comparative Ethics*, edited by Robin W. Lovin and Frank E. Reynolds, 225–50. Chicago: University of Chicago Press.

Butz, David, and John Eyles. 1997. "Reconceptualizing Senses of Place: Social Relations, Ideology and Ecology." *Geografiska Annaler: Series B, Human Geography* 79 (1): 1–25.

Campbell, Joseph. 2008. *The Hero with a Thousand Faces*. Novato, CA: New World Library.

Carney, 'Abd al-Hakeem. 2005. "Imamate and Love: The Discourse of the Divine in Islamic Mysticism." *Journal of the American Academy of Religion* 73 (3): 705–30.

Casto, Kira Lynn, Stanley Krippner, and Robert Tartz. 1999. "The Identification of Spiritual Content in Dream Reports." *Anthropology of Consciousness* 10 (1): 3–53.

Central Intelligence Agency. 2012. *The World Factbook (Egypt)*. Retrieved April 16, from, https://www.cia.gov/library/publications/the-world-factbook/geos/eg.html.

Cesari, Jocelyne. 2004. *When Islam and Democracy Meet: Muslims in Europe and in the United States*. New York: Palgrave Macmillan.

Chelkowski, Peter. 1979. *Ta'ziyeh: Ritual and Drama in Iran*. New York: New York University Press.

———. 1985. "Shia Muslim Processional Performances." *Drama Review* 29:18–30.

Chevannes, Barry, ed. 1995. *Rastafari and Other African-Caribbean Worldviews*. Houndmills, Basingstoke, Hampshire: Macmillan.

Chidester, David. 2008. "Dreaming in the Contact Zone: Zulu Dreams, Visions, and Religion in Nineteenth-Century South Africa." *Journal of the American Academy of Religion* 76 (1): 27–53.

Chittick, William C. 1989. *Sufi Path of Knowledge: Ibn Al-Arabi's Metaphysics of Imagination*. Albany: State University of New York Press.
———. 2007. *Science of the Cosmos, Science of the Soul: The Pertinence of Islamic Cosmology in the Modern World*. Oxford: Oneworld Publications.
Clarke, L. 2005. "The Rise and Decline of *Taqiyya* in Twelvers Shi'ism." In *Reason and Inspiration in Islam: Theology, Philosophy and Mysticism in Muslim Thought: Essays in Honour of Hermann Landolt*, edited by Todd Lawson, 46–63. London: I. B. Tauris.
———. 2011. *The Spirituality of Shi'i Islam: Belief and Practices*. London: I. B. Tauris.
Clifford, James. 1988. *The Predicament of Culture: Twentieth-Century Ethnography, Literature, and Art*. Cambridge, MA: Harvard University Press.
———. 1997. *Routes: Travel and Translation in the Late Twentieth Century*. Cambridge, MA: Harvard University Press.
Cohn, Bernard S. 1987. *An Anthropologist among the Historians and Other Essays*. Delhi: Oxford University Press.
Cole, Juan. 2002. *Sacred Space and Holy War: The Politics, Culture and History of Shi'ite Islam*. New York: I. B. Tauris.
Corbin, Henry. 1966. "The Visionary Dream in Islamic Spirituality." In *The Dream and Human Societies*, edited by G. E. von Grunebaum and Roger Caillois, 381–408. Berkeley: University of California Press.
———. 1969. *Creative Imagination in the Sufism of Ibn 'Arabi*. Translated by Ralf Manheim. Princeton, NJ: Princeton University Press.
Cordesman, Anthony. 1997. *Bahrain, Oman, Qatar and the UAE: Challenges of Security*. Boulder, CO: Westview.
Coutin, Susan Bibler. 2003. "Cultural Logics of Belonging and Movement: Transnationalism, Naturalization, and U.S. Immigration Politics." *American Ethnologist* 3 (4): 508–26.
Cox, James L. 1996. *Expressing the Sacred: An Introduction to the Phenomenology of Religion*. Harare: University of Zimbabwe.
Cox Miller, Patricia. 1994. *Dreams in Late Antiquity: Studies in the Imagination of a Culture*. Princeton, NJ: Princeton University Press.
Crapanzano, Vincent. 1973. *The Hamadsha: A Study in Moroccan Ethno-Psychiatry*. Berkeley: University of California Press.
———. 1980. *Tuhami: Portrait of a Moroccan*. Chicago: University of Chicago Press.
———. 2004. *Imaginative Horizon: An Essay in Literary-Philosophical Anthropology*. Chicago: University of Chicago Press.
Csordas, Thomas J. 1994. *Embodiment and Experience: The Existential Ground of Culture and Self*. Cambridge: Cambridge University Press.
Curiel, Jonathan. 2008. *Al' America: Travels through America's Arab and Islamic Roots*. New York: New Press.
Curtis, Edward E., IV. *Muslims in America: A Short History*. New York: Oxford University Press.
Dassetto, Felice, 1996. *La construction de l'islam européen: Approche socio-anthropologique (Musulmans d'Europe)*. Paris: L'Harmattan.
Daud, Wan Mohd Nor Wan. 1989. *The Concept of Knowledge in Islam and Its Implications for Education in a Developing Country*. London: Mansell.
Davidson, Christopher M. 2009. *Abu Dhabi: Oil and Beyond*. New York: Columbia University Press.

Davidson, Herbert A. 1992. *Alfarabi, Avicenna, and Averroes on Intellect: Their Cosmologies, Theories of Active Intellect, and Theories of Human Intellect*. New York: Oxford University Press.

Debrix, François. 2003. "Introduction: Rituals of Mediation." In *Rituals of Mediation: International Politics and Social Meaning*, edited by François Debrix and Cynthia Weber, xxi–xlii. Minneapolis: University of Minnesota Press.

Deeb, Lara. 2006. *An Enchanted Modern: Gender and Public Piety in Shi'i Lebanon*. Princeton, NJ: Princeton University Press.

Delaney, Carol. 1991. *The Seed and the Soil: Gender and Cosmology in Turkish Village Society*. Berkeley: University of California Press.

Denny, Frederick M. 1988. "Prophet and *Walī*: Sainthood in Islam." In *Sainthood: Its Manifestations in World Religions*, edited by Richard Kieckhefer and George Bond, 69–97. Berkeley: University of California Press.

Dilthey, W. 1976. *Selected Writings*. Edited, translated, and introduced by H. P. Rickman. Cambridge: Cambridge University Press.

Diner, Dan. 2009. *Lost in the Sacred: Why the Muslim World Stood Still*. Translated by Steve Rendall. Princeton, NJ: Princeton University Press.

Doumato, Eleanor Abdella. 2000. *Getting God's Ear: Women, Islam, and Healing in Saudi Arabia and the Gulf*. New York: Columbia University Press.

Dumont, Louis. 1986. *Essays on Individualism: Modern Ideology in Anthropological Perspective*. Chicago: University of Chicago Press.

Dupré, Louis. 1987. "Mysticism." In *Encyclopedia of Religion*, edited by Mircea Eliade, 10:245–61. New York: Macmillan.

Durkheim, Emile. 1965. *The Elementary Forms of the Religious Life*. New York: Free Press.

Eickelman, Dale F., and Jon W. Anderson. 2003. *New Media in the Muslim World*. Bloomington: Indiana University Press.

Eickelman, Dale F., and James Piscatori, eds. 1990. *Muslim Travelers: Pilgrimage, Migration, and the Religious Imagination*. London: Routledge.

———. 1996. *Muslim Politics*. Princeton, NJ: Princeton University Press.

Eliade, Mircea. 1957. *The Sacred and Profane: The Nature of Religion*. Translated by William R. Trask. New York: Harcourt, Brace & World.

———. 1959. *Cosmos and History: The Myth of the Eternal Return*. New York: Harper & Row.

Elkholy, Abdo A. 1966. *Arab Moslems in the United States*. New Haven, CT: College and University Press.

Eriksen, Thomas Hylland. 2002. *Ethnicity and Nationalism: Anthropological Perspectives*. London: Pluto Press.

Ernst, Carl W. 1993. "An Indo-Persian Guide to Sufi Shrine Pilgrimage." In *Manifestations of Sainthood in Islam*, edited by Grace Martin Smith and Carl W. Ernst, 43–67. Istanbul: Isis Press.

Esposito, John L., and Ibrahim Kali. 2011. *Islamophobia: The Challenge of Pluralism in the 21st Century*. New York: Oxford University Press.

Euben, Roxanne. 2006. *Journeys to the Other Shore: Muslim and Western Travelers in Search of Knowledge*. Princeton, NJ: Princeton University Press.

Evans-Pritchard, E. E. 1934. "Lévy-Bruhl's Theory of Primitive Mentality." *Bulletin of Faculty of Arts* (Egyptian University, Cairo) 2:1–26.

———. 1949. *The Sanusi of Cyrenaica*. Oxford: Clarendon.

Ewing, Katherine P. 1990. "The Dream of Spiritual Initiation and the Organization of Self Representations among Pakistani Sufis." *American Ethnologist* 17 (1): 56–74.

———. 1994. "Dreams from a Saint: Anthropological Atheism and the Temptation to Believe." *American Anthropologist*, n. s., 96 (3): 571–83.

el-Fandy, Muhammad Jamaluddin. 1961. *Min al-āyāt al-kawnīyah fī al-Qur'ān al-karīm*. Cairo: Supreme Council for Islamic Affairs.

Farrer, D. S. 2009. *Shadows of the Prophet: Martial Arts and Sufi Mysticism*. New York: Springer.

Featherstone, M. 1990. *Global Culture: Nationalism, Globalization and Modernity*. London: Sage.

———. 1995. Introduction to *Global Modernities*, edited by Mike Featherstone, Scott Lash, and Roland Robertson. London: Sage.

Flaskerud, Ingvild. 2005. "Oh, My Heart Is Sad. It Is Moharram, the Month of Zaynab: The Role of Aesthetics and Women's Mourning Ceremonies in Shiraz." In *The Women of Karbala*, edited by K. S. Aghaie. Austin: University of Texas Press.

———. 2010. *Visualizing Belief and Piety in Iranian Shiism*. New York: Continuum.

Flores, Alexander. 1993. "Secularism, Integralism and Political Islam: The Egyptian Debate." *Middle East Report* 183:32–38.

Foltz, Richard C. 2003. *Worldviews, Religion, and the Environment: A Global Anthology*. Belmont, CA: Thomson/Wadsworth.

Foster, George M. 1965. "Peasant Society and the Image of Limited Good." *American Anthropologist* 67:293–315.

———. 1973. "Dreams, Character, and Cognitive Orientation in Tzintzuntzan." *Ethos* 1 (1): 106–21.

Frank, Allen J. 1996. "Islamic Shrine Catalogues and Communal Geography in the Volga–Ural Region: 1788–1917." *Journal of Islamic Studies* 7:265–86.

Freud, Sigmund. 1950. *The Interpretation of Dreams*. Translated by A. A. Brill. New York: Modern Library.

Friedman, Jonathan. 1995. "Global System, Globalization and the Parameters of Modernity." In *Global Modernities*, edited by Mike Featherstone, Scott Lash, and Roland Robertson, 69–90. London: Sage.

Fuccaro, Nelida. 2005. "Mapping the Transnational Community: Persians and the Space of the City in Bahrain, c. 1869–1937." In *Transnational Connections and the Gulf*, edited by Madawi al-Rasheed. London: Routledge.

Fukuyama, Francis. 1992. *The End of History and the Last Man*. New York: Free Press.

Fuller, Graham E., and Rend R. Francke. 1999. *The Arab Shi'a: The Forgotten Muslim*. New York: Palgrave.

Gallois, William. 2007. *Time, Religion and History*. London: Longman.

Gangadean, Ashok K. 1998. *Between Worlds: The Emergence of Global Reason*. New York: Peter Lang.

Geertz, Clifford. 1960. *The Religion of Java*. Glencoe, IL: Free Press.

———. 1968. *Islam Observed: Religious Development in Morocco and Indonesia*. New Haven, CT: Yale University Press.

———. 1973. *The Interpretation of Cultures*. New York: Basic.

Gelvin, James L. 2005. *The Modern Middle East: A History*. New York: Oxford University Press.

Geoffroy, Eric. 2010. *Introduction to Sufism: The Inner Path of Islam*. Translated by Roger Gaetani. Bloomington, IN: World Wisdom.

George, Marianne. 1995. "Dreams, Reality, and the Desire and Intent of Dreamers as Experienced by a Fieldworker." *Anthropology of Consciousness* 6 (3): 17–33.

Gergen, Mary M. 1988. "Narrative Structures in Social Explanation." In *Analysing Everyday Explanation: A Casebook of Methods*, edited by Charles Antaki. London: Sage.

Ghanea Bassiri, Kambiz. 2010. *A History of Islam in America: From the New World to the New World Order*. New York: Cambridge University Press.

al-Ghazālī, Abu Ḥāmid. 1979. *Iḥyā' 'Ulum ad-Dīn*. Cairo: Dar al-Manar.

Gibran, Khalil. 2009. *The Khalil Gibran Collection: The Prophet and Other Works*. Alvin, TX: Halcyon Press.

Giddens, Anthony. 1984. *The Constitution of Society: Outline of the Theory of Structuration*. Berkeley: University of California Press.

———. 1990. *The Consequences of Modernity*. Cambridge: Polity Press.

———. 1991. *Modernity and Self-Identity: Self and Society in the Late Age*. Stanford: Stanford University Press.

Gill, Jerry H. 2002. *Native American Worldviews: An Introduction*. Amherst, NY: Humanity Books.

Gilsenan, Michael. 1982. *Recognizing Islam: Religion and Society in the Modern Arab World*. New York: Pantheon.

Glazer, Nathan, and Daniel P. Moynihan. 1975. *Ethnicity: Theory and Experience*. Cambridge, MA: Harvard University Press.

Godelier, Maurice. 1999. *The Enigma of the Gift*. Translated by Nora Scott. Chicago: University of Chicago Press.

Goldstein, David. 2007. Introduction to *Complicating Constructions: Race, Ethnicity, and Hybridity in American Texts*, edited by David Goldstein and Audrey B. Thacker. Seattle: University of Washington Press.

Goldziher, Ignaz. 1971. "Veneration of Saints in Islam." In *Muslim Studies*, edited by Ignaz Goldziher, translated by C. R. Barber and S. M. Stern, vol. 2, 255–341. London: Allen & Unwin.

Goody, Jack. 1977. *The Domestication of the Savage Mind*. Cambridge: Cambridge University Press.

Gottschalk, Peter, and Gabriel Greenberg. 2008. *Islamophobia: Making Muslims the Enemy*. Lanham, MD: Rowman & Littlefield.

Gouda, Yehia. 1991. *Dreams and Their Meanings in the Old Arab Tradition*. New York: Vantage.

Grace, Martin Smith, and Carl W. Ernst. 1993. *Manifestations of Sainthood in Islam*. Istanbul: Isis Press.

Graham, Laura R. 1994. "Dialogic Dreams: Creative Selves Coming into Life in the Flow of Time." *American Ethnologist* 21 (4): 723–45.

Green, Nile. 2003. "The Religious and Cultural Role of Dreams and Visions in Islam." *Journal of the Royal Asiatic Society* 3:287–313.

———. 2004. "Emerging Approaches to the Sufi Traditions of South Asia: Between Texts, Territories and the Transcendent." *South Asia Research* 24:123–48; *International Journal of Middle East Studies* 24 (4): 615–37.

———. 2006. *Indian Sufism since the Seventeenth Century: Saints, Books, and Empires in the Muslim Deccan*. New York: Routledge.

Gregorian, Vartan. 2003. *Islam: A Mosaic, Not a Monolith*. Washington, DC: Brookings Institution Press.

Griffel, Frank. 2009. *Al-Ghazālī's Philosophical Theology*. New York: Oxford University Press.

Griffin, David Ray. 1990. Introduction to *Sacred Interconnections: Postmodern Spirituality, Political Economy, and Art*, edited by David Ray Griffin, 1–14. Albany: State University of New York Press.

Grunebaum, G. E. von. 1955. "The Problem: Unity in Diversity." In *Unity and Variety in Muslim Civilization*, edited by Gustave E. von Grunebaum, 17–37. Chicago: University of Chicago Press.

———. 1966. "Introduction: The Cultural Function of the Dream as Illustrated by Classical Islam." In *The Dream and Human Societies*, edited by G. E. von Grunebaum and Roger Caillois, 3–21. Berkeley: University of California Press.

Haddad, Y. Yazbeck. 2011. *Becoming American? The Forging of Arab and Muslim Identity in Pluralist America*. Waco, TX: Baylor University Press.

Haddad, Y. Yazbeck, and Jane I. Smith. 1994. *Muslim Communities in North America*. Albany: State University of New York Press.

Haddad, Y. Yazbeck, Jane I. Smith, and Kathleen M. Moore. 2006. *Muslim Women in America: The Challenge of Islamic Identity Today*. New York: Oxford University Press.

Hall, S. 1990. "Cultural Identity and Diaspora." In *Identity: Community, Culture, Difference*, edited by J. Rutherford. London: Lawrence and Wishart.

———. 1992. "The Question of Cultural Identity." In *Modernity and Its Futures*, edited by S. Hall, D. Held, and T. McGrew, 273–326. Cambridge: Polity.

Halligan, Fredrica. 2001. "The Creative Imagination of the Sufi Mystic, Ibn 'Arabi." *Journal of Religion and Health* 40 (2): 275–87.

Halm, Heinz. 2007. *The Shi'ites: A Short History*. Translated by Allison Brown. Princeton, NJ: Markus Wiener.

Hamdon, Evelyn Leslie. 2010. *Islamophobia and the Question of Muslim Identity: The Politics of Difference and Solidarity*. Halifax, Canada: Fernwood.

Hansen, Thomas Blom. 2000. "Predicaments of Secularism: Muslim Identities and Politics in Numbia." *Journal of the Royal Anthropological Institute* 6:255–72.

———. 1996. *Beyond Eurocentrism: A New View of Modern World History*. Syracuse, NY: Syracuse University Press.

Sharabi, Hisham. 1988. *Neopatriarchy*. New York: Oxford University Press.

Hassoun, Rosina J. 2005. *Arab Americans in Michigan*. East Lansing: Michigan State University Press.

al-Haydary, Ibrahim. 1999. *Trajidia Karbala': Sociolojia al-khitab al-shi'i*. Beirut: Dar al-Saqi.

Heath, Brad, and Gregg Krupa. 2005. "Arab-Americans Wealthier, Better Educated, but Census Figures Find Metro Detroiters Are an Exception to This Nationwide Trend." *Detroit News*. http://www.detnews.com/2005/metro/0503/10/B01-112169.htm.

Hefner, Robert W. 2011. "Introduction: Shari'a Politics—Law and Society in the Modern Muslim World." In *Shari'a Politics: Islamic Law and Society in the Modern World*, edited by Robert W. Hefner, 1–54. Bloomington: Indiana University Press.

Heil, John. 2003. *From an Ontological Point of View*. New York: Oxford University Press.

Heinen, Anton M. 1982. *Islamic Cosmology: A Study of as-Suyūṭī's al-Hay'a as-sanīya fī l-hay'a as-sunnīya, with Critical Edition, Translation, and Commentary*. Beirut: Franz Steiner Verlag.

Herdt, Gilbert. 1992. "Selfhood and Discourse in Sambia Dream Sharing." In *Dreaming: Anthropological and Psychological Interpretations*, edited by Barbara Tedlock, 55–84. New York: Cambridge University Press.

Herman, Luc, and Bart Vervaeck. 2009. "Narrative Interest as Cultural Negotiation." *Narrative* 17 (1): 111–29.

Hermansen, Marcia K. 1997a. "Introduction to the Study of Dreams and Visions in Islam." *Religion* 27 (1): 1–5.

———. 1997b. "Visions as 'Good to Think': A Cognitive Approach to Visionary Experience in Islamic Sufi Thought." *Religion* 27 (1): 25–43.

Herzfeld, Michael. 2001. *Anthropology: Theoretical Practice in Culture and Society*. Malden, MA: Blackwell.

Hess, Andrew. 1976. "Consensus or Conflict: The Dilemma of Islamic Historians." *American Historical Review* 81:788–99.

Hiebert, Paul G. 2008. *Transforming Worldviews: An Anthropological Understanding of How People Change*. Grand Rapids, MI: Baker Academic.

Hoda, Qmar-ul. 2004. "The Remembrance of the Prophet in Surawardi's 'Awarif Al-Ma'arif." *Islamic Studies* 12:129–50.

Hoffman, Valerie J. 1995. *Sufism, Mystics, and Saints in Modern Egypt*. Columbia: University of South Carolina Press.

———. 1997. "The Role of Visions in Contemporary Egyptian Religious Life." *Religion* 27:45–64.

Hoffman-Ladd, Valerie J. 1992. "Devotion to the Prophet and His Family in Egyptian Sufism." *International Journal of Middle East Studies* 24 (4): 615–37.

Holes, Clive. 2005. *Dialect, Culture, and Society in Eastern Arabia, Volume 2: Ethnographic Texts*. Leiden: Brill.

Hollan, Douglas. 1989. "The Personal Use of Dream Beliefs in the Toraja Highlands." *Ethos* 17 (2): 166–86.

Horvatich, Patricia. 1994. "Ways of Knowing Islam." *American Ethnologist* 21 (4): 811–26.

al-Houdaleih, Hussein. 2010. "Visitation and Making Vows at the Shrine of Shaykh Shiāb Al-Dīn." *Journal of Islamic Studies* 21 (3): 377–90.

Howell, Signe. 1984. *Society and Cosmos: Chewong of Peninsular Malaysia*. Singapore, New York: Oxford University Press.

Hsu, Roland. 2010. "The Ethnic Question: Premodern Identity for a Postmodern Europe?" In *Ethnic Europe: Mobility, Identity, and Conflict in a Globalized World*, edited by Roland Hsu, 1–17. Palo Alto, CA: Stanford University Press.

Hudson, Leila. 2004. "Reading al-Sha'rani: The Sufi Genealogy of Islamic Modernism in Late Ottoman Damascus." *Journal of Islamic Studies* 15:39–68.

Hughes, Aaron. 2002. "Imagining the Divine: Ghazali on Imagination, Dreams and Dreaming." *Journal of the American Academy of Religion* 70 (1): 27–53.

Huntington, Samuel. 1993. "The Clash of Civilizations?" *Foreign Affairs* 72 (3): 22–49.

———. 1996. *The Clash of Civilizations and the Remaking of the World Order*. New York: Simon & Schuster.

Hyder, Syed Akbar. 2006. *Reliving Karbala: Martyrdom in South Asian Memory*. New York: Oxford University Press.

Ibn Bābawayh, Abi Ja'far al-Saduq Muḥammad ibn 'Alī. 1992. *Man lā yaḥḍuruhu al-faqīh*. Beirut: Dār al-Aḍwā'.

Ibn Hisham, 'Abd al-Malik. 1978. *aḷ-Sīrah al-Nabawiyah* (*Sirat Rasūl Allāh*). Cairo: al-Maktabah al-Tawfīqīyah.

Ibn Kathir, Isma'il Ibn 'umar. 1937. *Taftīr al-Qur'an al-'Azīm*. Cairo: Dar Ihaya' al-Kutub al-'Arabiyyah.

Ibn Khaldun. 1981. *The Muqaddimah: An Introduction to History*. Edited by N. J. Dawood. Translated by Franz Rosenthal. Princeton, NJ: Princeton University Press.

Ibn Sīrīn, Muhammad. 2000. *Kitāb Tafsīr al-ahlām (Muntakhab al-kalām fī tafsīr al-ahlām)*. Beirut: Dār al-arf al-Arabī: Dār al-Manāhil.

Izutsu, Toshihiko. 1964. *God and Man in the Koran: Semantics of the Koranic Weltanschauung*. Tokyo: Keio Institute of Cultural and Linguistic Studies.

Jacoby, Susan. 2004. *Freethinkers:A History of American Secularism*. New York: Metropolitan Books.

al-Jilani, 'Abd al-Qadir. 1992. *Revelations of the Unseen* (*Futūḥ al-Ghaib*). Translated by Muhtar Holland. Ft. Lauderdale, FL: Al-Baz Publishing.

Johansen, Julian. 1996. *Sufism and Islamic Reform in Egypt: The Battle for Islamic Tradition*. Oxford: Clarendon.

Joll, Christopher M. 2012. *Muslim Merit-Making in Thailand's Far-South*. New York: Springer.

Jones, W. T. 1972. "World Views: Their Nature and Their Function." *Current Anthropology* 3 (1): 79–109.

Juergensmeyer, Mark. 2005. "Religious Antiglobalism." In *Religion in Global Civil Society*, edited by Mark Juergensmeyer, 135–48. New York: Oxford University Press.

Julian, Roberta. 2004. "Hmong Transnational Identity: The Gendering of Contested Discourses." *Hmong Studies Journal* 5 (5): 1–23.

Jung, Carl G. 1961. *Memories, Dreams, Reflections*. New York: Vintage.

———. 2001. *Modern Man in Search of a Soul*. Translated by W. S. Dell and Cary F. Bayners. London: Routledge.

———. 2002. *Dreams*. Translated by R. F. C. Hull. London: Routledge.

Kamran, Tahir. 2009. "Contextualizing Sectarian Militancy in Pakistan: A Case Study of Jhang." *Journal of Islamic Studies* 20 (1): 55–85.

Kapchan, Deborah, and Pauline T. Strong. 1999. "Theorizing the Hybrid." *Journal of American Folklore* 112 (445): 239–53.

Kaplan, Caren. 1996. *Questions of Travel: Postmodern Discourses of Displacement*. Durham, NC: Duke University Press.

Karim, Jamillah. 2009. *American Muslim Women: Negotiating Race, Class, and Gender within the Ummah*. New York: New York University Press.

Karrar, Ali Salih. 1992. *The Sufi Brotherhoods in the Sudan*. Evanston, IL: Northwestern University Press.

Karsh, Ephraim. 2006. *Islamic Imperialism: A History*. New Haven, CT: Yale University Press.

Kaspin, Deborah. 1996. "A Chewa Cosmology of the Body." *American Ethnologist* 23 (3): 561–78.

Katz, Jonathan G. 1997. "An Egyptian Sufi Interprets His Dreams: 'Abd al-Wahhâb al-Sha'rânî 1493–1565." *Religion* 27 (1): 7–24.

Kaufmann, Fritz, and Fritz Heider. 1947. "On Imagination." *Philosophy and Phenomenological Research* 7 (3): 369–75.

Kayyali, Randa A. 2006. *The Arab Americans: The New Americans*. Westport, CT: Greenwood Press.

Kazim, Nader. 2009. "Hal al-Bahrain dawla mut'adidat ath-thqafat?" ("Is Bahrain a Multicultural State?"). *al-Wasat News*, 2356.

Kearney, Michael. 1975. "World View Theory and Study." *Annual Review of Anthropology* (4): 247–70.

———. 1984. *World View*. Novato, CA: Chandler & Sharp.

Kennedy, Paul. 2001. "Introduction: Globalization and the Crisis of National Identities." In *Globalization and National Identities: Crisis or Opportunity?* edited by Paul Kennedy and Catherine J. Danks, 1–22. New York: Palgrave.

Kennedy, Paul, and Catherine J. Danks, eds. 2001. *Globalization and National Identities: Crisis or Opportunity?* New York: Palgrave.

Kepel, Gilles.1994. *The Revenge of God: The Resurgence of Islam, Christianity and Judaism in the Modern World*. Cambridge: Polity Press.

———. 2004. *The War for Muslim Minds: Islam and the West*. Translated by Pascale Ghazaleh. Cambridge, MA: Belknap Press of Harvard University Press.

Khury, Fuad. 1981. *Tribe and State in Bahrain*. Chicago: University of Chicago Press.

Kiernan, J. 1981. "Worldview in Perspective: Toward the Reclamation of Discussed Concept." *African Studies* 40:3–11.

Kilborne, Benjamin. 1981. "Pattern, Structure and Style in Anthropological Studies of Dreams." *Ethos* 9 (2): 165–85.

———. 1987. "On Classifying Dreams." In *Dreaming: Anthropological and Psychological Interpretations*, edited by Barbara Tedlock, 171–93. New York: Cambridge University Press.

Kim, Hyung-Jun. 2007. *Reformist Muslims in a Yogyakarta Village: The Islamic Transformation of Contemporary Socio-Religious Life*. Canberra: ANU E Press.

King, Geoffrey R. 1997. "The Coming of Islam and the Islamic Period in the UAE." In *United Arab Emirates: A New Perspective*, edited by Ibrahim Al Abed and Peter Hellyer, 70–97. London: Trident Press.

Kluckhohn, Clyde. 1949. "The Philosophy of the Navaho Indians." In *Ideological Differences and World Order*, edited by F. S. C. Northrop, 356–84. New Haven, CT: Yale University Press.

Kulaynī, Muḥammad ibn Ya'qub. 1969. *Uṣūl al-Kāfī*. Tehran: Dār al-Kutub al-Islāmīyya.

Lakoff, G., and M. Johnson. 1980. *Metaphors We Live By*. Chicago: University of Chicago Press.

———. 1999. *Philosophy in the Flesh: The Embodied Mind and Its Challenge to Western Thought*. Chicago: University of Chicago Press.

Lane, Edward William. 1973. *The Manners and Customs of the Modern Egyptians*. New York: Dover Publications.

Langer, Susanne. 1953. *Feeling and Form: A Theory of Art*. New York: Scribner.

Lawson, Todd, ed. 2005. *Reason and Inspiration in Islam: Theology, Philosophy and Mysticism in Muslim Thought: Essays in Honour of Hermann Landolt*. London: I. B. Tauris.

Lecerf, Jean. 1966. "The Dream in Popular Culture: Arabic and Islamic." In *The Dream and Human Societies*, edited by G. E. von Grunebaum and Roger Caillois, 365–79. Berkeley: University of California Press.

Lee, Benjamin. 1993. "Going Public." *Public Culture* 5:165–78.

Lee, Robert D. 2010. *Religion and Politics in the Middle East: Identity, Ideology, Institutions, and Attitudes*. Boulder, CO: Westview.

Levi-Strauss, Claude. 1963. *Structural Anthropology*. New York: Basic.

Lévy-Bruhl, Lucien. 1985. *How Natives Think*. Translated by Lilian A. Clare. Princeton, NJ: Princeton University Press.

Lewis, Bernard. 2003. *What Went Wrong? The Clash between Islam and Modernity in the Middle East*. New York: HarperPerennial.

Lia, Brynjar. 2006. *The Society of the Muslim Brothers in Egypt: The Rise of an Islamic Mass Movement, 1928–1942*. Reading, England: Ithaca Press.

Lincoln, Bruce. 2003. *Holy Terrors: Thinking about Religion after September 11*. Chicago: University of Chicago Press.

Lings, Martin. 1975. *What Is Sufism?* London: Allen & Unwin.

Lockman, Zachary. 2004. *Contending Visions of the Middle East: The History and Politics of Orientalism*. New York: Cambridge University Press.

Louër, Laurance. 2008a. *Transnational Shia Politics: Religious and Political Networks in the Gulf*. New York: Columbia University Press.

———. 2008b. "The Political Impact of Labor Migration in Bahrain." *City and Society* 20 (1): 32–53.

MacLean, Stuart. 2009. "Stories and Cosmogonies: Imagining Creativity beyond 'Nature' and 'Culture.'" *Cultural Anthropology* 24 (2): 213–45.

Magnuson, Eric. 2005. "Cultural Discourse in Action: Interactional Dynamics and Symbolic Meaning." *Qualitative Sociology* 28 (4): 371–398.

Maḥmud, Abd al-Ḥalīm. 1981. *Qadiyat al-tasawwuf: Al-Munqidh min al-dalal*. Cairo: Dar al-Ma'arif.

———. 1993. *Aqtab at-tasawwuf: al-Sayyid al-Badawi*. 4th ed. Cairo: Dar al-Ma'arif.

Mahrer, Alvin R. 1989. *Dream Work in Psychotherapy and Self-Change*. New York: Norton.

al-Majlisi, Muhammad Baqir. 1965. *Bihar al-Anwar*. Tehran: Dar al-Kutub al-Islamiyah.

Malek, Alia. 2009. *A Country Called Amreeka: Arab Roots, American Stories*. New York: Free Press.

Mayeur-Jaouen, Catherine. 2004a. *Al-Sayyid al-Badawi: Un grand saint de l'islam Egyptien*. Cairo: IFAQ.

———. 2004b. "Holy Ancestors, Sufi Shaikhs and Founding Myths: Networks of Religious Geography in the Central Delta." In *Yearbook of the Sociology of Islam*, vol. 5, edited by Georg Stauth, 24–35. Bielefeld: Universität Bielefeld.

McDermott, Anthony. 1988. *Egypt from Nasser to Mubarak: A Flawed Revolution*. London: Croom Helm.

Melchert, Christopher. 1997. *The Formation of the Sunni Schools of Law, 9th–10th Centuries C.E.* Leiden: Brill.

Merten, Don, and Gary Schwartz. 1982. "Metaphor and Self: Symbolic Process in Everyday Life." *American Anthropologist* 84:796–810.

Metcalf, Barbara. 1996. *Making Muslim Space in North America and Europe*. Berkeley: University of California Press.

Mintz, Sidney. 1998. "The Localization of Anthropological Practice: From Area Studies to Trans-Nationalism." *Critique of Anthropology* 18 (2): 117–33.

Mitchell, Richard P. 1969. *The Society of the Muslim Brothers*. London: Oxford University Press.

Mitchell, W. J. T. 1986. *Iconology: Image, Text, Ideology*. Chicago: University of Chicago Press.

Mittermaier, Amira. 2011. *Dreams That Matter: Egyptian Landscapes of the Imagination*. Berkeley: University of California Press.

Momen, Moojan. 1987. *An Introduction to Shi'i Islam: The History and Doctrines of Twelver Shi'ism*. New Haven, CT: Yale University Press.

Moustakas, Clark. 1994. *Phenomenological Research Methods*. Thousand Oaks, CA: Sage.

al-Muqarram, al-Sayyid Abd al-Raziq. 1963. *Maqtal al-Husain*. Qom: Al-'Ali Publications.

Murray, Penelope, and John Cocking. 1991. *Imagination: A Study in the History of Ideas*. Florence, KY: Routledge.

al-Mutahhari, Murtada. 2003. *Al-malhama al-Husainiyya*. Beirut: al-Dar al-Islamiyya Press.

al-Nabulusi, 'Abd al-Ghanī. 1972. *Ta'tīr al-anām fī tabīr al-manām (wa-bi-hāmishihi kitāb Muntakhab al-kalām fī tafsīr al-aḥlām li-Muḥammad ibn Sirīn)*. Cairo: Dār Ihyā' al-kutub al-'Arabiyya.

Nacos, Brigitte L., and Oscar Torres-Reyna. 2007. *Fueling Our Fears: Stereotyping, Media Coverage, and Public Opinion of Muslim Americans*. Lanham, MD: Rowman & Littlefield.

Naff, Alixa. 1993. *Becoming American: The Early Arab Immigrant Experience*. Carbondale: Southern Illinois University Press.

Nakash, Yitzhak. 1994. *The Shi'is of Iraq*. Princeton, NJ: Princeton University Press.

———. 2006. *Reaching for Power: The Shi'a in the Modern Arab World*. Princeton, NJ: Princeton University Press.

Nasir, Kamaludeen M., Alexius A. Pereira, and Bryan S. Turner. 2009. *Muslims in Singapore: Piety, Politics and Policies*. London: Routledge.

Nasr, Seyyed Hossein. 1964. *An Introduction to Islamic Cosmological Doctrines: Conceptions of Nature and Methods Used for Its Study by the Ikhwan al-Safa', al-Biruni, and Ibn Sina*. Cambridge, MA: Belknap Press of Harvard University Press.

———. 1988. "Shi'ism and Sufism." In *Shi'ism: Doctrines, Thought and Spirituality*, edited by Seyyed Hossein Nasr, Hamed Dabashi, and Seyyed Vali Reza Nasr, 104–20. Albany: State University of New York Press.

———. 2009. *Sufi Essays*. Chicago: Kazi Publications.

Naugle, David K. 2002. *Worldview: The History of a Concept*. Grand Rapids, MI: Eerdmans.

el-Nawawy, Mohammed, and Sahar Khamis. 2009. *Islam Dot Com: Contemporary Islamic Discourses in Cyberspace*. New York: Palgrave Macmillan.

Netton, Ian Richard. 1989. *Allah Transcendent: Studies in the Structure and Semiotics of Islamic Philosophy, Theology and Cosmology*. London: Routledge.

———. 2000. *Sufi Ritual: The Parallel Universe*. Richmond, England: Curzon.

Newman, Andrew J. 2000. *The Formative Period of Twelver Shi'ism: Hadith as Discourse between Qum and Baghdad*. Richmond, Surrey: Curzon.

Nicholson, Reynold A. 2002. *The Mystics of Islam*. Bloomington, IN: World Wisdom.

Noyon, Jennifer. 2003. *Islam, Politics and Pluralism: Theory and Practice in Turkey, Jordan, Tunisia and Algeria*. London: Royal Institute of International Affairs.

Nyang, Sulayman S. 1999. *Islam in the United States of America*. Chicago: ABC International.

Ochs, Elinor, and Lisa Capps. 1996. "Narrating the Self." *Annual Review of Anthropology* 25:19–43.

Olthuis, James H. 1989. "On Worldviews." In *Stained Glass: Worldviews and Social Science*, edited by Paul A. Marshall, Sander Griffioen, and Richard J. Mouw, 26–40. Lanham, MD: University Press of America.

Ong, Aihwa. 1988. "The Production of Possession: Spirits and the Multinational Corporation in Malaysia." *American Ethnologist* 15 (1): 28–42.

Orfalea, Gregory. 2006. *The Arab Americans: A History*. Northampton, MA: Olive Branch Press.

Osanloo, Arzoo. 2009. *The Politics of Women's Rights in Iran*. Princeton, NJ: Princeton University Press.

Papastergiadis, Nikos. 2000. *The Turbulence of Migration: Globalization, Deterritorialization, and Hybridity*. Malden, MA: Blackwell.

Parmentier, Richard J. 1994. *Signs in Society: Studies in Semiotic Anthropology*. Bloomington: Indiana University Press.

Parry, Wayne. 2005. "Arabs a Portrait of Success in America, U.S. Census Says." Associated Press (March 9). http://www.adcnj.us/arabs-doing-well-ap-03-08-05.htm.

Parwez, G. A. 1968. *Islam: A Challenge to Religion*. Lahore: Idara-e-Tulu-e-Islam.

Peck, Malcolm C. 1997. *Historical Dictionary of the Gulf Arab States*. Lanham, MD: Scarecrow.

Peirce, Charles Sanders. 1931–1958. *Collected Papers of Charles Sanders Peirce*. Edited by C. Hartshorne and P. Weiss. 8 vols. Cambridge, MA: Harvard University Press.

Perry, Marvin, and Howard E. Negrin. 2008. *The Theory and Practice of Islamic Terrorism: An Anthology*. New York: Palgrave Macmillan.

Pieterse, Jan Nederveen. 2009. *Globalization and Culture: Global Mélange*. Lanham, MD: Rowman & Littlefield.

Pinault, David. 1999. "Shia Lamentation Rituals and Reinterpretations of the Doctrine of Intercession: Two Cases from Modern India." *History of Religions* 38 (3): 285–305.

Price-Williams, Douglass. 1987. "The Waking Dream in Ethnological Perspective." In *Dreaming: Anthropological and Psychological Interpretations*, edited by Barbara Tedlock, 246–62. New York: Cambridge University Press.

———. 1994. "Cultural Perspectives on Dreams and Consciousness." *Anthropology of Consciousness* 5 (3): 13–16.

al-Qardawi, Yusuf. 1966. *Mawqif al-Islam min al-ilham wa al-kashf wa al-ru'a wa min al-tama'im wa al-kahana wa-l-raqa*. Beirut: Al-Risala.

al-Qushayrī, Muslim ibn al-Ḥajjāj ibn Muslim. 1911. *Al-Jāmi' al-Ṣaḥīḥ*. Istanbul: Al-Maṭba'ah al-'Āmirah.

Rahman, Fazlur. 1966. "Dream, Imagination and the 'Ālam al-Mithāl." In *The Dream and Human Societies*, edited by G. E. von Grunebaum and Roger Caillois, 409–20. Berkeley: University of California Press.

———. 1980. *Major Themes of the Qur'an*. Minneapolis, MN: Bibliotheca Islamica.

Railton, Ben. 2011. *Redefining American Identity: From Cabeza de Vaca to Barack Obama*. New York: Palgrave Macmillan.

Rajaee, Farhang. 2007. *Islamism and Modernism: The Changing Discourse in Iran*. Austin: University of Texas Press.

Rambachan, Anantanand. 2006. *The Advaita Worldview: God, World, and Humanity*. Albany: State University of New York Press.

Rappaport, Roy A. 1979. *Ecology, Meaning, and Religion*. Richmond, CA: North Atlantic.

———. 1999. *Ritual and Religion in the Making of Humanity*. Cambridge: Cambridge University Press.

Rath, Sura P. 2006. "What Would Said Say? Reflections on Tradition, Imperialism, and Globalism." *Social Text* 24 (2): 21–33.

Raudvere, Catharina. 2008. "Between Home and Home Conceptions of Sufi Heritage in Bosnia-Herzegovina and in Swedish Bosniak Diaspora." In *Sufism Today: Heritage and Tradition in the Global Community*, edited by Catharina Raudvere and Leif Stenberg, 49–64. London: I. B. Tauris.

Redfield, Robert. 1941. *The Folk Culture of Yucatan*. Chicago: University of Chicago Press.

———. 1952. "The Primitive World View." *Proceedings of the American Philosophical Society* 96 (1): 30–36.

———. 1962. *The Little Community and Peasant Society and Culture*. Chicago: University of Chicago Press.

———. 1968. *The Primitive World and Its Transformation*. Ithaca, NY: Cornell University Press.

Renard, John. 1996. *Seven Doors to Islam: Spirituality and the Religious Life of Muslims*. Berkeley: University of California Press.

———. 2004. *Knowledge of God in Classical Sufism: Foundations of Islamic Mystical Theology*. New York: Paulist Press.

Richards, Alan. 1984. "Ten Years of Infitah: Class, Rent, and Policy Stasis in Egypt." *Journal of Development Studies* 20 (4): 323–38.

Ridgeon, Lloyd. 2010. *Morals and Mysticism in Persian Sufism: A History of Sufi-Futuwwat in Iran*. London: Routledge.

Robertson, Ronald. 1992. *Globalization: Social Theory and Global Culture*. London: Sage.

Robinson, Francis. 1997. "Ottomans-Safavids-Mughals: Shared Knowledge and Connective Systems." *Journal of Islamic Studies* 8 (2): 151–84.

Roseberry, William. 1989. *Anthropologies and Histories: Essays in Culture, History, and Political Economy*. New Brunswick, NJ: Rutgers University Press.

Rosensohn, William. 1974. *The Phenomenology of Charles S. Peirce: From the Doctrine of Categories to Phaneroscopy*. Amsterdam: B. R. Gruner.

Rouse, Carolyn, and Janet Hoskins. 2004. "Purity, Soul Food, and Sunni Islam: Explorations at the Intersection of Consumption and Resistance." *Cultural Anthropology* 19 (2): 226–49.

Roy, Olivier. 2004. *Globalized Islam: The Search for a New Ummah*. New York: Columbia University Press.

Ruffle, Karen G. 2011. *Gender, Sainthood, and Everyday Practice in South Asian Shi'ism*. Chapel Hill: University of North Carolina Press.

Sachedina, Abdulaziz Abdulhussein. 1981. *Islamic Messianism: The Idea of the Mahdi in Twelver Shi'ism*. Albany: State University of New York Press.

al-Sādiq, Ja'afar. 2001. *Tafsīr al-aḥlām al-musama bi taqsīm al-rū'īyā*. Wa-Yalihi al-Ta'bīr muyassar. Collected by Muḥammad Riḍā 'Abd al-Amīr al-Anṣārī. Beirut: Lubnā Dār al-Muḥajjah al-Beyḍa.

Said, Abdul Aziz, and Meena Sharify-Funk. 2003. *Cultural Diversity and Islam*. Lanham, MD: University Press of America.

Said, Edward W. 1978. *Orientalism: Western Conceptions of the Orient*. London: Pantheon.

———. 1979. *Orientalism*. New York: Random House.

———. 1981. *Covering Islam*. New York: Pantheon.

———. 1983. *The World, the Text and the Critic*. Cambridge, MA: Harvard University Press.

———. 1984. "Reflections on Exile." *Granta* 13:159–72.

———. 1993. *Culture and Imperialism*. New York: Knopf.

———. 1996. *Representations of the Intellectual: The 1993 Reith Lectures*. New York: Vintage.

———. 2001 (October 4). "The Clash of Ignorance."*Nation*. http://www.thenation.com/doc.mhtml?i=20011022&s=said.

———. 2002. *Reflections on Exile and Other Essays*. Cambridge, MA: Harvard University Press.

Salait, Steven. 2006. *Anti-Arab Racism in the USA: Where It Comes From and What It Means for Politics Today*. Ann Arbor, MI: Pluto Press.

Sanders, Jimy M. 2002. "Ethnic Boundaries and Identity in Plural Societies." *Annual Review of Sociology* 28:327–57.

Sanders, Mary Anne. 2007. *Nearing Death Awareness: A Guide to the Language, Visions, and Dreams of the Dying*. London: Jessica Kingsley.

Saniotis, Arthur. 2004. "Tales of Mastery: Spirit Familiar in Sufis' Religious Imagination." *Ethos* 32 (3): 397–411.

Schechner, Richard. 1985. *Between Theater and Anthropology*. Philadelphia: University of Pennsylvania Press.

———. 2006. *Performance Studies: An Introduction*. New York: Routledge.

Schimmel, Annemarie. 1975. *Mystical Dimensions of Islam*. Chapel Hill: University of North Carolina Press.

Schmidt, Garbi. 2004. *Islam in Urban America: Sunni Muslims in Chicago*. Philadelphia: Temple University Press.

Screiber, Jan. 1978. *The Ultimate Weapon: Terrorists and World Order*. New York: Morrow.

Sells, Michael A. 1996. *Early Islamic Mysticism: Sufi, Qur'an, Miraj, Poetic and Theological Writings*. New York: Paulist Press.

Shaery-Eisenlohr, Roschanack. 2009. "Territorializing Piety: Genealogy, Transnationalism, and Shi'ite Politics in Modern Lebanon." *Comparative Studies in Society and History* 51 (3): 533–62.

Shaheen, Jack G. 1997. *Arab and Muslim Stereotyping in American Popular Culture*. Washington, DC: Georgetown University.

———. 2001. *Reel Bad Arabs: How Hollywood Vilifies a People*. New York: Olive Branch Press.

El-Shamy, Hasan. 1977. "African World View and Religion." In *Introduction to Africa*, edited by P. Martin and P. O'Meara, 208–20. Bloomington: Indiana University Press.

———. 1995. *Folk Traditions of the Arab World: A Guide to Motif Classification*. Bloomington: Indiana University Press.

———. 2008. *Religion among the Folk in Egypt*. Westport, CT: Praeger.

Sharabi, Hisham. 1988. *Neopatriarchy*. New York: Oxford University Press.

al-Sharani, Abd al-Wahhab. 1965. *Al-Tabaqat al-kubra al-musamma bi Lawaqih al-anwar fi tabaqat al-akhyar*. Beirut: Dar al-Fikr.

———. 2004. *Al-'Anwar al-qudsiyya fi qawa'id al-sufiyya*. Beirut: Dar Sadi.

al-Sha'rawi, Muhammad Mutwalli. 1998. *Al-Ghaib*. Cairo: Dar Akhbar al-Yaum.

Sheehi, Stephen. 2010. *Islamophobia: The Ideological Campaign against Muslims*. Atlanta, GA: Clarity Press.

Shehadeh, Sophia. 2004. "Women's Religious Practices in Bahrain: Umm al-Darda." *MIT Electronic Journal of Middle East Studies* 4 (Spring): 26–41.

al-Shinnawi, Hasan Muhammad Said. 2003. *Fi riyad at-tasawwuf: Ruiya dhatiyyah*. Tanta, Egypt: Al-Shinnawiyya al-Ahmadiyya Order.

Shulman, David, and G. G. Strousma, eds. 1999. *Dream Cultures: Explorations in the Comparative History of Dreaming*. New York: Oxford University Press.

Silverstein, Brian. 2011. *Islam and Modernity in Turkey*. New York: Palgrave Macmillan.

Sindawi, Khalid Ahmad. 2004. "Al-Husain Ibn 'Ali and Yahya Ibn Zakariyya in the Shi'ite Sources: A Comparative Study." *Islamic Culture* 78 (3): 37–53.

Singer, Milton. 1984. *Man's Glassy Essence: Explorations in Semiotic Anthropology*. Bloomington: Indiana University Press.

Sire, J. W. 1997. *The Universe Next Door: A Basic Worldview Catalog*. Downers Grove, IL: InterVarsity Press.

———. 2004. *Naming the Elephant: Worldview as a Concept*. Downers Grove, IL: InterVarsity Press.

Sirriyeh, Elizabeth. 1999. *Sufis and Anti-Sufis: The Defense, Rethinking and Rejection of Sufism in the Modern World*. Richmond, Surrey: Curzon.

———. 2000. "Dreams of the Holy Dead: Traditional Islamic Oneirocriticism versus Salafi Scepticism." *Journal of Semitic Studies* 45 (1): 115–30.

Smart, Ninian. 1995. *Worldviews: Crosscultural Explorations of Human Beliefs*. Englewood Cliffs, NJ: Prentice-Hall.

Smid, Karen. "Resting at Creation and Afterlife: Distant Times in the Ordinary Strategies of Muslim Women in the Rural Fouta Djallon, Guinea." *American Ethnologist* 37 (1): 36–52.

Smith, Barbara Herrnstein. 1990. "Cult-Lit: Hirsch, Literacy, and the 'National Culture.'" *South Atlantic Quarterly* 9 (1): 69–88.

Smith, Jane I. 1980. "Concourse between the Living and the Dead in Islamic Eschatological Literature." *History of Religion* 19 (3): 224–36.

Smith, Jane I., and Yvonne Y. Haddad. 1981. *The Islamic Understanding of Death and Resurrection*. Albany: State University of New York Press.

Smyers, Karen A. 2002. "Shaman/Scientist: Jungian Insights for the Anthropological Study of Religion." *Ethos* 29 (4): 475–90.

Sokolowski, Robert. 2000. *Introduction to Phenomenology*. New York: Cambridge University Press.

Spiro, Peter J. 2008. *Beyond Citizenship: American Identity after Globalization*. New York: Oxford University Press.

Steinback, Robert. 2011. "Jihad against Islam." *Southern Poverty Law Center*, issue 142.

Stewart, Charles. 1997. "Fields in Dreams: Anxiety, Experience, and the Limits of Social Constructionism in Modern Greek Dream Narratives." *American Ethnologist* 24 (4): 877–94.

Stoller, Paul. 1989. *Fusion of the Worlds: An Ethnography of Possession among the Songhay of Niger*. Chicago: University of Chicago Press.

Sulayman, Kamil. 2004. *Yawm al-khalas fi zill al-Qa'm al-Mahdi*. Beirut: Dar al-Muhjjabah.

Suleiman, Michael. 1999. "The Arab Immigrant Experience." In *Arabs in America: Building a New Future*, edited by Michael Suleiman, 1–21. Philadelphia: Temple University Press.

Sullivan, Denis Joseph. 1994. *Private Voluntary Organizations in Egypt: Islamic Development, Private Initiative, and State Control*. Gainesville: University Press of Florida.

Sviri, Sara. 1999. "Dreaming Analyzed and Recorded: Dreams in the World of Medieval Islam." In *Dream Cultures: Explorations in the Comparative History of Dreaming*, edited by David Shulman and G. G. Strousma, 252–73. New York: Oxford University Press.

Swenson, Don. 1999. *Society, Spirituality, and the Sacred: A Social Scientific Introduction*. Ontario, Canada: Broadview Press.

al-Tabataba'i, Muhammad H. 1977. *Shi'ite Islam*. Translated by Seyyed Husein Nasr. Albany: State University of New York Press.

al-Taftāzānī, Abū al-Wafā al-Ghunaymī. 1974. *Madkhal ilá al-taṣawwuf al-Islām*. Cairo: Dār al-Thaqāfa.

———. 1975. *Al-Insān wa-al-kawn fī al-Islām*. Cairo: Dār al-Thaqāfa.

Takim, Iiyakat Nathani. 2009. *Shi'ism in America*. New York: New York University Press.

Tambiah, Stanley J. 1990. *Magic, Science, Religion, and the Scope of Rationality*. Cambridge: Cambridge University Press.

Tapper, Richard, and Nancy Tapper. 1986. "'Eat This, It'll Do You a Power of Good': Food and Commensality among Durrani Pashtuns." *American Ethnologist* 13 (1): 62–79.

Tax, Sol. 1941. "World View and Social Relations in Guatemala." *American Anthropologist* 43:27–42.

Taylor, Charles. 2004. *Modern Social Imaginaries*. Durham, NC: Duke University Press.

———. 2007. *A Secular Age*. Cambridge, MA: Belknap Press of Harvard University Press.

Tedlock, Barbara. 1987. "Dreaming and Dream Research." In *Dreaming: Anthropological and Psychological Interpretations*, edited by Barbara Tedlock, 1–30. New York: Cambridge University Press.

———. 1992. "The Role of Dreams and Visionary Narratives in Mayan Cultural Survival." *Ethos* 20 (4): 453–76.

———. 2007. "Bicultural Dreaming as an Intersubjective Communicative Process." *Dreaming* 17 (2): 57–72.

Thomas, Nigel J. T. 1997. "Imagery and the Coherence of Imagination: A Critique of White." *Journal of Philosophical Research* 22:95–127.

Thompson, John B. 1984. *Studies in the Theory of Ideology*. Berkeley: University of California Press.

———. 1999. *Globalization and Culture*. Chicago: University of Chicago Press.

al-Tirmidhī, Muḥammad ibn ʻĪsā. 1900. *Jāmi' al-Tirmidhī*. Delhi: Kutub Khānah Rashīdīyah.

Tomlinson, John. 1999. *Globalization and Culture*. Chicago: University of Chicago Press.

Torab, Azam. 1996. "Piety as Gendered Agency: A Study of Jalaseh Ritual Discourse in an Urban Neighborhood in Iran." *Journal of the Royal Anthropological Institute* 96 (2): 235–52.

———. 2007. *Performing Islam: Gender and Ritual in Iran*. Leiden: Brill.

Trimingham, John Spence. 1971. *The Sufi Order of Islam*. Oxford: Clarendon.

Troll, Christian W. 2003. *Muslim Shrines in India: Their Character, History and Significance*. New Delhi: Oxford University Press.

Tschirgi, Dan. 2007. *Turning Point: The Arab World's Marginalization and International Security after 9/11*. Westport, CT: Praeger Security International.

Tsing, Anna. 2000. "The Global Situation." *Cultural Anthropology* 15 (3): 327–60.

Turner, Bryan S. 2011. *Religions and Modern Society: Citizenship, Secularization, and the State*. New York: Cambridge University Press.

Turner, Edith. 1992. "Psychology, Metaphor, or Actuality? A Probe into Iflupiaq Eskimo Healing." *Anthropology of Consciousness* 3 (1–2): 1–8.

Turner, Victor. 1969. *The Ritual Process: Structure and Anti-Structure*. Chicago: Aldine.

———. 1982. *From Ritual to Theatre: The Human Seriousness of Play*. New York: Performing Arts Journal Publications.

al-Tusi, Muhammad ibn al-Hasan. 1970. *Al-Istibṣār fī-mā ikhtalafa min al-akhbār*. Tehran: Dār al-Kutub al-Islāmīya.

———. 1981. *Tahdhīb al-ahkām: fī sharh al-Muqni'ah*. Beirut: Dar al-ta'aruf.

———. 2004. *Kitāb al-Gaibah*. Qom: Mu'assasat al-ma'arif al-Islamiyyah.

Uddin, Sufia M. 2006. *Constructing Bangladesh: Religion, Ethnicity, and Language in an Islamic Nation*. Chapel Hill: University of North Carolina Press.

United Arab Emirates. 2007. *U.A.E. in Figures*. National Bureau of Statistics. Abu Dhabi, United Arab Emirates. http://www.mfa.go.th/internet/attachments/185.pdf.

———. 2009. *U.A.E. in Figures*. National Bureau of Statistics. Abu Dhabi, United Arab Emirates. http://www.government.ae/Documents/Federal_Statistics/Other/الإمارات%20في%20أرقام%202009.pdf.

———. 2011. "Population." National Bureau of Statistics (March 31, 2011). http://www.uaestatistics.gov.ae/ReportPDF/Population%20Estimates%202006%20-%202010.pdf.

United Arab Republic of Egypt. "Population." Central Agency for Public Mobilization and Statistics (July 23, 2011). http://www.capmas.gov.eg/?lang=2.

Valk, John. 2009. "Religion or Worldview: Enhancing Dialogue in the Public Square." *Marburg Journal of Religion* 14 (1): 1–15.

Varisco, Daniel Martin. 2005. *Islam Obscured: The Rhetoric of Anthropological Representation*. New York: Palgrave Macmillan.

Viveiros de Castro, Eduardo. 1998. "Cosmological Deixis and Amerindian Perspectivism." *Journal of the Royal Anthropological Institute* 4 (3): 469–88.

Voll, John O. 1993. "Islamic Issues for Muslims in the United States." In *Muslims of America*, edited by Yvonne Yazbeck Haddad, 205–16. New York: Oxford University Press.

Waardenburg, Jacques. 2003. *Religion and Reason: Muslims and Others: Relations in Context*. Berlin: Walter de Gruyter.

Wadud, Sayed Abdul. 1971. *Phenomena of Nature and the Quran*. Lahore: Khalid Publishers.
Wagner, Roy. 2001. *An Anthropology of the Subject: Holographic Worldview in New Guinea and Its Meaning and Significance for the World of Anthropology*. Berkeley: University of California Press.
Wahbi, Sayyid. 2000. *Al-Mausu'a al-Masiyya li-Muhafzat al-Delta: al-mugalad ath-thani, Awlyia Allah wa al-Athar ad-dineyya Gharbiyya wa Kafr al-Shaikh*. 2 vols. Cairo: Al-Ahram Press.
Wautscher, Helmut. 1994. "Social Issue: Dreaming and the Cognitive Revolution." *Anthropology of Consciousness* 5 (3): 1–2.
Weismann, Itzchak. 2007. *The Naqshbandiyya: Orthodoxy and Activism in a Worldwide Sufi Tradition*. London: Routledge.
Wensinck, A. J. 1916. *The Idea of the Eastern Semites Concerning the Navel of the Earth*. Amsterdam: Johannes Muller.
———. 1932. *The Muslim Creed: Its Genesis and Historical Development*. Cambridge: Cambridge University Press.
———. 1978. "Al-Khiḍir" (Al-Khiḍr), *Encyclopedia of Islam*, 4:902–5.
Werbner, Pnina. 1996. "Stamping the Earth with the Name of Allah: Zikr and the Sacralizing of Space among British Muslims." *Cultural Anthropology* 11:309–38.
———. 2003. *Pilgrims of Love: The Anthropology of a Global Sufi Cult*. Bloomington: Indiana University Press.
Werbner, Pnina, and Helen Basu. 1998. *Embodying Charisma: Modernity, Locality and the Performance of Emotion in Sufi Cults*. New York: Routledge.
Wiktorowicz, Quntan. 2005. *Radical Islam Rising: Muslim Extremism in the West*. Lanham, MD: Rowman & Littlefield.
Wilkens, Steve, and Mark L. Sanford. 2009. *Hidden Worldviews: Eight Cultural Stories That Shape Our Lives*. Downers Grove, IL: InterVarsity Press.
Wolf, Fred Alan. 1994. *The Dreaming Universe: A Mind-Expanding Journey into the Realm of Where Psyche and Physics Meet*. New York: Touchstone.
Wolters, Albert M. 1989. "On the Idea of Worldview and Its Relation to Philosophy." In *Stained Glass: Worldviews and Social Science*, edited by Paul A. Marshall, Sander Griffioen, and Richard J. Mouw, 14–25. Lanham, MD: University Press of America.
Woodward, Mark. 2010. *Java, Indonesia and Islam*. New York: Springer.
World Bank. 1997. *Egypt in the Global Economy: Strategic Choices for Savings, Investments, and Long-Term Growth*. Washington, DC: Middle East and North Africa Economic Studies.
Wuthnow, Robert. 1989. *Communities of Discourse*. Cambridge, MA: Harvard University Press.
Wright, Robin. 2010. *The Iran Primer: Power, Politics, and U.S. Policy*. Washington, DC: United States Institute of Peace.
Younis, M. Abdel Moneim. 1967. "The Religious Significance of Mi'raj." *Majallat al-Azhar* (*Al-Azhar Magazine*) 6, 5–9.
Younis, Mohamed. 2009. "Muslim Americans Exemplify Diversity, Potential: Key Findings from a New Report by the Gallup Center for Muslim Studies." http://www.gallup.com/poll/116260/muslim-americans-exemplify-diversity-potential.aspx.
Ziring, Lawrence. 1997. *Pakistan in the Twentieth Century: A Political History*. Karachi: Oxford University Press.

Index

Note: Page numbers given in *italics* refer to illustrations.

About the Author

EL-SAYED EL-ASWAD is professor of anthropology and chair of the Department of Sociology, Faculty of Humanities and Social Sciences, United Arab Emirates University. He is the author of several books, including *Religion and Folk Cosmology: Scenarios of the Visible and Invisible in Rural Egypt* (2002).

CPSIA information can be obtained at www.ICGtesting.com
Printed in the USA
BVOW032057050712

294340BV00002B/1/P